Mom, Can I Move Back in with You?

Mom, Can I Move Back in with You?

A SURVIVAL GUIDE FOR PARENTS OF TWENTYSOMETHINGS

*Linda Perlman Gordon
and Susan Morris Shaffer*

JEREMY P. TARCHER/PENGUIN
a member of Penguin Group (USA) Inc.
New York

Most Tarcher/Penguin books are available at special quantity discounts for bulk purchase for sales promotions, premiums, fund-raising, and educational needs. Special books or book excerpts also can be created to fit specific needs. For details, write Penguin Group (USA) Inc. Special Markets, 375 Hudson Street, New York, NY 10014.

JEREMY P. TARCHER/PENGUIN
a member of
Penguin Group (USA) Inc.
375 Hudson Street
New York, NY 10014
www.penguin.com

Library of Congress Cataloging-in-Publication Data

Gordon, Linda Perlman, date.
Mom, can I move back in with you? : a survival guide for parents of
twentysomethings / Linda Perlman Gordon and Susan Morris Shaffer.
p. cm.
Includes bibliographical references and index.
ISBN 1-58542-290-8
1. Parent and adult child. 2. Adult children—Family relationships.
3. Intergenerational relations. I. Shaffer, Susan Morris. II. Title.
HQ755.86.G67 2004 2003071155
306.874—dc22

Printed in the United States of America
1 3 5 7 9 10 8 6 4 2

Book design by Stephanie Huntwork

We dedicate this book in loving memory to our parents

JEANNE AND CHARLES MORRIS
and
JEANETTE AND HAROLD PERLMAN

We wish we could tell them how grateful we are for their unconditional love that became the cornerstone of our parenting.

Acknowledgments

The encouragement and support of many people saw us through the writing of this book.

First and foremost, to all of the parents and twentysomethings who so generously shared their personal stories with honesty, insight, and humor.

To Mark: We are grateful for his intelligence and wisdom and his willingness to read and re-read countless drafts, and for listening with patience on the many drives back and forth to New York.

To Arnie: We have been energized by his enthusiastic belief and faith in this project and appreciate his unwavering support and encouragement during these endless months.

To Susan Wechsler and Donna Shoom-Kirsch, for their invaluable counsel and psychological expertise. We could always count on them.

To Judi Deutsch and Dale Spector, for their wisdom, humor, and good words.

To Jean Bernard and Carol Rosenberg, for their excellent editing skills and quick turnaround time.

To Sheryl Denbo, for her vision and ability to make all things possible.

To David Miller, Elizabeth Shaffer, and Charo Basterra, for their intelligent contributions. David, for his understanding of the sociological issues regarding baby boomers and twentysomethings. Elizabeth, for her knowledge about gender and its importance to her generation. Charo, for helping to provide a multicultural perspective.

To our agent, Joelle Delbourgo, for her intelligent counsel and enthusiastic commitment to the project.

To our editor, Sara Carder, at the Penguin Group, for her insightful skill and support for the project.

To Kelly Groves, at the Penguin Group, for his energy and enthusiasm.

To Jeffrey Arnett, for his invaluable research and understanding of parenting twentysomethings.

To Sandy Kavalier, for her skills as a photographer, and for always making the "shoot" so much fun.

To Rabbi Joui Hessel, for making the past give voice to the present.

To our wonderful children, Emily, Zach, Elizabeth, and Seth, for their love, support, and encouragement, and for their willingness to contribute their stories and open up their private lives to public scrutiny. And to our new delicious sons-in-law, David and Josh.

Our deepest thanks to Arnie and Mark for putting up with our strangled, work-driven days and for providing infinite numbers of excuses as to why we were unavailable.

—*Linda Perlman Gordon and Susan Morris Shafffer*
   April 2004

Contents

To laugh often and much; to win the respect of intelligent people and the affection of children; to earn the appreciation of honest critics and endure the betrayal of false friends; to appreciate beauty; to find the best in others; to leave the world a bit better, whether by a healthy child, a garden patch, or a redeemed social condition; to know even one life has breathed easier because you have lived. This is to have succeeded.

—RALPH WALDO EMERSON

Introduction

When I was a boy of 14, my father was so ignorant I could hardly stand to have the old man around. But when I got to be 21, I was astonished at how much the old man had learned in seven years.

—*Mark Twain*

Most parents of adult children have heard, at one time or another, variations of the following statements:

"Mom, I don't have time to talk now but my paycheck hasn't come and I'm out of money!"

"I'm bringing home that adorable guy I told you about. Is it okay if we stay in my bedroom?"

"Dad, I'm going to be in court all day. Can you call the plumber for me?"

"After I get back from India, I really need some time to decide what I want to do next. Can I live with you guys for a few months?"

These statements are good examples of the disconcerting nature of the relationship between parents and adult children in the twenty-first century.

The parents of the 39 million twentysomethings in the United States face the unprecedented challenge of their children's prolonged adolescence. Unlike previous generations, our children are not moving directly into adulthood after high school or college graduation. Instead, they are following contemporary social norms by resisting or delaying the traditional markers of adulthood: choosing a career, leaving home, getting married, and starting a family. As a result, the line between adolescence and adulthood has become blurred, causing confusion for both parents and their adult children. As parents, we find ourselves in uncharted territory, requiring new skills to form successful relationships with our children who appear to be moving slowly toward adulthood.

While our children's lives are no more difficult than those of previous generations, unique experiences and labels define them, just like every other. We hear buzzwords such as *emerging adulthood, boomerang children,* and *twentysomethings* used to describe this generation. *Emerging adulthood* describes our children's prolonged youth, extended period of education, and deferred marriage and parenthood (Arnett 2000). *Boomerang children* refers to the 44 percent increase in adult children moving back home since 1970, reflecting how hard it is to become economically independent during a time when there is a shortage of good jobs, a high cost of living, and the burden of student loans. Commentator Richard Morin, in a *Washington Post* article "Much Ado About Twentysomethings," has used the term *twentysomethings* to describe this generation as "engaged in physical frenzy and spiritual numbness, a revelry of pop, a pursuit of high tech, guiltless fun . . . a generation weaned on minimal expectations and gifted in the game of life" (Morin 1994, p. 27).

Today's young adults tell us that they feel unsettled while shifting from a safe and structured environment to a complex world without a road map. Twentysomethings are uncertain and fearful. At the same time, they feel "judged" by their parents for not meeting their expectations. Twentysomethings feel pressured by the fact that they will be expected to support the largest number of senior citizens in history. This generation's plight is very different from our own. We believe that examining the circumstances of today's twentysomethings from the perspective of both generations will give parents and children a greater understanding and sense of confidence to renegotiate their relationships.

To begin, our adult children are using their twenties to explore options and to experience different relationships on their way to becoming adults. Here is an example of an average twentysomething's path: Debbie is a 30-year-old college graduate (1994) with a major in African history and a minor in special education. She attended the University of Massachusetts for two years and the University of Maryland for two years. After graduating, she traveled overseas to Africa, went home to Connecticut, and became certified as a massage therapist. To support herself, she took a low-paying administrative assistant job at the Connecticut School for the Deaf. She thought about becoming a physical therapist, did some part-time massage therapy work, and wondered, "What do I want to do with my life, as far as a career?"

Debbie is beginning a two-year master's program in physical therapy at the University of Minnesota in the fall of 2002. When asked whether she was looking forward to school, she replied, "Yes, I really enjoy school. Although it looks like I've been all over the map, my experiences have helped me to get to this point. I am relieved, however, that I have finally decided which career path to follow, so that I can get a *real* job!" Although this pattern of self-exploration and uncertainty has become the norm for many adult children, it is alien to most of their parents.

One mother shared with us the following observation: "Parenting adult children feels like stepping into strange territory. There is an absence of folklore and guidance to help us through this stage. How do I position myself to stay close to my daughter without being intrusive? I feel like I am always trying to guess what I should be doing." Another parent shared this concern with us: "I don't feel scared like I did with my teenage son. But I do feel a sense of loss. I don't quite know my place anymore. I wonder if other parents feel this way. Could I be the only one?"

The confusion of parents stems, in part, from major sociocultural changes. Our generation grew up knowing that once we reached our twenties, we were on our own. Whether we chose to follow the lore of the 1960s and 1970s to "tune in or drop out," or we decided to get married and start our own families, we did not continue to be dependent on our parents. Many of us did not stay single for an extended period of time after college, and our twenties started with the assumption that we would "live happily ever after."

Susie, a 55-year-old mother of two adult children, said, "I didn't have the experience of being single in my twenties. I was married at twenty-one and had a child by twenty-six. I often don't know how to help my daughter with the choices she faces. Should I allow my daughter to sleep with her boyfriend in my home? For my parents, the answer was simple: no. I need to know what makes sense for my kid as well as for me." Today's twentysomethings live a different life. They are taking longer to make career decisions and are putting off getting married and having children. Coming from such different experiences, parents have to learn to respond appropriately to these changing patterns.

Frances, a 53-year-old divorced mother, said, "I started working when I was fifteen, so by the time I was twenty, I had been working for five years. By twenty-six, which my daughter is now, I had been married, divorced, and had one child. I had bought my own home and opened my own business. And she has just left the nest. So there's a very big difference, and it's still kind of astounding to me, because I'm thinking, 'Gosh, how did I do all of that?' When I see her struggling, I wonder. I just did it. I didn't think too much about it, I just did it."

This new social dynamic of a prolonged adolescence requires that parents be informed and prepared to communicate and provide guidance on an array of issues that we handled without much parental input. Cheryl, a 51-year-old mother of one adult son, adds, "I would never have talked with my parents. They didn't understand anything about what I was going through. We were going to change the world, and my parents just wanted to go along with what was considered to be socially acceptable. My mother equated our following what she wanted my brother and me to do with love. If we rejected her recommendations, we were accused of not loving her. I didn't want that kind of relationship with my son." Cheryl understands that today's twentysomethings are not necessarily rejecting their parents' way of life; they are simply taking time to decide which options they want to explore.

These changes in family life are also becoming a topic for public debate, which may result in public policy changes. Some of these changes might include allowing parents to take tax deductions for children older than the current age of 21, providing low-cost health care and increasing access to unemployment benefits. Because many new employees are released before they have worked the necessary hours to be eligible for job-related benefits, adult children are now more frequently dependent on their parents for financial support (Leposky 2002).

In addressing these new changes, it is helpful to recognize that our two generations share many common experiences during their transition from childhood to adulthood, including individuating from childhood influences, forming peer relationships, developing job skills, and determining a purpose and path for future life. One

55-year-old mother described to us her feelings of despair when she finished college at 22. Although she was ready to leave college, she felt confused and anxious. Life was spiraling forward, leaving her no time for living. She always thought this struggle was unique to her, but she now realizes these thoughts are universal during this time of life, when we expect to cast off childhood and assume an instant adult identity. This, of course, is a fairy tale.

The Absence of Useful Conventional Wisdom, Literature, and Science

We have written this book because there has been little discussion of this period of parenting, and parents have nowhere to turn for advice or support. In contrast, while raising younger children, parents have the benefit of access to a wealth of conventional wisdom. Discussions with parents, family, and peers are commonplace. Even on the sidelines of a soccer game, parents talk about the trials and tribulations of child rearing. However, during this new stage of maturation, the parenting job is made more complicated by the loss of such a built-in support system.

There are very few books providing a road map for parenting adult children. Go to any bookstore and browse through the parenting section. You will find shelves stocked with books beginning with pregnancy and ending with adolescence. Experts on psychological theory have not offered parents much guidance on parenting their children after adolescence. Developmental experts, such as Erik Erikson, do not directly address the developmental stage of becoming an adult. Professor Jeffrey Jensen Arnett is researching a theory of development for what he calls "emerging adults." Arnett theorizes: "Emerging adults . . . have left adolescence but have not yet entered young adulthood. They have no name for the period that they are in—because the society they live in has no name for it—so they regard themselves as being neither adolescents nor adults, in between the two, but not really one or the other" (Arnett 2000, p. 476). Professor Arnett and other researchers can be used as a take-off point for discussing practical approaches to parenting twenty-somethings.

This is the period we call adult*escence,* the process of growing up. In this book, we'll explore what it's like to be ages 20 through 29 in this day and age and how we, the parents, of this "Quarterlife Crisis" (Robbins and Wilner 2001) generation can more effectively assist them on their way to becoming adults. Following are some of the issues we'll address:

- why this period is often a difficult and confusing time of life;
- the demographics of this generation of adult children and their parents;
- the historical, economic, social, and psychological factors that contribute to the changes in behavior and attitudes of this generation;
- the effects of the generation gap on the relationship between parents and children;
- the impact of gender differences (How have the changes and opportunities for women affected this phase of their lives? How do relationships impact this period for young men?);
- the markers of adulthood for this generation (For example, now that getting married and having children are delayed, what constitutes a "grown-up"?);
- the recent pattern of adult children moving back home;

- the need to renegotiate relationships with adult children and their significant others; and
- the expectation of emotional and financial support from parents.

Our Personal and Professional Experience

Each of us is a parent of a son who is a junior in college and a working daughter in her late twenties, so we have had personal experience with the transition to early adulthood. Like many other parents, we believed our children's developmental pattern would roughly follow our own. Although we know we live in a different world, we expected that once our children graduated from high school and were accepted to college, the hard part would be over. We viewed college as the rite of passage from childhood to adulthood. Our expectation has proved to be unrealistic. We now know that parental responsibility continues after high school and college, well into our children's twenties. We've all heard the expression "You're a parent until you die." And yet, people rarely discuss the complexities of parenting adult children.

As professionals who have built nationally recognized careers in education as well as in family, gender, and adolescent issues, and as parents of twentysomethings, we bring to this subject professional expertise and years of parenting experience. Using focus groups and interviews with mental health professionals, educators, and parents, we have developed a method for analyzing these issues that helps us to present accessible solutions to the problems of parenting twentysomethings. As a part of this method, we include "take-home messages" at the end of each chapter to highlight the salient points.

We acknowledge that many of the parents we spoke with have the luxury of discussing these parenting issues because they don't have to worry about basic needs, such as putting food on the table. In fact, many may remember the late sociologist Abraham Maslow's philosophy about hierarchy of needs. He taught us that when you're hungry or homeless you have more immediate, pressing issues than your adult children's self-esteem. Certainly, the issues shift, depending on one's socioeconomic situation. However, regardless of financial circumstances, parents want the same things for their children and worry about being good-enough parents.

We hope that this book will assist you in guiding your adult child toward a satisfying independence. We also offer you support in maintaining a connection with your twentysomething. The emerging relationship with your adult child should be one of connection to family while becoming self-sufficient. We have developed a set of guidelines for parenting adult children that provide the foundation for this book.

Building on Common Experience

In our focus groups with parents of twentysomethings, we have heard many of the same problems and issues repeated over and over. Although these parents describe universal experiences, there are no set formulas for success. Each child's uniqueness must be respected if we are to parent that child successfully. Every family has different circumstances and different cultural or religious roots. However, there is comfort in knowing that there are commonalities among our experiences. Regardless of background or circumstance, we can look to one another for guidance. We have to figure out a way to re-create the sideline discussions at athletic events that we relied on during our children's earlier years.

During this stage of development, parents also have to pay close attention to their own needs and values. It is very easy to be swallowed up in the drama of our children's everyday lives, and many parents are learning this the hard way. One mother told us, "It still surprises me how their ups and downs impact me. When things are not going as they expect, it's difficult for me not to jump in and try to make it better. Fortunately for all of us, I've learned I can't fix it. I've discovered when they call me and sound unhappy, they probably just need to talk and be listened to, not have someone—me—fix anything for them. I learned this the hard way, spending sleepless nights worrying and trying to figure out how to 'fix it,' only to call the next day and hear everything is getting better. They needed to talk, and I'm glad they chose to talk to me."

Another mother said, "You know, I find it kind of fascinating, because I have been really conscious of struggling to try to find a way to be right now. I don't quite know what that is, because when my daughter calls me for help, when she calls me for advice, it's a kind of hook for me to get pulled back into my old role of 'mother,' which is very comforting to me. I love being a mother, and I have to be so conscious not to just fall right back into giving the kind of advice that I would give to her when she was younger and living at home. It's almost like you have to learn a new vocabulary, and I don't know what that is quite yet."

While meeting with scores of parents in our focus groups, we heard several variations of the following story repeated. Nancy said, "I get a call on my way to work from my daughter, who lives in Ohio. I pull over before I get to my office building because the signal cuts off in the underground garage. Amanda is moaning over the phone, 'Mom. I don't feel well. My throat is killing me. I have a throbbing headache, and my cold has gotten worse.' I respond, 'Amanda, did you call the doctor?' 'No, because I don't want to go on antibiotics,' she answers. I respond, frustrated, 'Amanda, why are you assuming you know what the doctor will prescribe? By the way, if you have a secondary infection, the only way to clear it up is to go on antibiotics.'

"I was so frustrated that she hadn't tried to figure out how to help herself and then was resistant to what I suggested. I said, 'I have to go to my meeting now, people are waiting for me.' Amanda repeats, 'But I don't feel well.' 'Amanda, what do you want me to do from here? I'm three hundred and sixty miles away from you and can't drag you to the doctor myself. Why did you call me?' Amanda answers in a voice a decade younger than her age, 'Because you're my mom.' 'That's fine,' I say, 'but if you don't feel well, call the doctor. I have to go now. Bye.' My daughter was upset with me, but at that point I really didn't care."

Twentysomethings do expect us to fix things for them, and parents have to be ready to set appropriate boundaries. Again, what works for the parent of one child (even within the same family) does not necessarily work best for another. Our adult children are all different, and we urge you to tailor your responses and strategies to the complex person your child undoubtedly is.

Some Fundamental Truths

Unlike dealing with adolescents over whom parents still have some control, parents have no control over their adult children. A mother of five explains, "When they were little, providing a cookie, playing a game, or inviting a friend to play could turn tears into smiles and make their world right again. I had some control over what happened to them; I could soothe, encourage, cajole, suggest. Now when one of my [adult] children is experiencing pain, I feel that pain as intensely as I did when they were young. But more times than not, the only thing I can do to help is meditate . . . and remind myself that painful experiences often spawn the most growth and strength" (Stanley 2003).

Our children are older and want to be self-sufficient, but they generally still need some guidance and support. Our goal is to provide parents with a helpful set of ground rules to use during this transitional period. In brief, these elements include the following:

- listen completely before responding;
- respect each other's privacy;
- suspend judgment; and
- rescue with caution.

These basic principles allow parents to support their adult children without enabling dependency; to sustain a sense of connection without creating guilt or undermining their children's maturation and self-esteem; and to address their own personal and family needs as well as those of their children.

Parents must balance giving of guidance and support with encouraging their children's autonomy and sense of personal responsibility. They should expect to stay involved in the lives of their children during this extended period of exploration and frequent change. Although parents feel a need for guidance, without public discussion or historical, psychological, and popular literature to turn to, parents are left without a road map. In writing this book, our hope is to start a dialogue and begin to fill this void, enabling parents of twenty-somethings to construct their own path by which they can help their children reach independence.

One of the basic tenets of this book is the importance of modeling and teaching personal responsibility to our children. Accepting personal responsibility results in a more independent and competent adult. Being responsible means internalizing what one's rights and duties are and having a commitment to truth and a concern for others. It means accepting responsibility for one's actions and listening to the moral barometer within. Creating opportunities that help children to feel more competent will result in a more responsible child.

Our children's sense of responsibility is influenced by many factors, such as age, parental practices, achievement level, and peer influences. Developing a sense of responsibility includes the following:

- realizing one's own unique strengths and experiences;
- believing in doing more than what "passes";
- believing in the importance of behaving responsibly;
- making choices through thought and reflection; and
- owning up to mistakes and failures and attempting to make better choices as they become available.

As parents, we can help our children recognize that they have the ability to be responsible for their own lives. This recognition helps them to avoid blaming others for adverse life experiences and associated feelings of uncertainty and powerlessness. Such feelings often lead to avoiding personal responsibility. Integrity, taking responsibility for one's life and actions, self-awareness, critical thinking, and reflection can help them to create a more positive view of the world and how they can steer their own lives. To feel more responsible for their own lives, they need opportunities to practice making choices, reflecting on the outcomes and owning their successes and failures.

We influence our children negatively when we do not hold them accountable for their behavior. When we protect our children from natural consequences, we ultimately increase their sense of power-lessness and sense of entitlement. Having lower expectations for our children's competence contributes to their irresponsible and dependent behavior. Increasing their opportunities to accept more personal responsibility helps them on their way to becoming competent adults. We know how natural it is to want to protect our children, but as they get older, what was appropriate protection when they were children can become disabling as they enter into adulthood. As parents, we can provide them with our wisdom and insight as they move toward independence. At least we can try.

Maintaining connection with an adult child has to be learned in a culture that idealizes autonomy and believes that children should become instant adults at age 18. On the contrary, the parent-child relationship helps to guide the child toward self-sufficiency in incremental steps. This interdependence fosters a healthy independence in the adult child. In this relationship, the twentysomething has permission to express needs safely and have boundaries respected, while achieving self-reliance. Unfortunately, there is no recipe for this distinct transitional developmental stage. This book provides parents with information and skills to help them navigate through this period successfully, based on the principle of respectful interdependence and the core value of teaching and modeling personal responsibility.

This interdependence is to be expected because parents and children today experience less of a generation gap than did previous generations. Many share educational experiences and an interest in popular culture. This is a generation that grew up with working mothers and fathers. As a result of expanding parental roles, family life is more participatory and democratic, and parents are much more involved in their children's daily lives. Experiencing these changes for the first time, we have to forge a new way of parenting our adult children.

Practice, Practice, Practice

After discussing the culture, developmental processes, fundamental principles, and guidelines that affect our parenting, we present some proven strategies for identifying and implementing these principles, and answer many questions. For example, in chapter 9, we discuss strategies that apply our guidelines when addressing some common situations:

1. If your adult child is working and needs money to augment his or her income, do you contribute? If so, under what circumstances?
2. Do you provide a down payment on a house or condominium?
3. What if your adult child wants to bring home his or her significant other and to sleep in the same bed?
4. How do you handle living with your adult child?

Hang in There

Parenting is not easy, and it is never over. It just changes. Parents of twentysomethings who find themselves perplexed make avoidable mistakes. There is a learning curve at all stages of raising and/or parenting children. One mother told us the following story: "We were having Thanksgiving dinner, and my son said to me, 'Mom, my girlfriends know that you don't like them. They are very uncomfortable about coming to the house. I want them to be comfortable visiting me.' I responded with sarcasm and said, 'Josh, one of them has been married for two minutes and is divorced, and the other has two babies and an angry ex-husband. What do you expect from me?'

'Mom, I expect you to trust how I judge character. Who I see is really not your business, unless I ask your opinion.' When I saw the look on his face, I decided to think about what he said before I spoke. I realized that I needed to trust him and keep my opinions to myself."

This mother determined that maintaining a positive relationship with her son was paramount and that he was right: who he dates is his business. Their family values were not lost on their son, and anything she says now about these women could push him away from the family. To stay close with her son, she has to let go of her biases and her beliefs about what she thinks will make him happy.

We must work with our adult children to develop a solid sense of self that will allow them to make decisions in a world with so many competing and confusing voices and options. Parents need to teach their adult children that they may not always get perfect results from their first choice or effort. When the outcome of their effort is disappointing, they did not necessarily make a "bad" choice. There is something to be learned from every decision we make. Growing up, like parenting, includes both successes and failures.

We want parents to know they are not alone. Parents benefit from discussions with one another where they can receive support in recognizing how to respond to their children's needs with intentional strategies rather than with reactive impulses. We hope to initiate a conversation on parenting adult children, to help parents feel less isolated within this uncharted territory and to recognize the joy this period of development can bring. As psychotherapist Ginny Stanley explains, "Parenting is such an incredible life practice . . . it illuminates every secret corner of our souls, exposing all our warts and also finding the tiniest seed of beauty and nurturing its development" (Stanley 2003).

Part One

How Do You Parent an Adult?

1. Dazed and Confused

WHY IS THIS A DIFFICULT
AND CONFUSING TIME OF LIFE
FOR MY TWENTYSOMETHING?

WANTED: Recent College Graduate Seeks High-Paying Job, Supportive Work Environment, Opportunities to Travel, Meaningful Romantic Relationship . . . and Ridiculously Cheap Rent for a Phat Pad.

—*Catherine E. Toth*, Honolulu Advertiser
(posted on August 26, 2001)

The twenties are a transitional period for adult children. This is the time when many leave behind a structured and safe college environment (along with winter and spring breaks) to enter the world of alarm clocks, bosses, and bills. For many twentysomethings, it can often be difficult to see a clear path ahead with all of the choices and obligations pushing them in many different directions. One twentysomething said to us, "For sixteen years my job has been to be a student. I've worked hard and understood what it took to succeed at this job. I studied and partied, and all in all, I had a good time. Now that

I've graduated, in some sense I'm losing my old job, the only job I've ever had. I keep asking myself, What is it that I want? How do I decide what I want? I worry that when I figure out what I want out of life, I won't know how to get it." The associate dean of students at the University of Chicago believes this experience is common. He said, "At that stage in their lives, students can hardly remember a time when they were not in school, so they usually feel some trepidation about this extraordinary change. The abyss of freedom yawns" (Gutmann 2002).

The Society for Adolescent Medicine now covers people from 10 to 26 years of age. The MacArthur Foundation is currently studying emerging adults and considers age 34 to be the end of that transition (Stepp 2002(A)). This extended period of maturation leaves both parents and children perplexed. At a time of such confusion and uncertainty, the total absence of a road map increases stress for both twentysomethings and their parents. Parents are unsure about the best way to treat adult children, and kids are unsure about how to grow up. In previous generations, families more or less followed a structure. Expectations were more straightforward, and families relied on accepted rules. In today's society, both parents and children are faced with dualities of experience that create mixed messages and contradictions. This chapter explores some of these dualities and discusses how parents and children are coping and what parents can do to help in this complex process.

Understanding Your Twentysomething Child's Experience

TRAVELING A MORE VARIED COURSE

The transition from childhood to adulthood can be as shocking as a lightning bolt. Just as one can't prepare to be struck by lightning, many twentysomethings feel unprepared and experience this transition as startling. Many researchers now say that the journey from childhood to adulthood not only takes longer but is less defined, more complicated, and less straightforward as well. Unlike their parents, children no longer go directly from their childhood home to one they share with their spouses. They travel a more varied course.

Twentysomethings move to different cities, change jobs frequently, and experience a variety of living situations with assorted friends and significant others. One father describes his frustration knowing that his son was sleeping on the floor of a friend's apartment and was supporting his nomadic lifestyle by scalping tickets to rock concerts. One mother cannot believe how different her daughter's work experience is from her own. This mother has held the same job for more than 20 years, and her daughter has had six jobs within 2 years. The one thing that helps this mother understand her daughter's career indecision is the knowledge that her daughter worries that making a mistake might lock her into the wrong career. All this mother wants for her daughter is "one career path, right or wrong."

Mary, age 26, also observes, "Many kids my age are jumping, jumping, jumping from one job to the next. My parents have stayed in the same job for as long as I have known them. Their success is like magic, but it's hard to imagine that for myself." Beth, another twentysomething, tells us: "Until my sophomore or junior year in college, I wanted to be an anthropologist. After graduation, I wanted to be a psychologist, and found work at a sexual assault hot line. Then I changed my mind again. I decided I wanted to help victims, and realized that I should become a prosecutor. So, at the age of twenty-five, I applied to law school."

As part of an "instant-gratification" culture, twentysomethings have unrealistic expectations of both the length of time and the effort required to achieve their goals. While parents understand that meaningful goals can take years to achieve, children are not used to delayed rewards. Adult children are exposed to constant financial temptations that have grave consequences. An advertisement in a September 2002 issue of *Newsweek* for a wireless pocket PC phone reads: "Now you can call and access the Internet wherever you go. Yeah, instant gratification is cool, isn't it?" Psychologist Larry Gard says, "Twentysomethings are faced with messages that they should be able to buy what they want, without having the money first. It can be too much for a young person, especially if he feels needy by virtue of being alone and confused and on his feet for the first time" (Gard 2002). With such unrealistic expectations of entitlement, twentysomethings feel disillusioned. Matt tells us, "When I graduated *magna cum laude,* I thought doors would open, a red carpet would be rolled out, and employers would be knocking down my door. But, in this economy, I did the door knocking, and after six months, I was lucky to find an entry-level job."

The fact that twentysomethings may be working for years longer than their parents or grandparents makes them much more careful about choosing a meaningful career. Yet few professions seem to be stable because of the rapid pace of social change and economic uncertainty. They also have been exposed to ever-increasing and fast-changing information. Although twentysomethings have access to so much knowledge, they have less real-life experience to help them absorb and make sense of this information. Therefore, it is hard for them to feel confident when making choices.

Sara always identified herself as a student, and she was confused about how to transition into adult life. She doubted whether she could get up at dawn every day to go to work, after having scheduled all of her college classes to begin no earlier than 11 A.M. She couldn't figure out how to fit socializing into a 40-hour workweek. Sara would have been better off if she had known that many others felt exactly as she did. Knowing that other twentysomethings had the same experience would have made her less panicked about her own confusion. Support from friends provides comfort and validation during this unsettling time.

Sara didn't go to her parents for advice because they always said, "We will support you during college, and then you're on your own." However, Sara had been an art history major and was very disappointed with the lack of job opportunities and her inability to be independent. She wasn't ready to face the real world. Her self-doubt and insecurity are common during this transitional period. After feeling such a strong sense of community in college, twentysomethings lose their sense of belonging and knowing what comes next. They no longer have academic semesters around which to plan their lives.

Alison, a 24-year-old teacher, said, "A big part of the attraction to education was not that I had a passion to teach, but rather my not wanting to lose Thanksgiving, Christmas, and summer vacations." Twentysomethings often say it is difficult to find a career that satisfies their need for flexibility and gratification in their work. Alison is holding on to as much of her younger life as she can. Becoming an adult requires compromise and setting priorities; learning you can't have it all is a hard lesson. As a result, many twentysomethings are immobilized by the number of choices available to them. In a January 2002 issue of *Time* magazine, one twentysomething observes that "responsibility is always the price of freedom. But we are now responsible for so many decisions, requiring so much homework that many of us feel helpless and paralyzed" (Kadlec 2002, p. 24).

To respond to the varied choices available today, parents have to provide their children with opportunities to develop decision-making skills that will help them thrive in a more complex society. Adult children need our help with this transition, and yet this reality may be in conflict with our expectations as parents.

THE PROLONGED DEPENDENCE OF ADULT*ESCENCE*

Before becoming a twentysomething, teenagers anticipate independence as a long-awaited goal. But, today, independence can be a "virtual reality" experience. In contrast to past generations, today's adult children's dependency on their parents is frequently prolonged, and independence is illusory. In earlier generations, young adults became mothers and fathers and stable members of the workforce in their twenties. Today, parents must adjust to an extended education, fewer job opportunities, and the high cost of housing for their children. This reality creates a prolonged period of dependence on parents.

For most, finding a career doesn't happen instantaneously; it is a work in progress. Kelly's story is a good example of how a young adult can use transitional time to learn about herself in order to choose the right career. Kelly, a 25-year-old, tells us, "I still feel like I could be fresh out of high school and wish I could get a do-over on college. Now that would be great! I know how I would like to do it now, even though I feel the same today as I did a few years ago. I'm taking on a new career that may not be one that really fits me, and I don't feel as if I've moved forward career-wise. However, I finally have enough experience to know life is a series of stepping-stones.

"During this period, my parents have been the biggest emotional support for me. My dad always says, 'Just do what you love and the money will come. We will always support you.' He is just the greatest. I often respond to my dad with, 'Dad, that's a great philosophy for you, because you love chemical engineering, and that's a lucrative business. Not many people like chemical engineering, especially creating software for pulp and paper mills. I don't even know what to tell people you do.'

"Me, I love lying on the beach. Could you tell me how that's going to bring money to me, because that's what I love? My dad laughs with me when I tell him this, and then we take a serious look at why I love the beach and how to let that information guide me. For a while, I worked on a cruise ship. That job served me well, but it was never going to be a career, because I wasn't making enough money and I was just getting older. While I was on the cruise ship, my friends were talking about 401(k)s. I had no idea what they were, and I was twenty-four years old. I thought to myself, 'Oh, my God, what am I doing?' I needed to get back on land. I didn't know how to make this transition.

"I called my dad, and he said, 'I understand how you feel, Kelly, but I don't want you to worry about 401(k)s now. It's all going to come full circle. You're building skills and you have all these interests. You'll figure out how to use them to your advantage.'

"Now, I'm thinking about going back to get my MBA, and I called Dad to tell him. I felt so supported when he said, 'I think that's a great idea because you don't have the time to get your MBA on the job like I did. You'll be able to get the tools you need to get into an area that you will enjoy and be able to start your 401(k)! You'll find that all of your previous work experiences will serve you well.'

"My dad never made the choice for me. He stood by my side like a supportive coach. I knew I could believe what he said because he lived by his words. Because his life example speaks volumes, I often think to myself, what would my dad do?" Most helpful for Kelly during this time was the unconditional love and support her dad provided. Kelly's dad understands that transitions can bring feelings of anxiety and insecurity, but they almost always provide opportunities for growth.

Janice describes her anxiety at the end of college: "Everybody tells me it's supposed to be the best time of my life. Is it all downhill after that? Nobody told me how hard it would be to leave college and all of my friends who are now scattered all over the country. Who wants to be an adult? To be an adult means that the best time of my life is over!"

Kelly and Janice both express the confusion and transitory nature of the early to mid-twenties that many of our children experience. Another twentysomething puts this period into perspective with the following simile: "This period is like shedding one layer of skin at a time without knowing that another will grow."

COLLEGE IS NOT A SURROGATE PARENT

Today, parents often breathe a sigh of relief when they send a child off to college. One parent, Terry, expresses for us most parents' false notions about college: "Oh, my God, my job is over. He's an adult, thank goodness. I call him often to see how he is doing because I want to make sure he's happy and I don't want him to flunk out." Parents wrongly assume the university is watching over their children in addition to educating them and that they will mature without much further effort on their part.

For our generation, colleges assumed responsibility for children in the absence of their parents (*in loco parentis*). Colleges no longer take the place of parents, and students find themselves on their own without the skills necessary to take care of themselves successfully (Apter 2001). Randy tells us, "The month before graduation I already started to feel lonely. I became frustrated that I hadn't applied to graduate school. I have to admit, graduate school would have prolonged being on my own and provided me with a ready-made community." These emerging adults also lack the networks and traditional forms of support offered to earlier generations.

During these challenging years, the institutions that serve young adults do not seem to be meeting their needs. Although more young people attend college, retention rates, especially at community colleges, are poor (Steinberg 2001). Young people are told that going to college is the ticket to a better life, but many have too few financial resources to make it happen. For those who are able to get a higher education, not only do many leave school with a lot of debt, but they often do not have the skills to prepare them for life after college. Students get little help understanding the connection between school and work and often are uncertain what major will provide them with the best opportunities.

Colleges and universities often do not address the transition from school to work adequately. Donna Shoom-Kirsch, a psychologist working in "experiential education," has told us, "The students I work with tend to take courses for interest, rather than preparation for a career. As a result, too many graduates do not know what they want to do. When they flounder too long, they risk questioning where they belong. Universities should assist our children to make a connection between what they are learning in school and how they are going to use it." There is still a gap between offering activities and encouraging students to participate in them. Dr. Shoom-Kirsch suggests that parents and universities must promote career-oriented activities to facilitate more productive use of the college years. This recommendation is supported by Barnard College president Judith Shapiro, who advises, "Parents do best when they encourage their college-bound children to reach out enthusiastically for opportunities in the classroom and beyond" (Shapiro 2002, p. A23).

Dr. Shoom-Kirsch confirms that there is an emerging trend in some universities to make more of an effort to help students focus on their lives after college. She adds, "The university has a responsibility to communicate about what resources it has available to both the parents and the kids. When parents have this information, they could ask their children if they are interested in taking advantage of what the university has to offer. Possibly, the parents can just talk generically to their children. 'I know you're having a good time, but college is a stepping-stone to somewhere else. What are you doing, if anything, to get yourself to the next step?'" These discussions can assist our children in making better choices as they move through the college years.

We must not underestimate the fear that so many twentysomethings feel once they leave the structured and secure world of college and their friends. It is much easier to be independent within a protected environment, where they feel more in control of their choices and they have group support. Many graduates come out of college with debt and find themselves in a new city trying to create a new social life. Maggie recalls, "Besides the pressure of knowing what you're going to do, you don't know where you're going to live or with whom." Social life, geography, and identity are all in flux at the same time. Twentysomethings are beginning to sort out an overprotected childhood full of high expectations and mixed messages. This phenomenon makes it harder for twentysomethings to use their experiences to guide their new adult lives independently.

Parents must view the extended period of emerging adulthood through a wider lens to better contribute to their twentysomething children's mastery of the world of work and relationships. During the college years, young people cope with a truly complex set of developmental tasks. Later, they experience a series of transitions as they become independent of their families, develop intimate relationships, establish their own families, and explore job and career goals and options. The stress of these transitions is exacerbated as "they move in and out of the seemingly revolving door of higher education, and in and out of low-wage, dead-end jobs, often with no knowledge of how to get from where they are to self-sufficiency or a family-supporting income" (Steinberg 2001, p.1).

Today's twentysomethings do not have the economic freedom to be as autonomous as people their age were in previous generations.

Consequently, the transition from adolescence to adulthood requires continuing parental guidance, love, and understanding. One mother describes parenting as a "continuum, creating a broad spectrum of what is okay depending on the child's developmental age and individual needs, including the process of a child reaching adulthood." Many adult children agree with this assessment.

Understanding Your Own Situation as a Parent of a Twentysomething Child

OLD HABITS ARE HARD TO BREAK

As parents, we assume and expect that our college graduate will find his or her own way without much parental support. After all, our parents expected the same from us. While many of us continue to provide guidance, we often feel that we are the only parents whose adult children still need support. One mother we contacted for an interview says, "No, you wouldn't be interested in what my husband and I do. We are aberrant." Many parents think their experiences are atypical because they don't discuss these experiences with others.

Without the large number of support systems available while they are raising younger children, parents of adult children don't realize that their experience is universal. It is a unique time for parenting. Our children are well on their way to adulthood, but they are not there yet. They continue to call on us for emotional support and, sometimes, to solve problems for them. However, because both parties are adults, the parenting process is more complicated.

Our kids may look like they don't need help, but they often do. Kids grow up quickly—displaying their navels before middle school, pumping iron and hoping for a "six-pack," having early sexual experiences, and seeing sexualized and violent images on television and in movies. These experiences create in young people an aura of a pseudosophisticate, but that doesn't mean they are as mature as they appear. In reality, most of our children in their early twenties are not able to function independently of their families. Trying to find the optimal balance to promote growth and independence while maintaining connection is the most difficult challenge for this stage of parenting.

One parent shares this story: "I got a phone call from my son, the freelance writer, who complained to me that his laptop was broken. He was really frustrated and agitated, because it had just been fixed a few months earlier. I was frustrated because it took me hours of phone calls, angry letters, and follow-ups to resolve the problem the first time. So I knew what was in store for me. Rather than suffer my son's complaints, I decided to solve his problem and went into hyper-gear.

"I called the service department and waited through a series of recordings, until I finally found a live person, someone who had absolutely no interest in helping me. Unable to solve the problem, I called my son and told him that the company was of no help. He hung up, upset with me because I couldn't get it resolved. After all my effort, I was left with both his anger and my own frustration with the situation. Two days later, while talking to my son, I heard 'You've got mail' in the background. So I asked him whose computer he was using. He said, 'Oh, I forgot to tell you, Mom, my screen is working again.'"

It is not surprising that our twentysomething children unload their problems on us. Old habits are hard to break. We are used to holding their emotions and disappointments. But now our adult children move on without telling us how they have resolved their problems. In the meantime, we are saddled with their irritation and outrage until we are given further notice. This is, as Erma Bombeck points out, part of the "vice-president syndrome." Bombeck wrote:

"When mothers talk about the depression of the empty nest, they're not mourning the passing of all those wet towels on the floor, or the music that numbs your teeth, or even the bottle of capless shampoo dribbling down the shower drain. They're upset because they've gone from supervisor of a child's life to a spectator. It's like being the vice president of the United States" (Bombeck 2003). As parents of twentysomethings, we are both spectator and participant, without knowing which is most appropriate.

We believe parents must see this stage of parenting as a normal process of growing up if they are to be less confused and more tolerant by its unsettled nature. They must learn how to establish the boundaries needed to provide the guidance this age requires. For example, the mother of the son with the broken laptop could have told her son that he was capable of making the phone call himself and negotiating with the service department. At the same time, she might have guided him with information about a more effective way to handle himself when seeking assistance on the telephone. Because her son is a freelance writer, knowing how to get his own computer fixed is a critical skill. Parents must learn to foster independence while maintaining a strong connection with their children. These goals are complex, but not incompatible.

THE DUALITY OF OUR CHILDREN'S LIVES

As we listen to parents and adult children, many of their stories express a duality. Twentysomethings today have grown up being both excessively idle and overscheduled. On average, they have spent four and a half hours in front of electronic media each day, making passive observance a way of life. Therefore, many reach adulthood less disciplined and less able to organize the details of their daily lives. Parents are often required to remain their adult children's private "OnStar" navigational service.

One father remembers the night his son decided to drive to the beach, which was about three hours from home, at ten o'clock at night. The dad asked his 22-year-old son, Jason, if he knew the route and if he wanted a map. His son told him that he knew enough to get started and he could figure out the rest from there. It took some self-editing for the father to keep from giving his son a map and writing out the directions. But he figured he would let Jason do it on his own. The dad shut the door, waved good-bye, and went back into the kitchen, listening to the throbbing bass sounds from Jason's car radio as he drove down the street.

One hour later, the phone rang. "Dad, there's a bridge in front of me. I think I have to go over it. I don't know how it happened. I think I'm driving away from the beach. What do I do?" The dad told Jason to go to a gas station to get directions. Jason resisted, however; he wanted the information from his dad, and he didn't want to have to do any work to get it. Faced with, as the father described, "another emergency," he determined where Jason was and then went to the MapQuest Web site and read Jason the directions over the phone.

This father knew exactly what he thought he was supposed to do for his son. He wanted this to be an opportunity for his son to figure out for himself how to get to where he wanted to go, but his plan didn't work out. The dad ended his story by saying, "Maybe the only way to help Jason to grow up is not to answer the phone." Parenting is an inaccurate science, a mixture of success and failure, just as becoming a grown-up is for our kids.

Children must start thinking about their resumes before they are old enough to ride a bicycle. Typical schedules for college-bound teenagers include an impossible number of activities, such as wrestling, varsity baseball, weekly volunteering at a homeless shelter, religious school, and guitar lessons, all accomplished while maintaining a solid academic average. A soccer dad observes, "Kids don't play sports so much as work at them. They start athletic 'careers' before kindergarten and soon swear fealty to a single sport" (Lindsay 2002, p. 74). This hectic pace can continue into college, with swim practice at dawn, classes, school newspaper, school government, and work-study. Such a demanding program can have the opposite effect as well, where young adults don't want to participate in anything that may return them to such a frenetic world. This overscheduling provides little time for children to reflect or think about what they are doing and what they want.

Another duality is that twentysomethings grew up experiencing overinvolved parents who often did not have the time to spend with them during their teen years because so many parents were working. Our twentysomethings are the first generation of latchkey children. As a result, in the contemporary two- or single-parent family, time is at a premium. Parents make their children the center of the universe during the limited time they are together. We have bought into the palliative expression "It's the quality, not the quantity, of time" spent with our children that often makes the difference. Ellen Galinsky writes in her book, *Ask the Children: The Breakthrough Study That Reveals How to Succeed at Work and Parenting,* "Both the amount of time and what happens in that time matter. These aspects of time with our children cannot be separated" (1999, p. 309). In spite of this, many of us have tried to create "quality" time, something virtually unattainable on an everyday basis.

Often there is a discrepancy between how our children are treated at home and their experience outside of the home. Many find it difficult to go into the outside world where they are not recognized as the center of the universe. One mother told us a story about accidentally leaving her cell phone on while making a presentation to her company's board of directors. It rang in the middle of the meeting, and her daughter insisted on talking to her about her own job interview, even though the mother cupped her hand around the phone and kept whispering that she was in the middle of a presentation. It was as if her daughter couldn't believe that her mother couldn't stop what she was doing and instead attend immediately to her needs.

Another mother tells the story of her daughter's unrealistic expectation that the mother "of course" would be happy to take care of her daughter's baby when it came. This mother said, "The fact that I have a full-time job never entered the equation. I worked when my own children were small. I endured my own mother's referring to my children as her 'orphan grandchildren.' Why would she think I would stop working when her baby came?" Parents may unintentionally contribute to their children's unrealistic expectations.

We overinvolve ourselves in the lives of our young children and then expect to relinquish responsibility without warning or discussion. This change in parental behavior confuses adult children. They are used to parents who "scurry sons and daughters through their growing up years," and are not ready when parents "put on the brakes as they approach the finish line" (Ehrensaft 2001, p. 305). Some parents are ready for their children to be launched, yet their children require a transition before they are able to be independent without the same level of parental involvement.

One self-employed divorced mom has learned about the conflict caused by different expectations. She made a decision to give each of her engaged daughters a specific amount of money toward her wedding. She knew these boundaries would upset her daughters. However, her daughters' impending marriages made her think about her own future as a single woman. If she was going to take care of herself, she had to begin to set financial limits with her children. She said to us, "I set no controls on how my daughters could spend the money, and told them I would be happy to be a sounding board for any of their wedding ideas. Even though my daughters know I don't have deep pockets and an unlimited amount of money, they were still surprised at having to cope with limitations. Their own dreams for their weddings seemed more important than the reality of my situation."

When our children reach their twenties, many of us begin to re-assert our own needs. Our suspended priorities conflict with what our adult children may want. They may not like this change and feel unprepared to accept a more secondary role. As a result, they may be confused about what to expect from this new relationship. Again, our twentysomethings may look like adults but often want to be taken care of like children. Somehow, we are still responsible for the details of their lives.

Cheryl tells us that she and her husband feel like they are their daughter's "administrative assistants." She reports, "Our daughter is pretty independent. She drives around, manages her career and household. Yet she'll often call me and ask, 'What's Chris's address?' She doesn't know anybody's address, and she's not sure about the birthdays either. I've given her an address book with all of this in-formation. My husband has given her the pages, because he keeps a spreadsheet. We even have copies in the car. Do you know how many times she has called me for so-and-so's address? She says, 'One of these days I'm going to get the addresses.' And I think, what a novel idea!"

The transition from the teenage years to the twenties is not an easy one, and parents and children alike can be unprepared. Par-ents are ready for their adult children to be more independent, yet they still want to be involved in their children's lives and don't ex-actly know their place.

DR. SPOCK MEETS MR. SPOCK

The transition to adulthood is not simply a biological one; social, historical, and cultural constructs affect this developmental stage.

Examining the relationship among these constructs and their effect on twentysomethings helps us to understand our children's experiences. Our generation had a clear picture, a prescribed program for becoming an adult. We had only a few choices available to us, especially as women. One mother said she felt that she only had two career choices, teacher or dental hygienist. Today, twentysomethings have a broad range of career options—a full buffet versus just a continental breakfast! It should come as no surprise that many twentysomethings are having difficulties making choices. Many of them feel unsure about what they want to be or do.

Not only were the 1950s considered to be a more innocent time, parenting was more prescribed as well. From infancy until adulthood, cultural norms involving rules of behavior determined how children were raised. Some of these norms dictated when they were fed and how often, whether they could use a pacifier and for how long, when and how to comfort children, and precisely what to expect during each stage of development. It was not until Dr. Benjamin Spock published *Baby and Childcare* in 1946 that parents had permission to comfort their children on demand. This book is so influential that it is now in its seventh edition.

Arlene, a 58-year-old mother of two adult children, remembers, "My mother was amazed at the freedom I had to comfort my daughter in 1973." When Arlene's mother had her babies from 1947 to 1952, she was told not to pick them up when they cried; she hadn't read Dr. Spock in time for her last baby. She wanted to give her daughter a pacifier, but her doctor told her not to let the baby have one. Arlene's mother felt sad that she couldn't comfort her children, especially since one of them had been colicky and cried all the time. She always marveled at how confident her daughter was in soothing her granddaughter whenever the baby was upset. The early baby boom generation made different parenting choices. Within their historical and cultural context, they reacted to the rigidity of their own upbringing by creating a new set of rules.

For many, the 1950s were a time of great prosperity and optimism, "with limitless horizons" (Ehrensaft 2001, p. 312). We believed the world was our oyster. The 1960s' slogans "Do your own thing" and "We shall overcome" expressed our belief that we had the self-confidence to believe that we should follow our personal dreams and that we could correct past social wrongs. As parents of today's twentysomethings, we have extended our core beliefs and so-called counterculture values to our parenting. The world really is our oyster, and we have raised our children to feel like our pearls. In comparison, Jeffrey, a 51-year-old father, tells the story of how he applied to college without any outside guidance. What a concept! He did things on his own. Jeffrey's experience is in stark contrast to how overly involved today's parents are in the college admissions process. In his words, "We have been programming our children for years."

Jeffrey's parents, like many of his friends' parents, are the children of immigrants. They are first-generation Americans who believed that going to college would ensure their son's success. Jeffrey's parents begged him to go to a local state school and even offered him a car if he would do so. He was set on going faraway to a "real rah rah" university, one with a famous fight song that Jeffrey remembered singing in his high school music class. Jeffrey never visited the school and saw no photographs of it. He knew nothing about the school, except that *Playboy* magazine had featured it as a major party school. This was credential enough for him. Jeffrey took no SAT prep courses and received no assistance with any of his essays. He just filled out the application and waited. Jeffrey was accepted in the spring. He packed his own trunk, made his reservations, and flew, for the first time in his life, alone, to college.

Jeffrey often compares this experience with how he guided the education of his own children. From early in high school, he and his wife deliberately opened doors to opportunities that would help their children stand out from the others when they applied to college. They opened doors that Jeffrey never knew existed and never thought about when he was a young adult. Jeffrey hired a college counselor to smooth out the family fireworks that often occur when a normal 16-year-old high school junior will not focus on his future. The counselor counseled Jeffrey's son and edited his essays. The family took college trips to decide what kind of environment best fit their son. Jeffrey said he wanted to give his children the benefit of his knowledge of how the world works.

Jeffrey is not unique. Many of the parents in our focus groups are proud and happy to provide such guidance to their children. However, they are also aware that this involvement creates a very different twentysomething, a young adult who feels dependent on his or her parents' skills to navigate the adult world. Today's parents obsess about how to give their children all the opportunities they didn't have as children. This goal is not unlike their own parents' goals—to give them the financial security they never had growing up in *their* parents' new, adopted country. When this intense involvement suddenly ceases, many twentysomethings find themselves in a canoe without a paddle.

In previous generations, the pressure to comply with society's expectations directed young adults into a narrower range of acceptable options and life choices. Many married shortly after college or earlier and often had their first child by the age of 25. It was not uncommon for girls in the early 1960s to anticipate graduating with their "Mrs." degree. One parent recalls that after she had become engaged during the second semester of her senior year in college, her older sister had said to her, "Sherry, you just made it under the wire." Boys also felt the pressure to conform. One father recounts breaking up with his girlfriend of two years during their senior year because peers would assume they would marry after graduation if they continued to "go together." Delayed maturity and independence were not options for earlier generations.

HURRIED CHILDREN AND HYPER PARENTS

Today's parents assume the responsibility for molding their children into perfection. They are invested in wanting their children to make it in this world, even if that world is menacing and unsafe. It appears "as if we have created a generation of miniature adults deprived of play and, in the process, we have transformed children's formative years from a child's garden to a hard labor camp." Parents are "drill sergeants by day and fairy godmothers by night" (Ehrensaft 2001, pp. 304, 317).

Contemporary parents experience child rearing as stressful. They feel they are responsible for all of their children's positive *and* negative outcomes. When baby boomer parents were born, the dominant Western attitude likened children to plants that simply needed the opportunity to grow into healthy adults. Nature was considered the prevailing force in a child's unfolding. By the 1990s, children had been transformed into precious seeds in need of careful, prescribed, and consistent care from informed parents. The extent of parental involvement came to be seen as the principal factor in determining a child's outcome. As parents came to believe their actions alone could make or break their children's future, they became frantic. They accepted the notion that nurture had replaced nature as the most important ingredient in raising a child.

Diane, the mother of a 26-year-old son, laments the fact that "kids are so pressured for so many years to do things in order to get into college, especially in the big cities. Kids burn out from all the pressure. I think one of the reasons they're having trouble finding themselves is because they have to make so many decisions as young people, younger than they're really ready."

Joe responds to Diane's observation with the following story: "My son is an athlete. At one point, when he was only ten or eleven years old, he had to give up baseball, because his soccer coach forced him to choose between the two sports. He was only a kid. Why couldn't he play baseball anymore? Children are put into the position of making those kinds of choices before they are ready to do so. One of the consequences of this type of pressure is that people in their twenties just want some freedom from commitment and obligations, some relaxation, rather than planning or preparing for a career all the time. Children want time to just enjoy their lives."

Because we are so deeply invested in our children's competence, we overprogram our children. As parents, we are stuck on a treadmill, hoping to create a Renaissance child. Parents have become trapeze artists, juggling total involvement in work and total involvement with their children. Psychiatrist Alvin Rosenfeld says these are the same "hyperinvolved parents who get minivan fatigue from ferrying their kids to extracurricular activities and turned college admission into a competitive sport. They've convinced themselves they know how to lead a good life, and they want to get that for their kids, no matter what" (Tyre 2002, p. 4).

One parent of a high-school junior told us that he asked his friend, a college admissions counselor, to explain the requirements necessary for an applicant to stand out at his prestigious college. His friend replied, "I tell applicants, don't even think of applying if you don't have over fourteen hundred on your SATs, seriously play an instrument or a sport, and are fluent in another language." The pressure is tremendous. Many parents who are college graduates themselves would not be admitted now to their own alma maters with their high-school grades and SAT scores.

The parents of twentysomethings tend to be baby boomers and the first generation in their families to go to college. They have been focused on raising individual children who achieve, rather than promoting the well-being of the family unit (Doherty 1997). The accompanying expectations have raised the anxiety level for these children. Many adult children who spoke with us said they can't live up to their parents' expectations. Jason tells us, "My parents have higher degrees than I do. I will never be as good a student as they want me to be. I always feel that I disappoint them." Stacey says, "My parents have always pushed me to do better. If I get a B, they want a B plus; if I get a B plus, they want an A. I think this is about them, not about me. They seem so focused on my academic performance, and I have other things that are just as important to me."

In an article for the *New York Times* on the subject of children starting college, Barnard College president Judith Shapiro described the impact of these expectations on her students: "We are living in times when educational pressures on families begin when children are toddlers and continue relentlessly through the teenage years. Four-year-olds may face a battery of tests to get into a desirable preschool. As they face the college admission process, parents attuned to the barrage of media coverage believe that the best colleges accept superhumans . . . and strive to prepare their sons and daughters accordingly. One father even took a year off from his job to supervise the preparation of his daughter's admission portfolio" (Shapiro 2002, p. A23). After experiencing this level of involvement, twentysomethings can find becoming independent from their parents a difficult and treacherous process. By holding themselves responsible for their children's success, today's parents put themselves and their children in the proverbial pressure cooker.

PRESSURE COOKERS

The pressure cooker lifestyle leaves parents and children with little or no time just to *be*. As a consequence, many parents struggle to set limits and tend to raise more self-centered and indulged children, who feel a sense of entitlement. Parents who have insufficient economic means also feel pressure to provide their children with the latest consumer goods, such as athletic footwear and designer clothing. Soon after getting her citizenship, one mother thought very seriously about whether to bring her daughter to the United States during the girl's impressionable adolescent years. She remarked, "I am worried that much of my salary would go to keeping her dressed so she would fit in like a typical American teenager." As a new American, she is responding to the "status fad-crazed marketplace which extends its reach to very young children" (Mintz 2002, p. 4). Parents remark about constantly replacing a lost or broken Walkman, CD player, computer, or Playstation game. Everything is disposable, and most things don't last for more than a season.

Working parents give up most of their leisure time to be attentive to their kids. They don't want them to miss out on anything. In response to this practice, children give their parents mixed messages, as so aptly expressed by Anthony E. Wolf in the title of his book *Get Out of My Life, But First Can You Drive Me and Cheryl to the Mall?* They want their parents to chauffeur them to and from games and, at the same time, to "chill out." Our children still expect this level of commitment after they reach their twenties. One mother, Debbi, told us that she recently changed jobs to give her life more balance. Her three children are grown, the oldest is 29, and the youngest 21. Debbi deliberately chose to work part-time, three days a week. She planned to use the other days for herself. However, Debbi finds that she has less time now than she had when her children were younger and she also worked part-time.

In the past, Debbi had no trouble planning weekend getaways with her husband, finding child care for her children, and returning to work on Monday, refreshed. In her new role as the parent of adult children, Debbi has found herself canceling trips. She stayed in town when her son needed her assistance organizing the logistics of

his wedding and when her married daughter was in the neighborhood for a friend's wedding, even though she only had time to visit
with her mother for lunch. Debbi's three-day-a-week job, like most
part-time jobs, takes more than three days.

Debbi is surprised that she still feels like a pretzel, bending to
everyone else's schedule. When her children were young, she drove
the schedule; now Debbi feels like a parent-in-waiting. She thought
she could forfeit some of her salary to free up her time, the com-
modity that she had the least to give, but instead she finds herself
with less money and less time.

The stress of parenting twentysomethings can increase conflict
between moms and dads. One parent may be hyperfocused, determined to provide a safety net and give his child the opportunities he
never had, while the other parent may worry about being too engaged and creating a more dependent child. In some instances, parents hide things from each other to avoid constant battle. One dad
tells the story of giving his son money without his wife's knowledge.
The dad, Steve, permits his son, Aaron, to use his credit card to pay
for his son's health club charges. When asked why he doesn't share
this information with his wife, Steve's response is, "She thinks
Aaron should only go to the health club if he can afford it. I think
he works hard and doesn't make enough money to maintain a quality of life I can afford to give him." In this instance, the father is not
fearful of pampering his son, while the mother worries that continuing to indulge her son will hinder his ability to grow up.

Parents and adult children both struggle during this period. This
is the time when we must modify our behavior, perhaps slightly, to
allow our children to learn very important lifelong lessons. We
should emphasize those principles and lessons that will affect our
children's relationships and their ability to succeed in the world of
work. This is the time to evaluate the principles we teach at home
and consider how they apply to the world outside our home. The

ways in which parents approach this time is very relevant to how our children will experience and be able to apply these lessons.

It is helpful to draw parallels between today's behavior and tomorrow's goals. For example, one dad, Michael, said to his daughter, Laura, "You've exceeded your credit card allowance for two months, so I expect you to pay back the extra charges during the summer. I'm sticking to the budget for these reasons . . . But, trust me, you may thank me one day. You're going to find that if you pay attention to your excess spending now, it will serve you well when you graduate and you're on your own. I strongly believe it will help you to be more disciplined about how you spend your money."

Barbara said to her son, "Ben, it would be nice if you asked me how my day went every once in a while. It feels good to know that you're interested in how I'm doing. Plus, I think that when you partner with somebody, this is the way you should be with her." And Arthur told his son, Noah, "It really impacts my day when you are forty-five minutes late. I would have planned to do an errand before you and I met, if I had known you'd be late. I would really appreciate it if you would realize that my time is as important as yours. When you have a job, being on time will also be expected." It is important to draw parallels between what you are asking and how their behavior will affect their lives. Some of the confusion that twentysomethings experience may come from parents' not allowing their children to experience the benefits of being responsible and not holding them accountable for their actions.

STAND BY ME

Many twentysomethings experience their early twenties as culture shock. Until this time, their goals seemed obvious and the rules to follow to reach those goals easy to master. But after college graduation, when young adults enter the world of work, the merits of different career choices are often problematic, and the path from point A to point B is unclear. Life is no longer in linear form, nor does it have definite objectives. Twentysomethings worry that the choices they make will reverberate throughout their entire lives.

We can help our children by relaxing and coaching them while they become comfortable making their own choices. When twenty-something children find themselves overwhelmed by their choices, parents can tell them there may be more than one good choice. The important thing is to choose and put that choice into practice; this is how growth occurs. As parents, how do we help our children to make this transition as productive as possible? One answer is to instruct our children about the importance of going through a process when trying to reach a decision. Parents can teach their children about:

- setting a goal and creating an action plan;
- thinking about the decision, including time to reflect;
- applying what they learn; and
- understanding how their decisions will affect their lives as well as the lives of others.

Implementing such choices requires making a commitment, and honoring a commitment is part of being an adult. When they first confront this adult reality, many children are not yet economically independent. Their goals are no longer clear-cut, and the pathways to achieving them are blurred. However, how they make these early adult choices can positively influence their transition from school to work.

If we merely offer our children support and acknowledge that feeling confused is normal, we can help to make this period less overwhelming. How many times have each of us said, "If only I knew I wasn't the only one feeling this way, I wouldn't have felt so anxious"? It's the same with our adult children. Discussing the commonality of experience will help to lessen the anxiety and self-doubts that you and your adult children may be experiencing. One young adult, Alex, tells us that he was embarrassed that he didn't have it all together in his early twenties. For a long time, he would not discuss his self-doubts with his friends because they appeared so confident, and he assumed that they had it all together. When he finally shared his concerns with one of his friends, he found out that she and many others were experiencing the same fears and anxieties. He told us that it was a relief to realize that he was in such good company. Parents also can be comforted and increase their self-confidence by acknowledging and sharing their concerns with their friends.

Parents do their best parenting when they feel secure themselves. One parent educator has told us that when he teaches parent education to parents with young children, the biggest hurdle they face is dealing with their insecurity about knowing what is best for their children. Parent educators must remind parents that this self-doubt is normal. This attitude also applies to the parents of adult children. We all, at some time or another, ask ourselves, "Am I a good enough parent?"

Today's adult children are disillusioned with the twenties because, for many of them, these years are neither what they expected, nor easy. Because so many of their parents were married in their early twenties, twentysomethings feel they can't rely on their parents' personal knowledge or experience. Just as their mothers were the first generation to talk about and normalize other transition periods, such as menopause, twentysomethings are forging a dialogue that recognizes changing social patterns and identifies effective responses. If parents participate in this dialogue, they can normalize and lessen the anxiety for themselves and for their children.

Take-Home Messages

Renegotiate the parent-child relationship.

Build support networks with other parents of twentysomethings.

Be aware of society's complexities, which can overwhelm
twentysomethings.

Be mindful of the dualities of your adult children's youth.

Expect an extended period of dependence.

Have reasonable expectations for independence.

Understand that college does not fully prepare young people
for adulthood.

2. E-mail Versus Snail Mail

WHAT DOES THIS GENERATION LOOK LIKE? WHAT DO THEIR PARENTS LOOK LIKE?

> There's no place like http://www.home.com/.
>
> —*Ben Woodbridge, computer proverb*

Although the transition to adulthood is not a unique experience, every generation has defining qualities that affect the ways in which it lives. Twentysomethings are the children of the baby boomers. The oldest baby boomers were born in 1946 and are now in their late fifties and early sixties. Baby boomers grew up during a time of optimism and confidence, with two-parent families, and where the average 30-year-old white man could buy a mid-priced house with only 15 to 18 percent of his salary (Coontz 1997). Today, the age at which our children can support themselves, let alone support a family, has reached a new high (American Youth Policy

Forum 1998). Family patterns are changing
herent and strictly defined morality, and our
with unprecedented access to information.

This chapter covers some of the demogra
somethings and their parents. We examine so
and similarities between the generations and ide
that help to define them. To make sense of this ____, parents must
understand the economic, social, and psychological factors that affect
the attitudes and behaviors of their adult children. We also look at
the impact of the information age, occupational challenges and
choices, dating patterns and marriage, drug and alcohol use, the influence of the media, sexual preferences, sexual behaviors, and the
impact of AIDS.

Understanding the demographics of each generation and the in-
terplay of culture and sociology tells us much about the dilemmas
adult children and their parents face today. The number of twentysomethings is 39 million (U.S. Census Bureau 2000). According
to the 2000 census, one-fifth of all young people are children of
immigrants, and 26 percent of young people are Black, Latino, or
Asian, up from 20 percent in 1992. The proportion of children of
color is expected to be close to one-third of all children by 2005
(U.S. Census Bureau 2002). As our baby boom generation turns 65,
beginning in 2011, the elderly population will grow substantially. By
the year 2051, one in five Americans will be elderly (Fox 2002).

As parents, we must appreciate that our children live in the most
diverse society in U.S. history. Race, class, and culture affect the
ways in which our children interact with one another and how they
choose to live. Their options for developing friendships and forming
partnerships have created lifestyle choices that either were not
available to their parents or were not discussed. Work still needs to
be done, and our children have the opportunity to move civil and

ights to the next step. When parents understand the real
that their children live in, they can provide them with more
mpathy and insight.

Virtual Highway

Living in a world in which rapid change constantly revolutionizes
the process of gathering and receiving information has led, in many
ways, to a generation that expects instant gratification and has a
sense of entitlement. Being exposed to rapidly increasing levels of
information makes our children the most informed generation in
our history; however, they have less experience in exercising disci-
pline and focus. One lawyer told us that when she was interviewing
a first-year associate for her law firm, his only two questions were
"Can I leave the office early to ride my bike home before rush hour,
and how casual is casual Friday?" She said, "Who would ask those
kind of questions in an initial interview, when his starting salary is
more money than I made after twenty years of practice?" Because
everything is available instantaneously, this generation has little patience with delayed rewards. Their facility with technology also
makes twentysomethings less patient with their parents' reticence
to adapt to the twenty-first century.

The information age has made young people more suspicious of
adults as guides on the path to maturity because those same adults
are less comfortable with the explosion of technology. One mother
describes this difference: Phyllis remembers, "purple hands from
the ditto machines when I was teaching. If you couldn't get the
right book out of the library, then you were delayed in bringing your
students the most up-to-date information. In fact, I used to scribble
notes on yellow index cards because we weren't permitted to take
reference books out of the library. How I wish that we had Xerox

machines in the early sixties! Today, my kids can use the Internet and have access to hundreds of articles on the same topic. Not only don't they have to wait for anything, they don't even need to get out of their pajamas or leave their chair!" Parents of twentysomethings may still savor the feel of turning the pages of a book and browsing through the index to do research. Their children generally don't have as much patience for searching the library stacks and reading books to find information.

While the information revolution has created barriers between generations, other aspects of technology bring us together. The cell phone and Internet offer unprecedented opportunities for communication. This technology also has affected the expectations we have about how frequently we communicate as well as how we experience our adult children's lives with them in real time, even when they live in different cities. We have the capacity to connect with our adult children at any time, in every place—from an airplane on the tarmac, from the summit on the Grand Tetons, during happy hour at a bar, while walking to the subway, or when sitting in traffic. Lydia, who lives in the Midwest, refers to her son's cell phone as the "evolved Fisher Price" monitoring device, an adult walkie-talkie. In our focus groups, parents shared so many rich, detailed stories about the impact of the ability of adult children and their parents to communicate through technology. Some of their stories follow.

One father shared this story: "My daughter calls me many days on her way home from work, when she is relaxed in the car, before she gets home and reads the mail and starts dinner. She is much more focused during her commute, and we enjoy this time."

Another father told us about his son who lives in Seattle and sends his 93-year-old grandfather digital pictures of his new apartment, knowing that his grandfather will never be able to visit him. In this way, his grandfather can be a part of his new life in a way that was not possible before.

Pat, the 52-year-old mother of Abigail, told a story about cell phones and the consequences of not being able to reach her daughter. "The cell phone can be a great tool to stay connected, but it has its downside. While it is wonderful, the cell phone creates new expectations that can cause trouble, because you expect to stay connected to your children. If you don't hear from them or can't get in touch with them, you assume they're lying in a ditch somewhere.

"My husband and I went to Philadelphia for my sister-in-law's funeral. I spoke to Abigail in the early evening, because we were delayed in traffic and I figured she was going to be worried about us. When we arrived at my brother-in-law's home, we tried to reach Abigail again. There was no answer at her apartment and no answer on her cell phone. It is now two A.M., and still there's no answer anywhere. I'm convinced something happened because I can't get her on the phone.

"I finally resorted to calling her ex-boyfriend at three A.M. Of course, he had no idea where Abigail was. Finally, about three-thirty in the morning, I just called over and over and over again figuring that if she had fallen asleep, I would eventually wake her up with the phone. I was absolutely panicked. After my fourth attempt, a barely conscious Abigail moaned, 'Hi Mom, what's wrong?' I said, 'Sorry, sweetie. You know what a worry nut I am.'

"I think when you're used to being in touch so often, and you don't hear from them, your mind just goes off. Whereas, with my parents, I spoke to them every Sunday at ten-thirty A.M., whether there was something new or not. We didn't check in with each other on a daily basis."

Steven, a divorced father of two adult children, said, "When my son was in high school, I was happier with the cell phone than he was. I liked being able to call him ten minutes before his curfew. I would find out if he was near home and then be able to relax and fall asleep. My son felt like it was another way to exert control over him and would often refer to his phone as 'his dog collar.' I'm sure that there is some truth in that.

"Now that he is twenty-three, I have to renegotiate my relationship with the cell phone, and I find that I initiate fewer calls. However, to my surprise, I get calls all the time from my son. Yesterday, he called me from an exhibition football game because one of his favorite players was sidelined, and he wanted me to turn on the TV to see if the player was injured. Now the tables have changed, and I like being the one he calls. Even though our conversations are short and centered on sports or directions, I feel connected to him on a daily basis. I get to understand the rhythm of his life because he touches base so often. Maybe that's it: I'm home base, and he has to touch home before he runs around the bases again."

It's one thing to touch home base before moving on, but it's another thing to rely on your parents to tell you where the next base is located. One father, Michael, laughed when he told us a story about his 21-year-old son's first day of classes in his senior year of college. Michael was doing some paperwork at his desk when the phone rang. He answered the phone and it was his son, Matt, calling while walking to class. Matt said, "Dad, could you do me a favor? Log on to the net; go to the home page of my university, and then search for the location of this history seminar. I don't know where to go, and class starts in fifteen minutes." So, of course, Michael logged on, and with the aid of high-speed Internet access was able to get the information within three minutes. He told his son where to go and hung up, scratching his head and thinking about what just occurred. "Sure," Michael said, "I could have told him that I was too busy and that he needed to get all of the information for himself before he ventures out, but I didn't. I pay too much tuition to sit back and let him miss classes because he just can't get it all together. I also pick my battles. This one was just not important enough, and to be really honest, I like the fact that Matt knows I'm no farther away than the phone in his backpack."

Another father said, "The cell phone for me feels very much like an appendage. It's both an independence thing, but then at the same time, I almost feel like I've given my kid a digital chip, just like a tracking chip. My son calls from graduate school. He'll call on his way back from a class, just because he's got the cell phone in his hand and enough minutes to say 'Hi.' It's interesting to me, because in a way, it's kind of like that harness you used to see other parents have on kids in the mall. The kids may think they're independent, but the cell phone keeps them tethered to us; it's like an umbilical cord."

Numerous parents told similar stories describing the cell phone as an extension of them, something that draws their children physically closer and helps them to maintain connection on a daily basis. The connection to cell phones seems to be a universal experience for this generation. In a recent article, one twentysomething describes the cell phone as something she always wants near her. She said, "You take your phone even when you don't take your purse or your keys. It's like a little person" (Garreau 2002, p. C1).

Using the Internet also inspires stories. Paul, a first-time grandfather, said, "When our grandchild was born, we really liked getting the pictures, you know, getting pictures the day after he was born, on the Internet. It really made a difference. We saw him at infancy; we didn't have to wait. We watched him when he started to crawl; it was just amazing. Our son sent us a digital video on the Internet, and we were just as excited as if we were there. We actually spoke back to the screen saying, 'Stand up, Jesse, stand up.' It was so exciting."

Twentysomethings also tell how the Internet facilitates connection with family. Dan, a 23-year-old middle school teacher, said, "I really like instant messaging my eighty-eight-year-old grandmother in Cleveland. She wears a hearing aid, and it's hard for her to have a conversation, especially if more than one person is talking. When we IM each other, I appreciate how clear and insightful her thoughts are. I like this way of communicating better than E-mail because it's as if we're having a conversation." For Dan, the Internet helps to bridge the generational difference between him and his grandmother.

For another family, E-mail provides the best form of communication they have with their son, who has physical and emotional disabilities and lives in a group home. Karla, the mother of Alex, tells us, "Our son, who is twenty-four years old, discovered E-mail about a year ago. Now he writes beautiful E-mails. We hear from Alex when he takes a field trip; he'll tell us all about it. Alex will say, 'We went to the navy yard and saw a . . .' or 'We did this or that.' He also has E-mail pals. He never called us, and now he sends E-mails regularly. For someone who doesn't have mobility, like Alex, or for the elderly, who can't leave their homes, the Internet pulls them into the world. It is very powerful." The Internet cuts across physical challenges, age, distance, culture, and class.

As beneficial as it may be, the impact of technology also has its drawbacks. The same technological tools meant to make our lives easier are making them more complicated. Technology has adversely affected the family's ability to have uninterrupted time together. Cell phones ring anywhere at any time. At a family dinner of five people, each one might have up to three phone numbers where they can be reached. Multiplied by five people, numerous interruptions are possible. Ringing is ubiquitous; people even choose their own signature ring, such as "Take Me Out to the Ball Game" or the national anthem.

While all of these technological gadgets promised to free us from our offices and give us more time for activities and the people we love, such freedom is often illusory. With computers, the Internet, cell phones, PDAs, BlackBerrys, networking, digital photography, and fax machines, we are always one beep away from checking in or being pursued. All this access to information also results in twentysomethings' feeling disconnected and anxious.

One father shared how his daughter, Leslie, was feeling very apprehensive and unfocused about finding a job. Leslie's capacity to access information quickly was actually taking the place of her ability to be proactive and find a job. He said, "The idea of finding meaning in a career with value to her was overwhelming. Leslie needed a job, but was resistant to start just anything. She was looking for her dream job, and only that would do. I worried that Leslie was missing her day-to-day life. She spent hours hunting for jobs, researching careers via Internet and telephone, always searching for information she hoped would shine a light on her struggle to figure out who she was going to be when she grew up.

"I was pained by the constancy of Leslie's struggle, and wasn't sure how to help her. She finally said, 'Dad, this way of finding a job isn't working for me. I have to start living my life. So what if I make a mistake? My existential crisis doesn't have to get resolved as fast as I can access information on my high-speed modem. I need to step back, relax a little, and have time to think and process.'"

Leslie's dad responded, "That's right, honey. If you slow down, you'll find that you've got time on your side, not working against you." This father's life experience, as well as the years of advice he had given his daughter, helped her to gain perspective. Leslie realized that more is not necessarily better.

As Leslie's case shows, we are inundated with so much instantaneous information that it can be overwhelming. This generation has so much exposure to so many things at such a young age. Because of this exposure, parents tend to think young people are more sophisticated and more prepared for adult life than they actually are. We must remember that they still only become adults one step at a time. Because they have access to quick answers doesn't mean they make good decisions comfortably. Much of human life, especially with relationships, still proceeds at the rate of human emotion (Fraenkel 2001).

Karen, a 26-year-old accountant, explains her inability to slow down the pace of her life, even when she is having a meal: She talks on her cell phone while walking to lunch in downtown Chicago. Karen frequently balances her cell phone between her shoulder and her chin while she is ordering her lunch and sometimes talks while she is waiting for her food to arrive at the table. Although Karen attempts to end the call when her food comes, she often fails. Karen says, "I can't figure out how to be in the moment. My cell phone conversations may be about plans or appointments for the next day or week, or reviewing something that was done yesterday. I have one step in the past and one step in the future. I can't get a grip to be in the here and now." The technology that can alter the pace of human emotion has not yet been developed.

Digital Connection

Technology has transformed relationships and has been at the center of recent historical events. For example, the fax machine became the tool of democracy during the Chinese rebellion at Tiananmen Square. For the first time, a government without freedom of the press couldn't control the massive number of faxes sent from all over the world into China. In Indonesia, hundreds of thousands of civilians communicated via text mail to bring down the government. The Internet and cell phones also have had some unintended uses. One of the first things people did after the horrific terrorist attacks of September 11, 2001, was check in with one another, often via E-mail (Vogt 2001).

So many stories of heroism and compassion are told about the last phone calls made by passengers on the flights that were downed by the terrorists and by the workers in the World Trade Center. Men and women called their spouses to tell them how much they loved them and how much they loved their children. As a society, we were permitted to witness the most private and precious last moments of people's lives and to learn what was most important to someone faced with only seconds to say good-bye.

One twentysomething shared how she and her friends used E-mails as a way of letting one another know they were okay in the aftermath of September 11. Another twentysomething reached out to an ex-girlfriend who had worked in the World Trade Center. Jon recalled, "I found her E-mail address and wrote to her. She let me know that she was okay, and we decided to meet for drinks. We were able to resolve a terrible breakup and begin a new friendship." For parents who were desperate to know that their children were safe and couldn't reach them by phone, technology became a lifeline.

Risky Business

The risky behavior often associated with teenagers continues for some adult children into their twenties. Children have always experimented, but for adult children, risk-taking has become even more dangerous because the world has become a more violent place. Experimentation and risks have become life-threatening.

ALCOHOL AND DRUG ABUSE

Eighteen- to 39-year-olds account for almost two-thirds of the alcohol consumed in the United States (Wechsler and Wuethrich 2002). In an alcohol study of college students conducted by Dr. Henry Wechsler, director of the Harvard School of Public Health, many enlightening facts emerged regarding the amount of drinking on college campuses. Dr. Wechsler discovered that approximately 1,400 college students are killed each year as a result of drinking, and 500,000 more suffer unintentional injury because of drinking (Wechsler and Wuethrich 2002). Drinking games are a frequent form of social entertainment, and many parents are clueless about why their children participate in these games to the extent they do. Alcohol and drug abuse can play a negative role in your twenty-something's growing-up process, and it's important for you, as a parent, to watch for the signs of excessive use.

The alcohol industry develops messages that target young adults. The influence of these messages has not been lessened by harm-reduction strategies targeting the adverse consequences of drinking. For example, the ads are often stylish, intelligent, witty, and bold. Just think of the artistic and sophisticated Absolut vodka campaign. This so-called cool image is coupled with a relatively low price, easy availability, and messages that fail to mention alcohol's risks. Images and messages must be developed that will teach twenty-somethings about the danger of excessive drinking. At the same time, parents must be knowledgeable about the consequences of alcohol and substance abuse.

Many parents we spoke with revealed the pain of helping their children get off drugs and alcohol. Doris, the mother of a 27-year-old daughter, could barely talk about what it was like for her and her husband when they realized the severity of their daughter's substance-abuse problem. Their daughter couldn't hold a job, and she went through a series of destructive relationships. At first, they stopped sending her money, because she was using the money to buy drugs or alcohol. Doris said the hardest decision she made was to allow her daughter to sink so low because they wouldn't enable her habit. They went to Portland to take her to a rehab center. Her full recovery took almost two years. Doris said, "Whenever I think of that period of time, I have to fight back the tears. But what I know to be true is that we hung in there with her, and, on some level, she drew strength from that support." Many twentysomethings spoke about how much they appreciated their parents' involvement and support during their struggles with alcohol or substance abuse.

Doug, now 24 years old, started drinking with his friends when he was a sophomore in high school. He said he never worried about becoming an alcoholic, because there weren't any alcoholics in his family. During high school, all of his friends were either drinking or getting high. It just seemed like the normal way to have fun. However, Doug does remember his parents cautioning him about drinking before he left for college.

College was just more of the same, only alcohol became more accessible and everybody had fake IDs. Doug said, "Starting on Thursday, my friends and I would drink at our campus bar and then play intense drinking games on the weekend. I started to wonder about whether I was drinking too much when I couldn't remember what happened the night before. Were these lapses of memory blackouts?

"After college, there were bumps in the road, and my parents suggested I start therapy. With the help of a therapist, I gradually learned that I couldn't tolerate strong emotional feelings, so I drank them away. I know now that I was self-medicating. For me, my poison of choice was alcohol; for some, it could be drugs, for others— who knows! What helped me gain control over my drinking was therapy and my parents' honest reflection of what I was doing to my life. They realized something was wrong and supported me by getting me help."

As a result of risky behavior in their earlier years, adult children are at risk for psychological, social, and behavioral problems, including depression, substance abuse, eating disorders, and violence. Research shows that the key factor in protecting our children from these and other problems is connection to supportive adults (Wechsler and Wuethrich 2002).

SEX IN THE AGE OF AIDS

While we worried about getting pregnant, our children fear that having sex can kill them. For us, using birth control pills was enough to keep us safe. Michele, a 29-year-old administrative assistant, said, "Sex before marriage is the norm among my friends. For me, sex—although it's supposed to provide opportunities for intimacy and pleasure—also presents a big threat. I learned about AIDS even before I liked boys. From very early on, I learned that sex could kill me. I know I'm not alone; the threat of HIV/AIDS is always present; everyone is afraid of AIDS. As a woman, I am also saddled with the responsibility for protection against AIDS. I have to make sure my partner wears a condom."

AIDS has had a profound impact on twentysomethings and their families. Couples take blood tests to make sure they are not HIV-positive before beginning a sexual relationship. Today, intimacy requires a vigilance that our generation didn't need to have. Families have suffered the loss of children to this deadly disease. One mother tells the following story: "Our daughter, Abby, has had a difficult time growing up because her brother, Sean, died from AIDS when he was twenty-two years old. She was in denial while he was sick, and I think she was very angry with him for getting sick. Sean was the social one, the one to take charge. Abby was more reserved. But after Sean died, Abby took on his role; she took on those parts of him that were gone. His qualities became a part of who she was. Abby took it upon herself to fill in the empty spaces.

"Abby also started to act out a lot. She wanted to live at home and be taken care of after Sean died. I knew that moving home at that time would hurt her in the long run. However, I did let her come home for a while, but she had to pay rent. She is now getting on her feet, but going through her brother's death set Abby on a different path. I think that's true for other young people as well."

The possibility of AIDS has been a transforming experience for twentysomethings and their families. The idea that sex can kill our adult children has made intimacy different from what we experienced as young people. We didn't have to take tests in order to decide to sleep with someone. Our kids should. Regardless of their age, parents still have to intervene when their children are in danger, whether it is excessive use of alcohol, drug abuse, or having indiscriminate sex. Under these circumstances, we are still obligated to state our opinions, even if our twentysomethings choose not to listen. Emerging adults are most likely to avoid dangerous or destructive behavior when they are close to their parents. These connections help young people face today's difficult decisions and the serious risks to their well-being.

Rabbit Ears and Flat Screens

Twentysomethings have grown up with very different images to emulate. While we grew up with Donna Reed and June Cleaver, our children have experienced music videos and *Real World*. Twenty-six-year-old Lisa remembers fondly the day her family finally got cable. With cable, Lisa could watch uninterrupted music videos of Janet Jackson, Snoop Doggy Dogg, and Tupac Shakur. These images are as different from Perry Como, Dinah Shore, and the Partridge Family as possible.

Our children have grown up in a culture popularized and reinforced by mass media. Images of what to look like and how to act are everywhere, and twentysomethings often feel that their own status is determined by how closely they fit those images. Their lives as spectators began with *Mr. Rogers* and *Sesame Street* and continue today with reality television. Their experience is not only different from ours; television programming has changed dramatically since they were young children. They now have TV on demand.

Our generation believed that *Father Knows Best* and that *Leave*[ing] *It to Beaver* was a mistake. Many of us until we were adults didn't find out that Kitty, of *Gunsmoke* fame, was really a prostitute. The television shows of the 1950s and 1960s created a gap between the everyday realities of family life and our cultural images of how families ought to be (Skolnick and Skolnick 1997).

The media have such a powerful voice in today's society that they have created a more or less unified culture for our children. Television becomes a surrogate parent; it fills our children's time and minds with more information than any other source. As children, twentysomethings watched shows about both traditional and nontraditional families. They learned about the world and how to live in it from shows such as *The Brady Bunch, Different Strokes, The Cosby Show, The Wonder Years,* and *Family Ties,* while most of their parents' generation didn't have televisions until they were in early elementary school. Today, the average family owns three televisions, and children watch television 40 hours a week (Halstead 1999). Richard, a 51-year-old father of three, recalls falling asleep around midnight to the national anthem, which was followed by geometric test patterns on the screen. When his second child was born in 1982, Richard was ecstatic because cable came to his neighborhood. Richard endured watching *Grease* 19 times before his son was old enough to sleep through the night.

Barbara, a 52-year-old mother of three, said that the sanitized image of life as portrayed on television had a powerful impact on her: "I swear, *The Donna Reed Show* was a 'dangerous' show. It should be banned from reruns. I watched Donna, and I know that somewhere in my subconscious, I registered this family portrait as one that I thought was ideal. Donna had two kids—an older daughter and a younger son—and a professional husband who worked at home. She was so pleasant and wore dresses with crisp aprons to keep her shirtwaist clean and beautiful. All Donna had to do was untie one end of the apron string and she was ready to go from housebound housewife to . . . where? And that's where the image gets dangerous; big chunks of real life were left out. Where could Donna go? Did she even own a coat? Was there life outside her living room and kitchen?

"My life certainly didn't turn out like the images from the fifties and sixties. I'm a divorced, single mother raising my children with the help of their father. If I had followed Donna as a role model, I never could have imagined that I would be self-sufficient, working in a career that I'm proud of. I'm lucky. Maybe the complications in my life that presented me with 'sink-or-swim' situations gave me the opportunity to learn how resilient I am. I sure didn't learn this from the fictitious views of television family life of the fifties."

Whether art imitated real life or vice versa, family members in the 1950s and 1960s communicated only certain information to one another. It was important to keep up the image that everything was always okay. Our parents didn't share with us behind-the-scenes goings-on. In fact, hiding negative information became an art form. Communication was limited to happy times, logistics, and reporting. Children were included in discussions that only concerned them, so the image of *Happy Days* could remain intact.

Today's children have been less protected. Their television images range from MTV to *South Park* and *The Simpsons,* and movies vary from *Flashdance* and *Braveheart* to *Pulp Fiction, Boyz N the Hood,* and *Natural Born Killers.* This wide range of explicit images creates a very different childhood experience for today's adult children.

Dating Without Mating

The dating patterns of today's twentysomethings bear almost no resemblance to dating patterns of the past. They have more ways than marriage to pair off. The high rate of divorce and their education and careers delay forming permanent relationships. These were not our issues. Almost nothing stopped us from getting married. In the past, women waited for men to make the initial advance, sitting with trepidation by the phone.

Ellen, a 49-year-old mom, remembers, "When my girlfriends and I were dating, we used to sit and wait for the phone to ring. During the endless waiting, I would sometimes dial my boyfriend's phone number over and over again to see if he was home. If he answered the phone, I would hang up and stop calling. If I were dating today, I wouldn't be caught dead obsessively calling, because Caller ID would make me, and all my friends, look like stalkers."

Many twentysomethings don't really date; they seem more comfortable socializing in "packs." They are not confined to the phone or to being set up by friends. They have a number of other ways to "reach out and touch" someone. They can meet in singles' groups and bars, on the Internet, on theme cruises, and in personal columns. We didn't have these dating aids. In prior generations, young people paired off and married early. Careers and schooling were primarily concerns for men and did not delay marriage. Twentysomethings are less motivated to commit to a permanent relationship as early as their parents did, many of whom chose to marry right out of college.

The Internet has become the dating service of choice for many twentysomethings. They can maintain an objective distance and anonymity. One twentysomething explains, "Until I'm ready to meet him, I can keep whatever I want private. Our relationship unfolds a little at a time. I can commit when I'm ready, or not at all." It is common for twentysomethings to delay making decisions to commit. Virtually every kind of Web site is available—from those that identify prospective partners by religion or sexual orientation to those that focus on specific qualities such as a sense of adventure or high professional standards. Combing the bars and clubs is fine for meeting people and having fun, but less so for serious relationships. Twentysomethings go back to what they know—searching the Internet for the perfect mate. (By the way, our generation also uses the Internet to find eligible mates.)

As frustrating as the dating game is for parents who are worried that their adult children will never settle down, twentysomethings experience the disappointments of sustaining relationships first-hand. Extending childhood or adolescence into the twenties has adversely affected the ability of twentysomethings to establish committed relationships. Women complain that the pool of eligible guys who are willing to commit is small. Stephanie describes the challenge of trying to find a serious relationship: "There is a large group of guys who say, 'I'm not ready to grow up yet.' I know a huge number of guys, who, even in their mid-thirties, still want to play and are not ready to be involved in a serious way. My friend just started to date this twenty-eight-year-old guy who is a carpenter during the summer and a ski instructor in Jackson Hole in the winter. It's hard to maintain a relationship if a guy won't stay in one place for long." Monica agrees: "There are lots of guys who say, 'I'm not ready to settle down, you can't catch me. I'm exploring the world.'" While committed relationships are harder to come by, casual sex is still expected by both men and women.

There are still fewer pressures on men to make the relationship work. In our focus groups, men refer to marriage as "hard work," and they make the decision to "have fun" as long as possible. Men in our focus groups argue that women want the so-called "perfect guy." Both men and women discuss their frustrations with finding their soul mates, which are complicated by having fewer role models of what "good marriages" look like.

Baby boomers wanted to "settle down"; twentysomethings, either by choice or because of circumstances, are willing to spend the time looking for their soul mates. Our decision to settle down (and for most of us, it was in our early twenties) resulted in 50 percent of our marriages ending in divorce (Kalter 1990; divorcelawyers.com 2003). Perhaps in reaction to the high divorce rate of their parents' generation, twentysomethings are marrying later and living together before marriage more than their parents did. They date and marry cautiously because they have experienced firsthand their parents' or their friends' parents' failed marriages. The average age for a first marriage in 2000 was 26.8 for men and 25.2 for women, up from 24.7 and 22, respectively, in 1980 (U.S. Census Bureau 2000).

Twentysomethings want to find stable and happy relationships; however, because so many of them come from divorced homes, they are afraid to commit to one person. Scott tells us, "My parents were separated for one year when I was in seventh grade. They got back together when I was in the eighth grade to give their marriage one more try. It didn't hold. They finally got divorced when I was a freshman in college. Even though they waited until my brother and I were out of the house, the divorce still made me hesitant to be involved with just one person. I swore I wouldn't do to my kids what my parents did to me." As parents, we have to recognize the uncertainties our children face. Contemporary parenting requires flexibility and an understanding of why our children are making the choices that they do.

More and more twentysomethings are choosing to live alone or with people they are not related to, either by marriage or family. The number of women who have not married has doubled since the

1990 census. Another fast-growing group is single women with children (U.S. Census Bureau 2000). Unlike our generation, when getting married seemed to be the best economic hope for a future, twentysomethings see marriage as an economic risk. Both young men and women want to be economically independent and to be able to take care of themselves. Many women are no longer looking for Prince Charming to sweep them off their feet and take care of them. In fact, some women are preparing themselves for lives as single women and are also ready to have children on their own.

One parent gave her daughter the following advice: "My kids experienced the consequences of going through a divorce. My daughter learned that you can't depend on a partner to fill the bill, because she saw that it doesn't always work. That's why I always taught her you can really only count on yourself. She wanted to be an artist and majored in photography in college. I sat down with her to have a little talk. I advised her to keep up with her photography, but to take a more practical major. I wanted her to understand that she could do both. However, with a major in business, she could do anything she wanted. A business background would give her many more options. She decided to do both photography and business. She has always been able to support herself. She's already done the moneymaking thing, and she now can go back to her art."

Financial independence has become as important for women as it has always been for men. Moreover, women's goals to obtain financial independence have benefited the men in their lives as well. Women are contributing more and more to the economic support of their families. One mother explains: "My son, John, was talking about being a teacher. We told him he wouldn't make enough money being a teacher, and he needed to support a family. We told John that maybe he should be an engineer. John replied, 'Well, maybe I should marry an engineer.'" John is able to stay the course and become a teacher because there is a better chance he will marry someone who makes a good salary.

Both college graduates and those who did not graduate see living together as a way to, as one twentysomething describes, "sort out the good from the bad." Although they take the decision to live together seriously, they don't necessarily expect that the arrangement will culminate in marriage. A new relationship term has emerged as a result of these new circumstances of dating without mating: "24/7" (The National Marriage Project 2002). Lee, a 28-year-old medical resident, concurs: "You only know someone when you are with them day and night. Dating is more of a game, living together is more real." Many twentysomethings insist that, to avoid following in their parents' footsteps, cohabiting is a must. Now more than half of couples who marry cohabit before they make a lifetime commitment. The institution of marriage is one more example of the skepticism of twentysomethings about some traditions.

Many twentysomethings are willing to go against their parents' wishes because they feel so strongly about "trying it out" before marrying. Twenty-four-year-old Alexandra said, "I know how opposed my parents are to my living with a boyfriend before marriage. When Paul moved into my condominium, I first lied about it. Then my mom came over and wanted to see the new bedside tables that I had just bought. She started looking closely in the bedroom and opened up the closets. 'Whose shirt is this?' she asked. I answered, 'Dad's, you know how I love his old shirts. I just lounge around in them.' And I see that she's giving me that look, the one that says, 'Do you think I'm a moron?' Then I knew I was in trouble when she saw Paul's shoes. I couldn't say that Birkenstocks were Dad's shoes. Plus, my dad wears a size 10 and Paul is a size 13.

"So my mom figured out that Paul was living with me. I told her that it was just short term, until he found his own place. That story soothed her somewhat until he neglected to move out. But this was something that I needed to do for myself. I know my parents disagree, but they never say anything nasty or snide about it. They know their boundaries and never ask my boyfriend, Paul, 'When are you going to make our daughter an honest woman?' I realize that my choice offends their values, but I feel secure in my own values, and I am twenty-four years old.

"Even though my parents stayed together, I was surrounded by so many friends whose parents divorced. With all of those failed marriages, I thought it would be irresponsible to make a lifelong decision without knowing more about my relationship with Paul before marriage. My parents had one child and one on the way when they were twenty-four years old. I'm not anywhere near ready for those commitments, but on the other hand, I'm not casual about this decision to live with Paul. However, I am comfortable with it. Even though this is a hard dose of reality for my mom, she gave me one piece of advice that I find extremely valuable. She told me to make sure that, even though I was cohabiting, my condominium should remain in my own name. This is really good advice. I take comfort in knowing that when I choose to marry Paul, it's because, in my heart, I know that we are right for each other, not because we made financial decisions that seem too complicated to undo."

In contrast, Nancy, a 54-year-old businesswoman, remembers rushing back to her own college apartment to receive her parents' regular Sunday morning telephone call. She remarked, "I would never have told my parents that I was living with Allen, even when we were engaged to be married. When they came to visit, I would move enough of my things back to my apartment to make it appear like I lived there. I didn't confess my charade until I was the mother of two children. Now, with my own kids, we are very open about my son's living arrangement with his girlfriend."

The world of love and marriage is an extremely new one for our adult children, and it doesn't look like we'll be going back to our conventional ways any time soon. A lot of families are simply adjusting. One grandfather says it best. His granddaughter and her boyfriend were coming to stay with him and his wife for a few days. The grandfather called his son, Bob, and said he had to ask him a difficult question. Bob could tell that his father was very uncomfortable asking the question. The grandfather asked, "Will Sara and Jim cohabit when they stay with us?" Bob answered, "Only, if you're comfortable. If not, they can stay with friends." His 80-year-old father hesitated, and then responded, "With what I've had to adjust to in my lifetime, this is a piece of cake! And we do want to be cool."

Dot-coms Versus Brick and Mortar

JOB INSTABILITY

Twentysomethings tend to look for short-term rewards. They lack faith in the basic institutions and believe that long-term commitment is unlikely to produce dividends, as it did for their parents and grandparents. One twentysomething said, "My grandfather worked for the same company for thirty years and really did receive a gold watch when he retired. Today, so many companies change hands or fall apart that I can't assume that even if I do a fabulous job, I'll have job security." With a Bureau of Labor Statistics report in 2000 indicating that the average person now holds 9.2 jobs between the ages of 18 and 34, what he says really does ring true. More than half of these jobs are held between the ages 18 and 24.

Economically, the dot-com revolution has contributed to unrealistic expectations on the part of twentysomethings about earning a living. One mother reports, "My son was caught in the dot-com layoffs, and he was out of work in New York City for nine months. Because he was short of cash and without employment, we wouldn't co-sign a lease for him under those circumstances. So he found a way to stay there, rather than coming home. He paid rent in an apartment where several of his friends lived. He actually lived in a closet for the nine months to stay in New York. He told me, 'Ma, I couldn't even tell you or show you how I was living.' He didn't tell me this until he was able to get another job. I'm glad he didn't. A lot of his friends were laid off and were forced to go back to entry-level jobs." When the bubble burst, twentysomethings were the first to be let go.

Twentysomethings find themselves clinging to their jobs amid layoffs and hiring freezes. The recession has hit younger workers harder than their more senior counterparts, with unemployment rates for workers under 25 years old far exceeding the national average (Kersten 2002). As one twentysomething explains, "We were used to being wanted, being needed and courted. I have been sobered by a long period of unemployment after business school. I took an hourly wage type of job to keep afloat. This experience almost created a Depression-era mentality in me. I'm not stealing ketchup from restaurants, but that's kind of my outlook" (Emert 2002, p. G1). Twentysomethings are learning lessons from this downturn. They no longer take getting a job for granted, and they are dressing in suits, networking, and joining professional organizations to help them through the process.

Before the economic downfall in 2001, there were twentysomething millionaires in greater numbers than ever before (Lewis 2002). Many twentysomethings assumed they had a chance at making it big, and making it young. In contrast, many parents thought that chances had passed them by. One mother describes her own experience of looking for a beach house with a group of twentysomethings. Cathy says, "My husband and I have been looking for a beach house for twenty years. We stayed in a small house so that we could save for a second home. We met with a realtor and spent our

Sundays going to open houses that were filled with young couples our daughter's age. They were looking for houses twice as expensive as the ones we were looking at, and at bigger, much bigger, homes than we currently owned. It seemed amazing to me that they didn't have to save or have a goal in mind to work toward. They just happened to be in the right industry and made it big so quickly. I wonder how they can appreciate what they have without ever really having worked for it. Our way of earning a living seemed so devalued. Fee for service was no longer profitable. Until the bubble burst in the stock market, I was feeling very antiquated."

DEBT FOR TWENTYSOMETHINGS

Although the number of college graduates has remained consistent over the past few years, the number of unemployed college graduates has increased by 20 percent (Fleming 2002). Many of these graduates, who would normally be in the job market, are looking for alternatives, such as unpaid internships and graduate school. This reality keeps twentysomethings more financially dependent on loans and parents for a longer period of time, prolonging their inability to become self-sufficient.

Twentysomethings enter their twenties with debt, from both school and credit cards, in greater amounts and more often than ever before. The National Association of Student Financial Aid recently reported that the average student graduating from a private four-year college owes $15,000; for a public-school education, they owe $12,500. Some who go to a graduate or professional school can end up with a six-figure debt. In contrast, one father remembers paying $500 a semester to go to law school in the 1970s.

Some parents blame themselves for the credit card debt accumulation. Cindy says, "I never really taught my kids to manage money. There is some delayed learning going on. Instead of holding my son responsible for his debt, I bail out the overcharged credit card." Another dad shares, "My daughter's condo is really too expensive for her. I am willing to supplement what she earns in order to help with the payments. But then the other bills start creeping up, and I wind up helping her with those, too. I told her that I wasn't going to bail her out anymore. This was the last time. I know I have to stick with what I say."

Another mother tells the story of her son's coming home for a high-school reunion. She knew he wanted to discuss bills with her. She explains, "It was a busy weekend. His friends were all over the place. We had company all of the time. We were supposed to sit down and talk about the credit card bill. He left to go to the airport before we could have a conversation. When I returned home from the airport, there was a folder sitting on my kitchen counter with his bills in it. He expected me to help pay the bills. I, at least, expected a conversation."

Living above their means seems epidemic among twentysomethings, and our bailing them out is expected. When we were twentysomethings, many of us didn't have credit cards. For women, in particular, the cards were in our husbands' names, even if we were paying the bills. One mother remembers, "We didn't have credit card debt. If you were lucky, you had money in your checking account, and you wrote checks against it. And that was it." If we did overspend, going to our parents was not an option for most of us.

For some twentysomethings, leaving home doesn't mean their bills don't still live at home with their parents. Julia tells the following story: "I only recently developed a concept of money management. After I graduated from college I had a make-believe grown-up life with an entry-level job. I didn't have bills to pay, because they were sent to my parents' home. It was scary not knowing about money. It was a 'don't ask, don't tell policy.' I didn't have to face the bills. I knew it was bad, but I didn't want to deal with it. Now that

I'm twenty-seven years old, I've learned that you have to face it, because then you can learn the tools to take care of it. I now feel I have control, and I know what I need to do to make things happen.

"I know my parents were trying to help me. But I wish they would have taught me about money at an earlier age, so I wouldn't have had huge panic attacks when I didn't know how to deal with money. I would be up all night worrying how I was going to get along."

Stepping in to save our adult children when we know they are scared and clueless about money could have been avoided if we had taught them money-management skills earlier. Now, developing an appropriate balance between support and rescue is our challenge.

The Juggling Act

Currently, many twentysomethings feel they have to choose between work and family. Research demonstrates that twentysomethings are putting a greater emphasis on relationships, health, and balancing work and home life. They have watched their parents work 60-hour weeks and exist on 13 days of vacation (Fraenkel 2002). In just 16 years—from 1973 to 1988—the average workweek jumped from just under 41 hours to 47 hours, a 14 percent increase. Professionals are estimated to work 50 hours a week or more (Ehrensaft 2001).

One mother explained, "The women's movement told us we could have it all. We juggled more than we could handle, and our kids watched us struggle. I'm not surprised that they are making a different choice and looking for balance." One twentysomething told us, "I watched my mother come home from a full day of work and start her second job without going upstairs to change out of her work clothes. I don't want that same stress. While I'm preparing myself for a career, my generation's task is to make sure the workplace is more family friendly. Our mothers took care of opening the doors."

Life Ever After

The events that took place on September 11, 2001, are a collectively shared historical moment between parents and children. It was a common experience that may well define this generation in much the same way Pearl Harbor and the Kennedy and King assassinations affected previous generations. While the full impact of this tragedy is not yet known, we do know that our children's, and our own, sense of safety has been altered. A recent Roper Poll shows that the group whose confidence has been most undermined by the events of September 11 is people in their twenties.

September 11 and subsequent events have provided an opportunity for parents and children to come together and share, as one young woman explains, "a renewed appreciation for their families" (Moore 2002, p. 14). In a post–September 11 *Washington Post* article, a 25-year-old woman is quoted as saying, "I never thought at 25 our friends would write about witnessing the loss of thousands of lives . . . That at 25, we would want mom and dad to wrap their arms around us, stroke our hair, and soothe us and make us believe that everything is okay." Media and technology made it impossible not to feel a part of September 11. Perhaps it also created a desire for long-term, rather than short-term, rewards, and the need to develop and maintain stable relationships. Parents can't fix everything, nor should they be expected to, but they can provide comfort and reassurance based on their experience with tragedy and loss.

Take-Home Messages

Appreciate that access to technology can facilitate communication and connection.

Realize that contemporary health issues, such as alcohol abuse, drug abuse, and AIDS, have the potential to be life-threatening. Keep an open dialogue with your twentysomething about these enormous issues.

Balance the tremendous influence of the media and popular culture with communication.

Respect the fact that the dating and coupling patterns of twentysomethings are different from yours.

Juggling education and career is a challenge, but, at the same time, twentysomethings are more thoughtful about choosing their life partners because they are older and have more experience. They are also aware of their need to be financially independent.

Be aware of the adverse impact of the 2001 economic downturn on twentysomethings.

Understand that the events of September 11, 2001, are having both traumatic and motivating effects on our adult children.

3. The Way We Were

IS THERE A GENERATION GAP?

> They have execrable manners, flout authority, have no respect
> for their elders. They no longer rise when their parents or
> teachers enter the room. What kind of awful creatures will
> they be when they grow up?
>
> —*Socrates, c. 470–399 B.C.*

In order to parent our twentysomethings well, we must have an understanding of the differences and similarities between our two generations. Among the questions we must address are the following: How do we define a generation? What is a generation gap? Is there a generation gap? What common experiences connect our two generations? By applying the principles of generational theory and examining modern family life, we hope to enable parents to better understand and meet the challenges of parenting twentysomethings.

Different Starting Points—Us

We grew up in a stable and certain world. The United States was dominant; we experienced unprecedented wealth; we saw the end of polio and smallpox; the United Nations was established; and television brought us June and Ward Cleaver and Ozzie and Harriet Nelson. Our children have grown up in an age of constant change and virtual communities, including the development of the personal computer, CDs, DVDs, and video games; violence in schools and neighborhoods; early and easy access to drugs and alcohol; eating disorders; AIDS; the post–Watergate era; the *Challenger* explosion; and the Internet.

Change creates a natural tension between generations. However, as each generation matures, it shows a common concern for the well-being of its children. Involved parents are preoccupied with common questions about their children. Do they have integrity? Do they have the heart to make this world a better place? Do they have the skills to be successful? Do they have what it takes to care for themselves? Committed parents worry about almost all aspects of their children's lives.

These are challenging times, but regardless of the time in which they raise their children—the 1930s, the 1960s, or the beginning of the twenty-first century—parents worry about whether their children will end up "going to hell in a handbasket." Parents are parents, and no generation gap should stop us from being appropriately involved in our adult children's lives.

As with previous generations, we too want to pass on wisdom to our children. It's not unusual for every generation to worry that families are not what they used to be. We look back to our childhood as being simpler and less problematic. We struggle with how to integrate our past and present lives in order to make the lessons relevant to our kids. As parents of twentysomethings, we have attempted to apply the values we learned as children and young adults to our children, who are moving targets in our rapidly evolving society. We must recognize that parenting is part of our own effort to achieve a sense of purpose, and in this exploration we must address some fundamental questions about the basis of maturity. What sacrifices did we make in our struggle for maturity? What sacrifices will our children be required to make?

During the twentieth century, it appears that each generation developed a shared identity and connection to the next when confronting a worldwide crisis. Our grandparents sacrificed material comforts merely to eat during the Great Depression. Our parents were separated from their families for years at a time as they fought and died to defend humanity during World War II, then lived with the constant threat of nuclear weapons during the Cold War. Our generation struggled with national divisions caused by the civil rights, women's, and anti-war movements.

Until September 11, 2001, twentysomethings had escaped the anxiety of a unifying national or international crisis that forced them to define themselves and to mature. It is too soon to determine the battles our children will be called upon to wage. However, we do know that the truths that emerged on September 11 will require millions of young Americans to make sacrifices they never could have anticipated.

Different Starting Points—Them

Every new generation believes it is more enlightened than its predecessor. Today, however, twentysomethings appear to be more disillusioned than arrogant. They are trying to master the world we have given them. In turn, we are concerned that they may not be able to accomplish the goals that we have set for them, through no fault of their own. They may be the first generation to be unable to attain a lifestyle comparable to or better than their parents'.

Our adult children grew up during the post–Watergate era. Their "youth was full of oil shortages, televised war and starvation, hostage crisis, AIDS, inner city decay, divorce, stagflation, political assassinations, and nuclear threat" (Miller 2002, p. 1). However, none of these events produced a "defining moment." Until the attacks on September 11, 2001, twentysomethings' experience with such events had been secondhand, through our stories about Vietnam and civil rights, and our parents' stories about the Depression, World War II, and the Cold War. Our defining moments are so strong in our consciousness that, decades later, their evocative power has not faded. Without their own defining moment, twentysomethings appear to us to be adrift. Rather than gaining strength and certainty of purpose from confronting their challenges, they seem to be reactive and cowed by political corruption, community dislocation and corrosion, and the corporate meltdown.

Facing an explicit threat to our way of life, we now find many of our adult children, for the first time, thinking about country, patriotism, mortality, and religion, and not taking either freedom or family for granted. However, this newfound awareness of their mortality and fundamental values does not mean that our adult children are about to adopt the same attitudes and conclusions that we did during the crises of our youth.

Baby boomer parents became empowered by wrestling with the complex issues of their youth. The crises of our youth made us stronger, indeed self-righteous. Until September 11, twentysomethings displayed edginess, weariness, and insecurity while confronting a seemingly unending list of intractable, but very personal, problems, including AIDS and drugs; latchkey adolescence without adequate supervision or support; unprecedented academic competition in school; step- and blended families (e.g., *The Brady Bunch*); and the end of lifetime relationships between businesses and their employees.

As parents, we have the opportunity and duty to help our adult children to perform their societal and international responsibilities. With the crisis at hand, the September 11 attack on our society and value system, we must teach them that, even in the midst of fear or even horror, there exists an all-too-rare opportunity to gain the certainty of purpose that stems from being forced to focus on the basics. Many personal stories emerged from our focus groups about the impact of September 11.

Carol, a 51-year-old mother of three, recalled, "My daughter was on the road near the Pentagon. She was on Route 110 . . . and the plane came right over her car, and the debris fell around her. She started screaming, 'Oh my God! Oh my God!' She's had some real difficulty getting past this trauma; it has had a major impact on her. My daughter lost patience with some of the decisions she was struggling to make and is more concerned with trying to live her life to the fullest now. She said to me, 'I better figure out how to enjoy my life, because I may not have a life tomorrow. I still see the plane diving into the side of the Pentagon. I can hear the deafening noise and sometimes smell the smoke in the air.'"

This catastrophic moment has awakened our adult children from their natural, but in their case prolonged, self-indulgence of childhood. It has made them more interested in historical events, including our own experiences as children and young adults.

Another mother, Frances, said, "I know nine-eleven affected my children, too. They all arrived at my house after the tragedy. I think the urgency for them was because my father was killed in World War Two, and so my children have known about my story, and my history, and the pain of losing a parent in a war. They were reminded about stories of my growing up in Liverpool, which was so badly bombed that my mother ran with us from air-raid shelter to air-raid shelter to keep us safe. They know my stories, and I think when the hijackers hit America, it brought my history back home. I have felt that my son, especially, seems to be a lot more verbal about his love, telling me often that he loves me.

"When my son went off to his trip in Germany, where my father is buried, he said, 'I really love you, Mom.' I think this disaster taught us the importance of remembering that every time you leave the house, you let your loved ones know how much you love them. You might not see them again. My son really understands that I never saw my father again . . . that my mother never saw her husband again.

"My daughter and I also talked about nine-eleven shortly after it happened, maybe the next day or so, and she asked me what the deeper meaning was of it all. I couldn't come up with an immediate answer. Instead, I told her that people need time to search for the deeper meaning of events such as these, or something along those lines. She said, 'I don't expect everybody to come up with an expla-nation, just you, Mom.' It's hard to have answers for our children when we have none for ourselves."

Sarah, a mother of two adult children, said, "You know, we had already been through losing my twenty-one-year-old son, Lenny, from AIDS. So I think we had already been looking for deeper meanings in things. I've always shared my spiritual experiences with my daughter, Molly, and with the rest of my family. I think nine-eleven probably didn't affect us as much as it did other people, be-cause I have thought about life and death for a long time.

"My son, Lenny, was sick for three and a half years. I went through that with him, and when your child is dying, in a way, you are, too. Life is very uncertain, fragile, and we already knew that. A lot of people I know were surprised that life wasn't safe. I mean, if you lose a child, that's about the most unsafe thing that can happen, and we had already lived through that. September eleventh was traumatic for all of us, but bad things happen every day, and all over the world, and you never know when it's going to be traumatic in your life."

While September 11 may forge a bond between our generations, we shouldn't lose sight of the differences between our world and theirs. We can't discount the difficulties they face from lesser events than September 11. The bursting of the tech bubble and the resulting economic downturn are real. Twentysomethings see their options reduced. Some are going back to graduate school because they can't get jobs. At the same time, we have suffered a reduction in our own resources. Parents who at one point could afford to help their adult children with financial support now must watch their resources more closely. It has become a challenge to explain to our adult children why our financial help is no longer available. Many of our children aren't prepared to take care of themselves or to do without.

"Talkin' 'Bout Our Generation"

We commonly define generations in 20-year cycles. Generational theory is a hypothesis that helps us to recognize that the qualities of generations occur in repeating patterns. In this theory, each generation is defined by the historical realities that surround it. Therefore, just as all the markers of our history are cyclical, so are the attitudes and characteristics of each generation, as it responds to, and creates, its own history (Strauss and Howe 1993). Strauss and Howe are authors of several books that explain the differences between the generations and how they affect history. Our American story resounds with wars, economic booms and busts, racial conflicts, religious and spiritual revivals, and technological progress. By viewing the baby boom generation and its adult children through this lens, we are able to see and evaluate patterns.

Boomers can be classified as *idealists* who, as children, grew up in an optimistic era with a general sense of well-being. America had just emerged from the Great Depression and won World War II to become the premier nuclear superpower. Our economy became, by far, the most dominant in history. The suburbs exploded with highways and affordable housing, and consumer spending surged (Strauss and Howe 1993).

In this environment of wealth, power, and self-confidence, boomer children were raised on the permissiveness espoused by Dr. Spock. With the advent of the birth control pill and greater acceptance of marijuana, many boomers experienced the excesses of the sexual revolution and drug use. Although it is difficult to acknowledge, our value system changed from one based on a sense of community to one based on narcissism.

The certainties of the post-war boom ultimately were undermined by a series of events: the Cold War, civil rights struggles, the Kennedy and King assassinations, and Watergate. As young adults, baby boomers entering college and the workplace in the 1960s and 1970s rebelled against many of the institutions they found stifling and corrupt. However, their failure to make fundamental changes left them conflicted, both committed to and disillusioned by our political system.

Baby boomers turned inward during the Reagan Revolution. The 1980s saw them abandon the flower power revolution to embrace solid middle-class values and an upscale lifestyle with enthusiasm. "Instead of marching," as one father remarked, "we decided to go shopping." Before we "burned out," our generation fought for social justice—protesting the Vietnam War; marching on behalf of civil, women's, and gay rights; and preserving the environment.

As with all previous generations, we have left our unfinished business to our adult children. Our preoccupation with our own individual upward mobility interfered with our efforts to achieve social justice. Our children observed the disparity between our rhetoric and how we implemented it—or didn't—and became somewhat cynical.

We boomers are self-righteous in our opinions. We believe we have cornered the market on moral imperatives. We tend to be judgmental and intolerant of dissent and disagreement. We have failed to implement the very truths that we held so dear in our youth. This failure exacerbates the differences between the generations.

Our adult children have grown up hearing us speak passionately about the importance of commitment but have seen us divorce in unprecedented numbers. They have heard us espouse the essential nature of tolerance and plurality, while we continue to live in segregated neighborhoods. We have tried to control every detail of our children's lives, thinking they should live each life event exactly as we would have them do. We present ourselves one way, while thinking of ourselves in another. We are forever young, with our identities stuck in who we were in the 1960s and 1970s. One father explained how, when he looks in the mirror, he asks, "How did this young person get in this middle-aged body?"

As middle-age, and mostly middle-class, adults we unwittingly have adopted a more traditional lifestyle. We forget what it is like to live with the uncertainties of childhood. Our children live in a world defined by ambivalence. Technology has created so many realities that there are very few fundamental truths. Neighborhoods and communities have given way to virtual communities. Families must also contend with the range of values presented on the information highway. These realities create a schism between the generations. We think we know what is right, yet our adult children are accustomed to uncertainty and ambivalence. Modernization has produced widespread confusion and alienation. Some twentysomethings shy away from the complexities of modernity by turning to the certainty and security of religious fundamentalism. For those who seek contemporary answers, the path to forming a clear identity and creating and integrating meaningful values is very challenging.

The World of Ambivalence

Ambivalence is fundamental to the twentysomethings' experience. These young people are members of what Strauss and Howe's generational theory refers to as the *reactive* generation, the generation that historically follows an *idealist* generation (baby boomers) (Strauss and Howe 1993). This *reactive* generation grew up in a world filled with freedom but coupled with chaos and confusion. Even though twentysomethings yearn for some clear path to follow, they don't blindly accept direction from the adults who came before them because of the ambiguity of our message—personal freedom versus fundamental values, and order and social justice versus materialism. Even adults in authority, such as parents, teachers, clergy, executives, and presidents, don't automatically receive respect because of their positions. We were willing to tear down belief systems and institutions, and, as a result, our adult children are less trusting of those who are in charge of the very same institutions.

When we explore the childhood family lives of our adult children, they were less than perfect. Many twentysomethings have experienced divorce and second marriages, resulting in blended families, step-siblings and half-siblings, single parents and multiple parents and grandparents. The women's movement, economic necessity, and materialism produced the two-working-parent family in unprecedented numbers. Children "went to school every day with house keys on a shoelace so that they could come home to find their own entertainment and snacks" (Miller 2002, p. 2). The risk of separation and the fear of divorce were ever present, making reliance on social order and family security problematic. These circumstances created chronic anxiety.

Many of the generational characteristics of twentysomethings that trouble us are probably a reaction to our failure to model reliable relationships for them. Their experience as children of divorce may explain why twentysomethings marry later and cohabit more frequently than their parents' generation did. In Laurie Graham's novel *The Future Homemakers of America* (2002), one of the characters describes this phenomenon: "She's in another relationship now. . . . That's what people were starting to have, instead of getting married: relationships" (p. 260).

One 25-year-old explains, "After my parents divorced, I never felt safe in relationships. Dating is exhausting after a while, and I never feel that I quite measure up. I learned that nothing is permanent, although that's what I keep searching for." These feelings of uncertainty create a need for safety, stability, and connection for many twentysomethings. This insecurity manifests itself as ambivalence and excessive caution before making personal commitments.

Twentysomethings grew up with very little faith in society's institutions. Historically, today's 29-year-old was born during Watergate, which burst any fantasy he or she could ever cherish about the integrity of the institutions that previous generations had been taught to revere. Parents were supposed to be in charge, but weren't able to control their own personal lives. Therefore, our children learned very early that nothing was safe: not family, not jobs, not institutions, not government. They refused to take our generation's interpretation of the state of things at face value and were left to figure it out for themselves. Our children were never able to feel there was a clear way to success, because the economy of the 1980s created economic dislocation, resulting in mergers, acquisitions, and layoffs.

The old world order of starting at the bottom of one company and working one's way to the top has become outdated. Paying dues is no longer rewarded with long-term job security. Twentysomethings have learned to value the short-term gain, and they choose short-term goals requiring them to switch gears, change jobs, and move on. Because they know they can't count on loyalty from their employers, the relationship among work, career, and life changes. This sense of uncertainty creates a feeling of impermanence and a shift in priorities. Twentysomethings are putting more emphasis on relationships, healthy lifestyles, and a successful balance of work and personal life.

Today's parents may not fully understand their adult children's insecurity and its impact on their lives. Take their music, for example. When we reflect on the effect of all this change, we can understand more easily the appeal of artists such as Madonna, a continually changing chameleon. Nothing could be counted on more than change. "Madonna always offered us something different. She might be the Virgin Mother or a sweet socialite or a strong single woman or a slutty boy toy or a devoted wife and mother. She was multidimensional and changing. Our reactive personalities yearned for the opportunity to take risks and create new worlds . . . in an always changing world that owes nothing to anyone" (Miller 2002, p. 7). This constantly changing reality causes twentysomethings to be more cynical, because it is hard to hold on to truth when the ground beneath your feet is constantly shifting.

Where's the Gap?

At the same time that the generations seem worlds apart, there are great opportunities for friendship and enjoyment of common interests. The cultural and political rebellion, so common to the experience of the baby boomers during the 1960s and 1970s, seems to be missing from the experiences of the twentysomethings we interviewed. In many ways, they share similar interests and aspirations with their parents. We live in a time when mothers and daughters shop for the same clothes and Madison Avenue uses Beatles music to sell Nikes and cars.

Both boomer parents and their adult children watch *The Sopranos, Sex in the City, That '70s Show,* and many of the reality shows. Hallmark sells cards inscribed "To my Mother, my best friend." Most young adult children can come home with a tattoo, blue hair, or a modest piercing without fearing a parental explosion. Nowadays, the lines delineating a distinct youth culture from the prevailing adult culture are disappearing rapidly.

We may no longer be living in an era in which children necessarily will rebel against their parents by becoming alienated and rejecting their families. Generational conflicts in the American past emerged as a phenomenon of the age of immigration, when parent and child embodied real collisions between the values of the old and new worlds. Stan, a 49-year-old dad, remembers, "I always felt like my parents were kind of remote figures. They didn't really relate all that well to me, and they sure didn't have a clue as to what I was thinking. I think it's because of the way they grew up. Life was tougher for my folks; they didn't have money, and they lived through the Depression and World War Two. My parents were the ones that had to learn the ropes, because my grandparents' cultural context was entirely outmoded and different from theirs. I feel like my kids are more in touch with me, and I'm more in touch with them. I definitely feel less of a generation gap than I did with my parents."

Phyllis, a 56-year-old mother of two adult children, reflects, "We are so tied into our children. Maybe our parents were not tied into us in the same way because they were so different from us. The differences gave us something to rebel against, something to walk away from, not to want to be like. This increased our independence. It's harder to walk away from us. Our children look at our lives, and they look pretty good. It's harder for both of us to separate, and more difficult for our children to create an identity separate from ours."

Common Ground

It may be that baby boomers' difficulty in accepting their age also has something to do with compatibility with their children. Baby boomers prize youth and continue to define themselves through memories and music. Thirty years after they first gave voice to their experience, the most successful musical groups or artists on tour are still the Rolling Stones, Paul McCartney, Billy Joel, Elton John, Crosby Stills Nash & Young, James Taylor, Bob Dylan, Tina Turner, Patti LaBelle, and Aretha Franklin. These aging boomers outdraw Eminem, Britney Spears, and other contemporary performers. These oldsters' concerts are filled with aging, graying boomers yelling and singing lyrics memorized decades ago and still dancing in the aisles, and their adult children are there as well.

Our orientation toward youthfulness creates a comfort level with our own adult children. It gives them the confidence that they can rely on us for opinions about a movie, concert, or cultural event. Twentysomethings assume that we can connect with them and will happily talk about their experiences with us.

In contrast, baby boomers surrounded themselves with politics, music, clothing, values, and a sex- and drug-oriented lifestyle that their parents often found frightening and alien. Every aspect of youth culture seemed to develop in opposition to the values and lifestyles of mainstream America, which incorporated most of their parents. Boys grew long hair when it wasn't fashionable. Girls went braless when their mothers still wore girdles. We watched sexually explicit movies and listened to music that advocated drugs and un-restrained sex. "Mr. Tambourine Man" didn't just play music, and "Lucy in the Sky with Diamonds" was not about an engagement ring. "Never trust anyone over thirty" was more than a slogan; it was the watchword of a generation.

Judy, a mother from Norfolk, Virginia, said, "I can't imagine call-ing my mother and father at midnight to ask if they saw *The Joy Luck Club,* but my daughter needed to connect with me imme-diately after she saw the movie. Oddly enough, or maybe not oddly, I had just seen the movie and knew just how she felt!" Adam, a 25-year-old accountant, calls his father Sunday night at 10, right af-ter *The Sopranos,* to discuss the nuances of the show. In response to this ritual, Adam's dad said, "I had no desire to call my parents to discuss the characters in *The Godfather* thirty years ago."

Susan, the mother of 23-year-old Michael, said, "Michael burns me CDs of his favorite alternative hip-hop groups and mails them to me. I would never have dreamed for a millisecond that my parents would be interested in the Grateful Dead or the Rolling Stones. Last week he left me the message 'The new Springsteen album is great, Mom, you'll love it.'" Most of the personal stories that de-scribe today's adult children's connection with their parents through television, movies, or music end with the parents saying, "I never would have thought to call my parents like my child calls me."

CULTURAL ADAPTABILITY

Our institutions have proven to be adaptable to challenges to their basic values, whether they are political, economic, social, or cul-tural. Rather than trying to defeat or destroy alternative beliefs or lifestyles, our system absorbs them, embracing what is most valu-able and pushing to the margins what is most extreme. The result is a society that constantly transforms itself, continually adapting to the needs of its population, whether it's using baby boomer music for marketing products or recycling comedy routines on *Saturday Night Live* or *Comedy Central* to appeal to both baby boomers and their adult children.

As a society, we have become more tolerant, more flexible, and more inclusive about differences. We may not approve, but we are more accepting of our adult children's expressions of self-identity, whether it's a third ear piercing, dreadlocks, or a tattoo. Our experience with rebelliousness makes it very difficult for our twentysomethings to shock us. We realize that this, too, shall pass, giving our children less to rebel against. We find ourselves with a generation of twentysomethings that did not grow up adopting values or lifestyles just because its parents would disapprove. Indeed, as a generation, we approve of, or at least understand, the need to rebel.

Our children feel more connected to our values and culture, are comfortable relying on us for our opinions, and are more receptive to accepting our help and guidance during life's challenging moments. Connie, a mother of three daughters, said, "My daughters know I am always interested in what they have to say, and they know that I respect their input. We have always talked about everything. They come to me with their broken hearts, angst, and joy. I always say to them, 'I want to make sure we talk about whatever issue is confusing you so it doesn't get to be anything really big.' And we do.

"I also listen to their music; we can discuss art, exercise together, and try on lipstick at the makeup counter. I try to keep up. My parents would never have had many of the conversations that I have with my children. Last Thanksgiving, when my sixty-one-year-old brother came to the table, my eighty-nine-year-old mother still asked, 'Larry, did you wash your hands?'"

Parents who tolerate differences and practice flexibility may help to create an adult child who is more self-directed and is not defined by one rigid set of cultural mores or expectations. The conflict comes when we determine that it is time to "settle down," and our adult children are not quite ready yet.

There is an interesting analogy between the pre-boomer generation, born in the early 1940s, referred to as "rock and rollers," and today's twentysomethings. The rock and rollers grew up in the immediate post-war culture of unprecedented wealth, prosperity, and U.S. international power. There was little for the rock and rollers to achieve that their parents had not already mastered. The cultural icons of this group were Elvis; James Dean, the "Rebel Without a Cause"; and Chuck Berry. The object of their rebellion was the smugness and certainty of this period of economic nihilism as portrayed in *The Man in the Gray Flannel Suit* and Ayn Rand's *The Fountainhead*.

Like the rock and rollers, twentysomethings had just been born or they were toddlers during the Reagan Revolution, when the so-called Red Menace collapsed with the Berlin Wall, and greed became honorable. They grew up during the Clinton era, with its technology bubble, and the following recession, which pushed international affairs to the back of our consciousness. Like Oscar Wilde's analysis of the British and Americans, we are two generations separated by the same language (Bartleby.com 2003).

Reinventing Gender Roles

When baby boomers were in their twenties, feminism of the late 1960s and early 1970s profoundly transformed the lives of women in the United States. This struggle brought about upheavals in both law and the customs of everyday life and altered the consciousness of women themselves. The women's movement redefined roles, attitudes, and values, because the traditional definitions of men and women were so at odds with women's actual experiences. Women no longer would be confined to "girdles and poodle skirts, and stymied by a 'Men Only' economy" (Paul 2002, *The Starter Marriage*, p. 19).

The women's movement also uncovered knowledge about and appreciation for gender identity. Women joined together to fight for equality with men in employment, law, education, and politics. They began to realize many problems that seemed personal were common and due to social conditioning; we learned "political" was "personal." Communities were created, and these dialogues, or "consciousness-raising groups," were effective in compelling many Americans to rethink their lives. Today's twentysomething women don't have the time to meet with other women the way we did. This kind of support and camaraderie is missing from many of their lives.

Our generation became engaged in a common struggle to carve out a place for ourselves in a society that left many of us feeling, at worst, stranded and desolate and, at best, disillusioned. We wanted to connect with one another through friendship and family relationships and to be of consequence in the world. Our children watched us trying to have it all, and they did not see a pretty picture. Brenda, a 28-year-old department store buyer, said, "I watched my mother struggle raising me and my two brothers while juggling the stress of her more than nine-to-five job. I don't want that same amount of stress. I know when I decide to have children, I'm going to have to give up something. I am going to have to find a better balance." Jon, a 26-year-old publicist, adds, "I want to have kids and spend time with them. I don't want to kiss them goodnight after they're already asleep, like my dad did for my sister and me."

We didn't engage in this struggle perfectly or equitably. As with any struggle, there are compromises to be made. In addition to the choices we made to balance our work and home lives, our generation learned that gender is something people have in common and that it has an impact on the choices we make, the expectations others have, and how we see ourselves. The role of gender is also influenced by race, class, and culture (Shaffer 1996).

For many women of color, choices have been limited, and this reality has an impact on all important life decisions. The majority of women of color have always worked because their income was needed to maintain a standard of living for their families. African-American women are often the sole breadwinners in their families. Women of color still are frequently relegated to low-paying, dead-end jobs (U.S. Department of Labor 2000). For the baby boomer generation, as well as for twentysomethings, most women of color have either supported themselves or, as single parents, have been primarily responsible for the support of their families (Browne 1999).

Annie, a 56-year-old legal secretary, who is responsible for her children and her daughter's five-year-old son, remarks, "I have never had the luxury of simply having to care for my home and my family. I do what I have to do, like so many others in my community." Traditionally, African-American women took care of their own children and those of other family members; this concept of "extended kin" is a long-standing custom. But even for African-American communities, this is changing, and women of color are operating in more autonomous ways than they did in previous generations (Brewster and Padavic 2002).

Balancing work and family is made that much more difficult when there are limited support systems in place or fewer opportunities available. We fought for the right to work and still have families. Of course, for people without economic means, this option remains a choice for the privileged.

Both generations talk about gender and racial equality, but our shared language does not necessarily reflect either a universal understanding of that language or a common lesson derived from it. Our generation grew up at a time when women had few options, and people of color "knew their place." We devoted much of our youthful energies to addressing these inequities. Although twenty-somethings agree that they have benefited from the women's movement, many seem unaware of its history. One mother tells the story about talking to a young woman in medical school: Linda Shevitz, an education equity specialist at the Maryland State Department of Education, was talking to one of her daughter's friends about the celebration of the thirtieth anniversary of Title IX. The young woman responded with, "I know about Title IX. It gave girls the right to participate in sports, just like the boys." Linda explained that Title IX encompassed much more than just athletics. To make her point, Linda asked the young woman how many women were in her medical school class. The young woman answered, "Sixty percent are women." Linda smiled and reminded her that this transformation was the result of Title IX and the struggle for educational equity for women. Unfortunately, this history is frequently taken for granted.

Today's expectation that a "woman's place is in the House, Senate, and Oval Office" did not just happen; our generation fought to make this a reality. The little girls who wore T-shirts in the 1970s with this expression silk-screened on them may be tired of hearing how indebted they should be to their mothers' generation. But, at the same time, twentysomethings need to understand the vigilance that is still necessary to maintain their options and choices and to move ahead. Happily, many of the rigidly defined gender roles we grew up with no longer apply to today's twentysomethings.

The women's movement opened doors, but there is still work to be done. Ellen, a 26-year-old teacher, said, "Having choices is worth all the confusion. I'm happy as a teacher, but I like having the choice to be one. We have so many more doors open to us than our mothers did. It's also easier to get where we want sooner. For my mother's generation, even if they finally got to where they wanted to go, it was so much harder for them to get there. They had to fight for everything. I remember when my mom went back to get her Ph.D., her mom was so angry with her. Like, what could she be thinking when she already had children? Isn't that everything?"

In addition to more job and career options for women, their contemporary relationships have changed. Without the rigidly defined gender roles of the past, our adult children's relationships are very different from many of their parents'. Certainly, both young men and young women today expect to have an equal partner. However, this equality creates its own stresses. Equality has produced logistics issues. The mobility of twentysomethings requires that partners negotiate their career moves when they involve either geographic relocation or long-term commitments. It is no longer unexpected or unusual for young men to give up their jobs to follow their wives or significant others to a different city.

Ross, a 27-year-old, told us, "I was happy living in Philadelphia with my girlfriend, Amy, who was finishing her MBA at Penn. I was working for a local ticket broker handling sales for all kinds of major sporting events. It was a dream job for a sports nut like me, but I knew that it wasn't a career. When Amy finished her degree, she got a job offer from Microsoft in Seattle. At first, I was reluctant to encourage her to take the job because I couldn't imagine moving across the country to a city I never even visited. Plus, I don't drink coffee and love the sunshine, so why would I want to move to Seattle? But, ultimately, the offer was too good to pass up, and I knew, because I was committed to the relationship, that I had to make this move.

"For months before we moved, Amy felt guilty and nervous that I was making such a sacrifice for her, without a job or friends. But we both understood that it would have been unfair for me to try to persuade her to pass up the opportunity. Amy's work is as important as mine." The assumption can no longer be made that the woman's career automatically defers to the man's.

This shift in gender-role expectations requires that both young men and women must learn skills for the home and skills for the workplace. Mothers no longer are solely responsible for nurturing and taking care of the children. Twentysomething men are increasingly focusing on the family, and fathers can now be seen changing diapers in the men's room at restaurants and shopping malls.

Wanted: A Sense of Belonging

Not until the events of September 11, 2001, did twentysomethings share a collective experience that challenged their formerly autonomous way of life. They were a generation of individuals without any reason to rebel against the institutions that, in decades past, had disillusioned their parents. Why would they rebel against the institutions in which they never had much stake to begin with? Unlike their parents, who gained a sense of political power engendered by the anti-war movement, twentysomethings aren't disillusioned with belief systems or institutions. Twentysomethings haven't grown up believing in the infallibility of these institutions. Their detachment from the political system creates, instead, a sense of the futility and irrelevance of politics.

In contrast to the boomers' generational sense of unity and empowerment, the lives of twentysomethings seem fragmented and cut off from their community. Twentysomethings are even more mobile than their parents were. They often move to attend college, then move again to pursue careers. They change jobs more frequently to take advantage of opportunities or because they are laid off. They don't live in a community; they have to create one.

The television show *Friends* is an idealized version of the world of the twentysomethings. "In a world where most people live in scattered single-dwelling vestibules, *Friends* provides the ultimate fantasy. It's what we all long for—a social realm that feels a lot like . . . family. Most of us don't even know our next-door neighbor, let alone cook dinner with them. Most of us have to travel across town to see our friends; we can't just ring a doorbell across the hall and flop down on someone's sofa to watch a video together when we feel lonely. But we wish we could" (Paul 2002, *The Starter Marriage*, p. 82). Twentysomethings are searching for a sense of belonging, being part of a community. This is particularly difficult when they are leaving one world (school) and are not yet settled in the next.

The World Is Not Enough

More than anything, we embraced the right to achieve. We became the "me" generation. It is no wonder we concentrated on raising achievers. Susan, a 52-year-old mother of two adult children, couldn't agree more. She explained, "I think my parents' goal was just to raise me to be a good person and send me off. I should get married and have kids, and that would be enough for them. I think it's something about our generation. We want our kids to have so much. When I went to college, I went to a state school, and everybody I knew went to a state school. Now we are so invested in how wonderful our kids' lives should be. It feels so narcissistic on our part."

Judy, a 57-year-old mother, agrees with Susan. She added, "We feel compelled to provide our children with every opportunity that we can. We are very invested in our kids' being successful in a way that our parents were not. We are willing to do anything to make this happen."

Our children have shared our stress and have come to reject some of the imperatives that drove us. We ferried them from one activity to the next and sacrificed time for ourselves and time to be a couple. We expected them to achieve. Work and children came first, and marriage became a distant third. High expectations for career, achieving children, and marriage overwhelmed a couple's ability to cope at a time when divorce was losing its social stigma (Doherty 1997). Divorce became a more acceptable way for solving dissatisfaction. Even couples who have stayed together tell a similar story.

Barbara, married for 32 years and the mother of two adult children, shared this: "I'm glad we're still together, that we're still a family. My husband and I never had time to be together. Between our careers, the kids, and other family and social obligations, there wasn't any, as we used to say, 'quality' time to spend together. There are only so many hours in a day. I don't know if we intended for this to happen, but our children and careers were so much more compelling than anything else in our lives, including one another. Now that the kids have left, we finally have the time to try to recapture why we married each other in the first place."

Another long-term married man affirms this description of married life. Jim, married for 30 years and the father of two grown sons, said, "Everybody makes sacrifices in life. We all have to compromise. After homework, activities, work, chores, and other social obligations, being a couple had to suffer. It isn't that we didn't spend time together, but by the time we could, we were too exhausted to spend that 'quality' time. I don't know how we could have done it differently with both of us working."

Our generation fought for the right to be who we were, to take care of ourselves, not disadvantaged by gender, race, or national origin. We gained a tremendous amount in education and in the workplace. But, as with any fight, we had to let go of something. We taught our daughters, in particular, and our sons that we could have it all. We, and our children, have learned that this is impossible. We suffered losses and, as is usual between generations, twentysomethings wish to avoid our mistakes. What did we lose?

Fifty percent of us ended up divorced, and we experienced unprecedented and frequent depression and loss of community. We raised the bar impossibly high, not only for ourselves but also for our adult children. We gave them choices, to have children or not, to work or not, and to create different types of families. But among these options was, as one father puts it, the alternative between "the top of the ladder or failure." The challenge now for us as parents is to manage our own feelings when our children take advantage of these choices, and to support them when they make decisions different from the ones we think they should make.

Reconfiguring Families

Parents of twentysomethings grew up with one choice for creating a family—marriage or marriage. We lived in nuclear families, consisting of two parents and two to three children. Today's twentysomethings enjoy unprecedented freedom to define their own families. The lack of stigma attached to divorce and alternative family units creates both choices and challenges. Thus, while families continue to share common experiences, such as providing a sense of belonging, emotional and material needs, a sense of security, and a belief system, twentysomethings are being exposed to values and influences different from their parents. When they lack agreed-upon rules for marriage, child rearing, and other aspects of family life, contemporary families must define principles and values for themselves.

In this new environment, consisting of many types of families, critical and complex issues emerge about how to parent adult children. When divorce became easier, after no-fault divorce laws were instituted, couples no longer needed to demonstrate Draconian reasons for divorce, such as desertion, infidelity, or abuse. This change in the law made it much easier for couples to divorce, and many chose to take advantage of this.

The number of single-parent and blended families has mushroomed, and single-parent families comprise a significant percent-age of American households. The U.S. Census Bureau estimates that single-parent families account for 27 percent of families with children, a proportion that has been increasing rapidly over the last few years (Cohn 1998). A comparison of single-parent households by race/ethnicity indicates that this type of family is even more prevalent among communities of color (Federal Interagency Forum on Child and Family Statistics 1999). While it is statistically true that women head the vast majority of these single-parent families (16.6 million), the number of households headed by single fathers has grown from 1.7 to 3.1 million (Cohn 1998).

One 50-year-old psychotherapist who specializes in blended families told us about her experience with the decision to divorce her husband when their daughter was two years old. She said, "I'm still incredulous about how casual I was when I divorced Sam. I really thought that we could raise our daughter, Jenny, without her feeling the loss of us as a family. Jenny spent equal time in her dad's house and my house. We thought that, because we both loved her, it would be enough. While I know that we did our best to raise Jenny together, while living apart, I think it was so naive to discount the impact it would have on her. If I understood then what I know now, as a professional who works with divorce, I'm not sure I would do it. I don't remember what was so wrong with our marriage." Many twentysomethings would agree with this conclusion, and, as a result, they are much less casual about divorce.

With the increase in nontraditional family configurations comes new challenges for both adult children and their parents. One mother shared the following story about preparing for her daughter's wedding: "When I got married, there were two sets of parents, mine and my husband-to-be's. With my daughter, as they say, 'It is a horse of a different color.' There will be me, my daughter's stepfather, her biological father, and his partner. In addition, I have one daughter, and my husband has two sons. My daughter's fiancé has two parents and two stepparents, one brother, and two sisters. Trying to coordinate the wedding is like planning the invasion of Normandy! I know our situation is a little unusual, but I have been to too many weddings with multiple families to know that we are not unique."

The New York Times and *The Washington Post* are currently announcing gay and lesbian commitment ceremonies in their Sunday wedding announcement sections. In the *Times,* the heading of the section has changed from "Weddings" to "Weddings/Celebrations." This inclusiveness was unimaginable in the days of *Ozzie and Harriet.*

Life Today Is More Dangerous

We live in an era of high divorce rates, daily random violence, juvenile mass murderers, terrorism, economic instability, and a redefinition of *world order.* As has always been the case, we remember the past as a better time. We look back to the 1950s, 1960s, and 1970s with nostalgia. We idealize those times as simpler and posing fewer threats and risks. We forget that those times were marred by sexism, racism, and anxiety about family life, especially the threat posed by the new youth culture (Strauss and Howe 1993).

One dad, Frank, remembers how his older brother, John, looked and dressed so tough. John and Frank grew up in Brooklyn in the 1950s, when many of the boys congregated on the front stoops of their apartment buildings. Frank said, "I loved the way John rolled up the sleeve of his Fruit of the Loom T-shirt; it made his muscles bulge. When my parents weren't looking, he even placed a pack of unfiltered Camels in the sleeve. He looked so cool. Our big fear was meeting up with boys from another block, and our roughest weapons were brass knuckles or baseball bats. This is a far cry from children falling asleep while listening to gunshots in their neighborhoods or worrying about a sniper when walking to school. We just didn't have access to real deadly weapons. What seemed so threatening then seems so innocent now."

We have given our adult children the most dangerous world in history. In the past, the risk of violence was generally external, the consequence of war. Of course, there have been exceptions: the enslavement of West Africans, the slaughter of Armenians, the Russian pogroms, and Hitler's Holocaust. While we are experiencing increased threats from terrorism, in contemporary society the primary threat to our safety is domestic. The proliferation of weapons in society has replaced the 1950s' knife fights with a population that is better armed than the police. Today, mistakes can be fatal. Fistfights and honking a horn can lead to automatic weapons fire. Bill Cosby's son was killed when he agreed to change a motorist's tire. Children kill other children over a new jacket or backpack. Alienated youths kill their classmates and teachers. Anybody can make a bomb from liquid fertilizer. Who knew from this growing up in the 1950s and 1960s?

Unlike our children, many of us lived a much more protected life and had the luxury of remaining innocent longer. Every generation faces risks; for twentysomethings, these risks are life-threatening. A diet consisting of relentless messages and experiences that highlight our vulnerability creates general anxiety in our children.

Forming Partnerships with Our Adult Children

As parents, we know that child rearing is complex. The analogy of molding clay or writing on a blank slate to raising children is too simplistic. The parent-child relationship is a two-way process in which both of them try to influence and shape each other. This does not change when the child becomes an adult.

Parents in our focus groups presented the same message about learning from their children in a variety of ways. Judy, a 50-year-old mother, explained, "I feel like I learn a lot from my kids' experiences. They are teaching me things all the time. I don't know if my parents ever felt they were learning from me. If they did, they never shared it with me."

Susan, a 54-year-old mother, agreed: "I'm always learning from my children. I use the information they give me to help guide them. We are so much more emotionally honest with our children than our parents were with us. My husband and I are not afraid to communicate our mistakes to our children, or go through a process explaining why we are deciding to do things differently from the way we did before. We don't feel like we will lose our credibility as parents if we do that. I don't remember my parents admitting when they made a mistake about something they did with us." Each generation has the capacity to learn from one another. Indeed, it is the only way we can move forward.

Contemporary American families now come in all sizes and shapes and reflect cultural diversity. They are fluid and open to what each member of the family has to contribute. There are single parents, two working parents, stay-at-home moms, stay-at-home dads, couples with and without children, blended families, gay parents, and grandparents acting as parents. But, despite all this diversity, there is a striking uniformity in values. Even without the advantages of built-in communities and the rigid social norms of the past, today's families value stability, unity, rootedness, and continuity. This democratizing endeavor extends across families of all kinds and means that, whatever our differences, we are all involved in the age-old quest for relationships that are caring, supportive, and enduring (Gillis 1996). The American family is like a kaleidoscope, consisting of many colors and shapes, yet resilient, even if it is uneven or ragged around the edges.

Pay It Forward

As a result of September 11, 2001, we have heard a constant refrain among the parents and the twentysomethings in our focus groups: "We are trying to live without regrets." For a period of time, more mundane concerns have been given their proper perspective. We are a bit less concerned about the new sofa, the new car, and the plans for Saturday night. Our thoughts are dominated by new and bigger concerns: terrorism, Al Qaeda, classroom safety, holding on to a job, fear of getting on an airplane, and trying to figure out why some people hate the United States and all it stands for. The parents and adult children are in this together. They are forging an alliance to make sense of the unthinkable and working together for the common good.

As parents, we must evaluate both the lessons and wisdom that we can share with our adult children and the proper way to communicate with them. This latter concern may be the most critical. We must address issues as presented and avoid trying to mandate a definition of the problem and our solution. Adulthood is best defined by a number of characteristics, such as integrity, empathy, and persistence, not milestones. As parents of adult children, our challenge is to guide them in applying these characteristics to the process of becoming adults.

Take-Home Messages

Cultivate an understanding of the reasons for the similarities and differences between generations.

Learn to count on change.

Be flexible, listen, and avoid knee-jerk responses, as we are all ambivalent by nature.

Be aware of the expanding roles of young men and women and how these new roles impact the quality of their lives, both positively and negatively.

Be open to the kind of family your adult children may choose to form.

4. From *Sesame Street* to *Sex and the City*

HOW CAN WE USE WHAT WE ALREADY KNOW FROM EARLIER PARENTING EXPERIENCES?

Listen to the MUSTN'TS child,
Listen to the DON'TS
Listen to the SHOULDN'TS
The IMPOSSIBLES. The WON'TS
Then listen close to me
Anything can happen, child,
ANYTHING can be.

—*Shel Silverstein*

As we focus on communicating with and guiding our emerging adults, examining what worked in the past when our children were younger can be invaluable. Like all of us, our children are the sum of their individual life experiences, and sometimes we forget that they only have the accumulative knowledge of 20-plus years. In the early 1970s, many young parents craved knowledge about raising their children. We bought countless how-to books by authors such as Rudolf Dreikurs, John Gottman, and Haim Ginott; took classes; and joined parenting groups in the hope that we would better understand the challenges posed every day by our new families. We are a generation that couldn't read enough about every aspect of child rearing, from *Solve Your Child's Sleep Problems* to *Helping the Fearful Child* and *Keeping the Baby Alive till Your Wife Gets Home.* While our lack of knowledge about raising adult children takes us into new and at times uncomfortable territory, exploring earlier lessons we learned can help guide us through this latest developmental phase.

This is not a book about psychological theory; however, it is important to look briefly at the psychological concepts generally associated with effective parenting before we address specific issues about parenting adult children. Reexamining the lessons we learned while raising young children helps to guide us as they become adults. As parents, we confront similar questions and issues, but they are played out differently at various stages of parenting. As our children grow older, we should continue to seek answers to questions about where we draw boundaries, how we encourage independence while remaining connected, and when we pull back or push forward. In this chapter, we will help parents to recognize what they already know that can be useful when guiding young adults. We address the following questions:

- How has sex-role socialization influenced this generation of twentysomethings?
- How do we continue to build our twentysomethings' resilience?
- What constitutes maturity?

- How can we adapt earlier parenting experiences to meet the needs of our adult children?
- What lessons have we learned as parents up to this point?

"Free to Be You and Me": Sex-Role Socialization

Baby boomer parents influenced our twentysomethings by reading them picture books like *William's Doll* and presenting concepts such as "Take Our Daughters to Work." Susan, the mother of a 27-year-old daughter, remembers watching *Mr. Rogers* with her then-6-year-old daughter. Mr. Rogers was taking one of his friends to the pediatrician, who happened to be a woman. Susan told us, "I remember saying to my daughter, 'Look, Nicole, even Mr. Rogers goes to a woman doctor.' As I looked at Nicole's face, I realized that she didn't understand my point, and I wanted to bite my tongue. She had only been to female doctors, so for her, it was normal. For me, seeing a woman doctor was still a new experience."

Connie, a 59-year-old mother of two adult children, remembers a similar story: "Our female dentist and her female partner both recommended that my eight-year-old daughter see an orthodontist about her overbite. Just before we left for our appointment, I tried to explain what the new doctor would do. 'He'll look in your mouth and ask you to bite down,' I said. 'He?' my daughter exclaimed, shocked. 'You mean men can be dentists?'"

Early childhood experiences set patterns for adult behavior. During these years, children develop perceptions of themselves and form relationships with others. Children learn that society's perceptions of and expectations for them are often defined and assigned on the basis of gender. They learn that individuals sometimes may be expected to engage in certain types of behavior and to refrain from others, to possess certain skills and aptitudes, and to exhibit certain emotional characteristics based on their gender.

These expectations can be suffocating. Boys may be accused of being a "sissy" or a "mama's boy" if they are perceived as being too emotional or overly dependent. Girls may be accused of being aggressive if they appear to be too opinionated or strong. When a kid behaves "outside the box" according to predetermined gender-role expectations, they are exposed to ridicule and rejection. Such negative early experiences restrict children's ability to make choices free from gender-role expectations and impact their lives as they mature into adulthood.

Paul, a 27-year-old sales representative, remembers the negative impact of sex-role stereotyping. He recalled, "As a young boy, I was slow to learn how to throw a baseball. One day, my frustrated father yelled at me, 'You throw like a girl!' There was such a negative twist to that statement; I still hear it in my mind whenever I go to throw a ball. Needless to say, I never did learn how to throw very well."

Even though we have acknowledged for years the damaging influence of sex bias, our society lags behind this intellectual knowledge in practice. Sherry, a 55-year-old mother of 20-year-old David, told us, "I always said that if I had a boy, I would offer him the same opportunities that I offered my daughter. I had been pretty vocal, so when my son was born, my older sister sat me down and wanted me to promise that I would not make him the only boy in ballet class. I bristled at her ignorance, because I believed that both girls and boys should have the same choices. I reminded my sister that Lynn Swann of the Pittsburgh Steelers took ballet to enhance his agility and said that it helped his skills on the field.

"But, much to my own surprise, as David got older, I edited out some of his opportunities. I was not going to push my values on him and make him 'the only one.' I became pretty sensitive to wanting

David to fit in and wasn't willing to risk his being called names by the other boys because of ballet. I must admit my own bias surprises me to this day. I was a big talker who thought I would be unaffected by our culture's gender straitjackets, until it came to my own son. The truth is, I don't know what parts of David didn't develop, because I edited out what I thought wouldn't help him to fit in."

Many of us are finding that we are still affected by the restraints of cultural forces and stereotypes when we try to guide our adult children. Kyle, 29 years old, called his mother with the following complaint: "I don't understand why I can't have the same options as women. Why is it a given that I shouldn't consider trying to establish a balance between my career and family? I would love the option to stay home, work part-time, and have time for my kids. I'm frustrated that I'll look like a weak slacker if I'm not out there working like a caveman hunting for food. I wasn't raised like my girlfriend, Jess, who has all this support from her parents to find a satisfying job that gives her flexibility."

We believe Kyle makes an important point. There is the reality factor to consider, but we should guide our kids to make choices that work for them, regardless of whether they are males or females. Young couples need to sit down, discuss their values, and decide what is fair and what solution best meets their needs. They shouldn't have to make their decisions on society's expectations based only on gender.

Even though our adult children witnessed and were products of dramatic social changes in family life, gender expectations still remain a critical part of understanding their lives. Their mothers and fathers often worked, many children were raised by single parents, and gay and lesbian parents came out of the closet. The rigidly defined sex roles that baby boomer parents grew up with still exist, but they are more subtle for twentysomething children. Baby boomer parents had to counter iconoclastic media messages with honest discussion, diverse role models, and alternative experiences. We struggled to give our children opportunities to plan their lives based on their passions, abilities, and individual hopes and dreams, rather than on whether they were male or female.

Parents blazed the trail for their children, and, as a result, career choices expanded, family configurations evolved, and relationships became more equitable. It is no longer unusual for new fathers to change their children's diapers or for young men to move across country for their partner's new job. Women work in every field, and marriage is not their only dream. This freedom from specific gender roles is part of our challenge as parents of adult children.

By raising our children to believe that they can make career and life choices based on passion and interest, we must be prepared for the conflict between how we see the universe and what our children choose to do in this universe. If, after years of education and employment, our daughters decide to stay home with their children or our sons decide to be their children's primary caretaker, we have to support their freedom to choose for themselves. That is, after all, what we fought for. We certainly can alert our adult children to the necessity of protecting themselves economically, but the choice remains with them.

Continuing to Build Family Resilience

Why do some children thrive in spite of difficult challenges in their childhood, and why are some more resilient than others? Research on family resilience has noted that families can manifest certain strengths that protect their children (Moore et al. 2002; Sears and Sears 2002). Family strengths are measured by how family members interact with and treat one another, and what families actually *do* as a group and as individuals to support one another.

Regardless of their socioeconomic status or other contributing factors, families strive to develop positive resources for their children, which gives them the ability to adapt effectively to crisis and change, to demonstrate positive and open communication, and to build a stable and reliable environment. The following story demonstrates one family's ability to adapt to crisis and change:

Michele, a 27-year-old administrative assistant, said, "When I was eleven, my parents divorced. I was raised in a small town and was embarrassed that everyone seemed to know the intimate details of my parents' lives. I felt like people were whispering about my 'poor' mother or 'bad' father whenever I ran into someone who knew my parents. The situation was made worse in school, where I was one of a handful of kids whose parents weren't married. After my dad left town, we struggled with money, and I worked at a grocery store throughout high school.

"For a long time, I blamed myself for my parents' breakup. I always thought that if only I were a better child they would have stayed together. Thankfully, my mom was very candid and encouraged my sister and me to tell her our feelings. She never made us feel embarrassed or guilty after we poured out our hearts and laid our anger and sadness at her feet. She told us it wasn't our fault so much that it finally rang true. We knew that Mom appreciated how hard my sister and I worked around the house, and I also understood the importance of my contribution to my family's well-being because of my part-time jobs.

"During my senior year in high school, my mother encouraged me to apply for loans and attend the local community college. Like a broken record, she repeated, 'Michele, when there's a will, there's a way.' After two years, I transferred to the state university and graduated with honors. Now, I can savor my successes, and I'm happy that I'm not scared of hard work. Was it a struggle as a kid? Absolutely, but I think I turned out pretty well."

Michele's story demonstrates that children who grow up in families that exhibit strengths, such as positive communication, respect for one another, and personal responsibility, are better able to deal effectively with difficulties. Parents cannot prevent bad things from happening. But if children are raised with honest and consistent messages, they develop the resilience to meet life's challenges.

By providing children with sensitive and reliable care in early childhood, we create positive attachments, which demonstrates to our children that they are worthy of our care. The bond that children form with their parents and other loving caregivers as they grow has a powerful influence on their mental health and all future relationships. One 20-year-old said, "The measure of a resilient family is how it sticks together when its members don't need each other." This self-trust and faith in other family members build children's self-confidence in a way that can help them when they struggle with adversity later in life. Ideally, families reproduce themselves by raising children who are able to establish a stable and harmonious family unit for themselves.

Positive communication, which includes being warm, respectful, and interested in your child's opinions, is one of the most important family strengths. When our children were younger, positive communication was enjoyable and satisfying to parents and children, and it gave family members a sense of well-being. Every parent can recall soothing a fearful toddler with words of comfort that taught our children that expressing feelings is both reassuring and soothing. As our children become young adults, this same two-way communication in a trusting atmosphere is essential to encourage healthy relationships between parents and children. Erica, a 28-year-old lawyer, told us, "I called my parents sobbing when I broke off my engagement with James. I had been so mixed up about what to do and needed to sort through my feelings with the people I trust the most." Many parents have helped their twentysomethings recover from failed relationships or career disappointments by reassuring them that they will emerge from this period stronger and wiser. Parental warmth and support contribute to our younger children's healthy development and continues to offer additional benefits to our adult children. In fact, positive communication is essential to staying connected to young adults.

Providing children with a stable and reliable home environment enhances their feeling of safety and security. Children need to be able to count on the predictability of their parents' behavior, values, and personalities. If the structure of the family changes through divorce or death, children need to be reassured that, regardless of the shape or form of their family, the messages that they learn will remain consistent. Michele's mom's constant message that her divorce was neither the fault of Michele nor her sister gave Michele the confidence to believe in the truth of her mom's words. The family form changed, but the message remained consistent.

When our children are young, family dinners provide a perfect daily ritual that enables every family member to connect, express opinions, and be heard at the end of the day. As our children get older, the advice parents offer should reflect the same values learned around the dinner table. Parents who fear that they failed to provide their children with a stable and supportive environment can find some comfort in knowing there is no statute of limitations on emotional intelligence. Many parents gain wisdom about their parenting and experience less daily stress when their children are older. This new stage provides them with the opportunity to engage in important conversations with their adult children. We believe it is never too late to communicate love, support, and warmth to older children. People never stop growing.

Laying the Groundwork
for Adult Maturity

Children learn to have a good relationship with themselves by internalizing the healthy parts of the relationships they have with their parents and other caregivers. The objective of successful parenting is to help our children grow into functioning, well-adjusted adults. This continues into their twenties. When you're overwhelmed by your twentysomething and what feels like the boundless gap between the two of you, remember that there are strong foundations for you to rely on.

It's not too late to help your twentysomethings gain the skills they weren't able to learn in childhood or to assist them in enhancing the solid foundation they may already have. As you raised your child, you probably thought about nurturing maturity and fostering resilience. At this critical juncture in your adult child's life, you can continue to do some of the same things you did when your child was young.

SELF-ESTEEM: LIKING YOURSELF DESPITE
YOUR LIMITATIONS AND IMPERFECTIONS

When our children were young, we didn't critique their drawings before hanging them on the refrigerator. Instinctively, parents seem to understand that their appreciation and praise will build their children's self-esteem regardless of the quality of their drawings. This instinct is just as important to remember when our children are in their twenties. For instance, Sandy, the mother of 28-year-old Zoe, said, "My daughter has never sewed a thing in her life, and her first project was kitchen curtains for her apartment. Zoe's technique was crude, and it sure looked like a first effort, but I smiled and complimented her attempt when she proudly showed them to me." Sandy understood that this was not the time for constructive criticism. It was important for her to support her daughter's pride in her accomplishment.

Self-esteem is the basis for a secure sense of self. Low self-esteem can cause children to feel ashamed or have a false sense of superiority. Parents need to provide their children with personal experiences that validate who they are in order to give them the message that they are lovable and valuable.

SELF-AWARENESS: KNOWING WHAT YOU THINK AND FEEL AND BEING ABLE TO SHARE IT

Being self-aware permits an adult child to weigh the pros and cons of important decisions and avoid plunging into situations without realizing the consequences. Without self-awareness, a child may either "flake out" (dissociate) or get stuck trying to be perfect.

When our children were young, we enthusiastically applauded their dancing, singing, painting, and athleticism. Without restraint, we cheered them on, hoping they would feel confident about their accomplishments. However, when they are older, we want them to appreciate their strengths while at the same time accepting their limitations. It's one thing to support your sweet little star in the elementary school play, but quite another to respond well when your twentysomething says he or she is considering a life in the theater.

Barry, the father of 22-year-old Amanda, said, "Amanda wants to be a Broadway actress, and while I think that she's talented, I know that for everyone who makes it, there are countless other talented kids waiting tables in anticipation of their big break. I need to be supportive, but not unrealistic. I'm there to listen and point out things that I think are problematic. However, I don't express my opinion in a way that dampens her enthusiasm. I know this is ultimately her choice, but as her dad, I need to give her some perspective from my vantage point."

Barry understands that even though his daughter's chances of making it on Broadway are small, it is not his role to diminish her dreams. He can soften Amanda's fall, but as an adult, she ultimately must learn to gauge her success or failure accurately herself, not depend on her parents' opinions. A parent can point out some of the obstacles likely to be encountered along the way, while at the same time being supportive and positive. Parents need to guide their adult children by expressing their concerns, while accepting that the advice they offer might be disregarded.

According to psychologist Donna Shoom-Kirsch, "Parents should support their children as they learn to fly and when they don't make it, show them that there are other paths. When kids are little, they run ahead and parents rein them in. When they are older, we need to let them run, even if they hurt themselves. Our job is to say it's okay, and if it doesn't work, go out there again. Children have to learn from their failures" (Shoom-Kirsch 2002). This lesson remains equally important for twentysomethings.

BOUNDARIES AND INTERDEPENDENCE: BEING ABLE TO PROTECT YOURSELF AND TO STATE YOUR NEEDS, WHILE RESPECTING THE NEEDS OF OTHERS AND REMAINING CONNECTED TO OTHERS BY BOTH GIVING AND RECEIVING ASSISTANCE WHEN APPROPRIATE

Knowing how to maintain appropriate boundaries is essential to becoming a mature adult. This characteristic is integral to creating privacy, building personal integrity, setting protective limits for ourselves, and engaging in appropriate behavior with other people.

In dysfunctional families, boundary violations can produce barriers between family members or a complete disregard for privacy and personal space. In Terrence Real's book *How Can I Get Through to You?* (2002), he discusses how young adults re-create familiar themes from childhood and tend to treat themselves the way they were treated, because that's all they know.

Robert Frost said, "Good fences make good neighbors." The same message is true for boundaries. Finding a balance and setting limits are tricky. Appropriate boundaries permit us to voice our wants and needs without self-reproach. Stephanie, a 26-year-old physical therapist, said, "I always feel responsible for everyone else. Sometimes I don't answer the phone, because when I have plans for an evening I feel guilty excluding anyone who calls me. I actually avoid people, because I can't say no without feeling selfish. I wish I could just say what I want without obsessing how the other person feels. It's not that I want to be rude; I just want to be able to spend my time with whom I want." Stephanie illustrates that, as a result of poor boundaries, a child may be unable to say no without feeling guilty.

Parents can guide their adult children in maintaining healthy boundaries by showing them when it is appropriate to say no. They must also demonstrate the importance of good boundaries by showing respect when their adult children create boundaries for themselves. Josh, a 23-year-old graduate student, said he didn't want his parents to drop by his apartment unannounced. His parents let him know that they understood his request and promised to respect his privacy by calling before they came over. Appropriate boundaries require balance. All mature adults need to establish suitable boundaries for themselves and respect the boundaries of others.

BALANCE: BEING ABLE TO EXPERIENCE LIFE AND
EXPRESS YOURSELF WITH MODERATION

In this age of instant gratification, many children expect their desires to be met immediately. Expecting to get what they want when they want it results in a low tolerance for frustration. Reflecting on old parenting skills helps us to understand why our twentysomethings experience a high level of frustration, entitlement, and little patience. Jenny, a 27-year-old teacher, said, "I think I must have been a tyrant. My parents rarely said no to me, and I always knew that I could use my baby voice and flash my dimples to get anything that I wanted. After college, I worried about how I would be able to handle living on my own. I didn't think that I could pass up a cute pair of shoes without charging them to Mommy and Daddy. Trust me, I was stuck between my impulse to indulge and my desire to find some moderation. I hope that when I have children, I'll figure out when to say no as well as yes." Jenny's parents didn't do her any favors by giving her everything she asked for, even though they apparently were financially able to do so. Their inability to balance when to indulge and when to restrict made Jenny fear that she might always be too dependent on them and not be able to control her own impulses.

At the opposite end of the spectrum, parents who give their children too much responsibility may contribute to their children's growing up with a lack of understanding about their true needs and desires. James, a 25-year-old lawyer, is the oldest of five children. He said, "Both my parents worked, and I would come directly home after school to help my sister and brothers with their homework. There were countless times when I wanted to be out with my friends or just hanging out staying after school, but I knew my siblings needed me. I became very good at ignoring my own needs because I had no choice." At 25, James understands that he doesn't know how to get what he wants, because he didn't have the opportunity to think about his own needs as a child. He appears to be very mature, but on closer examination, James expresses some concern about being too independent, unable to know what he wants or to ask for help when he needs it.

Balance is essential. Without it, a child may be excessively dependent or inappropriately detached. Parents provide the initial framework for understanding how balancing independence and dependence impacts their children's ability to get what they want. Parents should remain available to provide their twentysomethings with a reality check by giving them honest feedback, such as preparing a new college graduate for an entry-level job although he or she might feel deserving of a higher-paying job.

Working Guidelines for Parents to Assist Children on Their Way to Adulthood

PERSONAL RESPONSIBILITY, NOT ENTITLEMENT

When our children are older, obviously we can no longer restrict them the way we might have done when they were very young. However, we still need to set limits for them. Joan, the 51-year-old mother of 21-year-old Stuart, said, "Give me a scratched knee anytime; dealing with my son now is much more complicated. Stuart has champagne taste when it comes to eating out. He will fall in love with a trendy new restaurant and think nothing of charging his meals and his drinks to us. It's usually a restaurant that we would think was too expensive for ourselves. Stuart knows that his spending is over the top, but he chooses to act irresponsibly and satisfy his immediate desire no matter how often we ask him to watch his spending. Last month we canceled his credit card. Now he will have to experience more of the real world by resisting his impulses and adjusting his spending to what his finances can afford. We hope that, in a way, he might feel relieved."

Many parents talk about making their children happy and are reluctant to set limits. Often parents feel insecure and worry about establishing limits because they anticipate their children's anger and the consequent battles. Young children push against their parents' rules, until sometimes it may feel as though limits have evaporated. When parents defer to their children, the children suffer because they fail to learn that they are not the center of the universe.

When the sky is the limit, a young adult may have a hard time exercising control. The ability to exercise restraint is critical to self-discipline and maturity. Limits have been and always are valuable regardless of your child's age. In fact, "failure to supply appropriate guidance and limits does a grave disservice to your child, and represents a serious breach in parental responsibility" (Real 2002, p. 93). Limits are the antidote to misplaced entitlement.

Children of all ages need to appreciate rules and limits and opportunities to develop personal responsibility. Again and again, the goal is to attain balance. Establishing open communication between the generations has many benefits. However, when parents make decisions based solely on what children want, the power shifts inappropriately to the children. When children have too much power, they develop a sense of entitlement, which may continue into adulthood. Accepting personal responsibility means that our twentysomethings hold themselves accountable and accept limits. Without limits, twentysomethings have a hard time accepting the world as it is.

EMPATHY, NOT INDIFFERENCE

Most people value empathy in their relationships because they associate it with sympathy, warmth, and compassion. Empathy is actually a more comprehensive concept: awareness of the impact of one's behavior on others and a sense of responsibility for this. Empathy is the foundation for mature relationships; it promotes connection by inviting intimacy. When 22-year-old Michael was young, he and his parents frequently visited his grandfather who lived in a nursing home. On Thanksgiving and other holidays, including frail Grandpa Harry in the festivities required carefully transporting him by wheelchair from the nursing home. Throughout Michael's early childhood, he watched his parents lovingly include his grandfather in their daily lives, and this sensitivity to the well-being of another had a profound impact on him.

Recently, Michael's friend, Peter, found out that his mother was seriously ill. Peter told Michael this upsetting news on New Year's Eve, while Michael was eagerly getting ready to go to a party. Instead of celebrating with his friends, however, Michael decided to have dinner alone with Peter. He told us that he knew how much Peter appreciated his comfort, illustrating perfectly the concept of empathy. Michael knew that his desire to party and have fun with his friends was not as important as providing support to his friend. In retrospect, Michael thought about how his mother always said, "You reap what you sow." We can safely assume that when Michael has a trying time, he will receive the same support he offered his friend.

For parents of adult children, an important strategy for obtaining empathy is to remember to be quiet and just listen. We believe this skill has lifelong application, what John Gottman, author of *The Heart of Parenting* (Simon & Schuster 1997), refers to as "emotional coaching." An emotional coach can allow a range of emotions, including sadness, anger, and fear. Parents who function effectively as emotional coaches are able to train their children to identify, understand, and tolerate complex feelings. Emotional coaches are more successful at setting and maintaining healthy boundaries. This kind of parent permits children to express emotions and is patient with them. The emotional coach doesn't try to fix the feeling but mirrors the emotion back to the child and, by doing so, facilitates the child's growth and sense of self.

This style of parenting is particularly helpful when responding to twentysomethings' frustrations and doubts. Janet, the mother of 24-year-old Scott, told us, "My proudest moment of parenting was subtle, and it required more restraint than intervention from me. Scott signed up to take the LSATs for law school and was extremely anxious about taking the test because he was a poor test taker. He had his heart set on getting into a law school located in the city that his girlfriend worked in. She had a good job and was not in a position to relocate if he had to leave Chicago.

"During the time Scott waited for the test score, his anxiety was so high it was palpable. If I could have made it go away, I would have intervened, but there was nothing I could do to help him to feel better. Scott was so scared that he refused to call and get his scores, instead waiting for them to come in the mail. Finally, he got his scores and they were just average. Scott was feeling pretty low and told me he was stupid. My instinct was to cheer him up and tell him exactly why he wasn't stupid, but I figured he'd just counter all my success stories with stories of failure.

"Instead, I sat next to Scott and repeated his phrase, 'So you're feeling stupid.' I really didn't know what to say and remembered learning that just sitting with a child's strong feelings could be consoling. I was surprised at how comforted he seemed, and that my ability to tolerate his sadness provided an opportunity for intimate conversation about his feelings of inadequacy."

Janet didn't tell her son how he *should* feel. She also didn't try to *fix* his problem. By listening to Scott's fears and frustrations and acknowledging how he felt, she showed him that he could sit with his sadness without having to act on it. Her restraint in this situation helped Scott to trust his own feelings and regulate his own emotions to get through his disappointment.

Many parents told us they learned to listen to their children and "bite their tongues" from early on. One mother said, "Besides biting my tongue, I learned how to end the conversation with my son before it became destructive. Now that he's older, I say, 'What you say makes sense, even if I don't feel the same way.' I believe that it's not what you say; it's what you don't say." Steve, the father of a 26-year-old daughter, said, "I pick my issues and I edit out much more now that my daughter is in her twenties. My wife and I have read many books on raising children, and the most useful information we learned is that listening and understanding without judgment is critical."

CULTURAL COMPETENCE, NOT INTOLERANCE

The concept of the United States as a melting pot is no longer quite apt. Cultural differences are currently seen as sources of strength. We believe that parents can honor diversity for themselves and their children by identifying common values and beliefs between different races and cultures. At the same time, individual differences should be valued and preserved.

In order to raise our children to function successfully in today's world, parents need to communicate an attitude of inclusiveness and tolerance. Positive attitudes toward people whose cultures are different from our own can only be demonstrated through words and actions, which provide our children with a model for developing cultural competence. Cultural competence is the essential ingredient that allows children to appreciate their own culture and use this knowledge to understand others. Cultural competence is a crucial ingredient in adult children's self-esteem, and it will help them to function better in the world, while contributing to further breaking down barriers.

Most of us did not grow up in a world as culturally and racially diverse as that in which our children live. Our challenge as parents, therefore, is to grow and change with the times, while supporting our children by modeling tolerance for others and speaking out against discrimination. Cultural competence is an essential skill for young adults in today's diverse world. As the parents of twenty-somethings, we, too, need cultural competence to enjoy the richness of the world in which we live.

Perfect Parents Need Not Apply

After caring for and guiding your child so closely for twenty years, it may seem that the rules you learned up to this point no longer apply. Remember, even when your child is twentysomething, you remain the most significant influence in your child's life. Support can be given to children of all ages; for example, "When a baby learning to walk takes a tumble, what to do? They set her back on her feet, applaud her progress and urge her to try again. Wouldn't the same understanding and encouragement work with adventurous youths only a few years older and just as eager to learn?" (Stepp 2002(B), p. C10b).

Parents should remember that the parenting techniques that worked for them while their children were young can still be useful in guiding adult children. One mother told the story of having taken her adult daughter shopping for what she called her "work trousseau." Friends and colleagues criticized her for being overly involved in her daughter's life. Her response to this criticism was, "I trusted my instincts and knew that these purchases were good for me *and* for my daughter. It was my pleasure to launch my daughter into the workplace." This mother used her experience with her daughter and her inner wisdom to parent her child, rather than succumb to outside pressure.

Part of the challenge of parenting our grown children is that we assume they are adults because they are physically large. Marlene is more than a foot shorter than her 22-year-old son, Robby. She said, "My son looks like he should command authority. Robby is not only tall, he's really big. I have to remind myself he's still the same boy who is scared of spiders. Sometimes he gets the broom and clears the spiderwebs before he walks through the archway on our porch." Twentysomethings still need the encouragement and support required by all children, yet the type of encouragement may differ.

To be effective parents, we need to understand the characteristics we want our adult children to acquire. These qualities include self-esteem, balance, respectful interdependence, personal responsibility, and empathy. Bearing this in mind, our first job is to provide emotional coaching and to maintain boundaries and support connection. This gives us the framework for our parenting road map. If these parenting structures and objectives are in place, we are prepared to assist adult children to develop into mature adults. We have to remember that children will integrate the qualities of adulthood incrementally. As one mother said, "Life is not a race."

We want our children to be free to spend these transitional years between 20 and 30 improving their emotional lives, rather than repairing them. In a perfect world, parents provide their children with everything they need to become successful adults. However, in the real world, parents can only provide children with the best possible childhood, which is never perfect. The truth is that our children don't need ideal or perfect parents; they need honest, loving, flexible, and thoughtful parents who recognize the value of staying connected to their children. Parenting certainly does not end when our children reach age 20; however, this transitional stage requires continuous connection coupled with a keen sense of restraint. With adult children, we must stand back and hope that much of how we have parented them during their childhood has been absorbed. The truth is, our children are a work in progress.

Take-Home Messages

Respect your adult child's attitudes and choices despite gender-role expectations.

Continue to teach your adult child respect for cultural differences.

Value your adult child's opinion.

Create a trusting atmosphere.

Remember that you are still helping to mold and support the characteristics of maturity: self-esteem, self-awareness, healthy boundaries, interdependence, and balance.

Expect your twentysomething to assume personal responsibility.

Continue to promote empathy in your twentysomething.

Become an emotional trainer by listening to your twentysomething express a full range of emotions, including sadness, anger, and fear.

Part Two

How Do We Renegotiate Our Relationship with Our Adult Child While Remaining Connected?

5. The Turning Point

HOW DO WE DEFINE ADULTHOOD?

The conveyor belt that once transported adolescents into adulthood has broken down.

—*Dr. Frank Furstenberg, sociologist and researcher*

I n previous generations, there have been specific markers of adult-hood: a career, economic independence, marriage, home, and children. For this generation of twentysomethings, many of these markers are elusive and delayed. Young adults attend school longer; change jobs more frequently; switch careers; and delay getting married, having children, and buying a home until they are well into their thirties. Because of dramatic cultural changes, these markers are not as useful a standard for either parents or adult children to measure the maturity we associate with achieving adulthood. Because social scientists and mental health professionals have not yet tackled this issue, parents and adult children are being forced to address measures of maturity in a vacuum, an anomaly in the information age. A helpful standard for measuring maturity must be based on emotional characteristics that can be associated with adulthood, rather than with the traditional milestones of past generations.

A Different World

The traditional values and rules of appropriate social behavior that we grew up with are now overshadowed, if not obscured, by media bombardment and pop culture. Both parents and their adult children are confused about what constitutes adulthood and how adult behavior manifests itself. This confusion is exacerbated by the fact that many of the traditional markers we have identified with adulthood are delayed because adult children live in a more complex world with more options from which to choose. The traditional markers are unconvincing because they no longer work well as signs of maturity.

In our society, young people are raised in a tumultuous, overwhelming, and, at times, baffling environment. Novelist Ann Patchett (2002, p. 19) wrote a compelling article about this confusion in a *New York Times Magazine* article entitled "The Age of Innocence." She explains:

> Gone are the days when we all kept getting older; the bar for youth is now raised with every birthday. College feels less like a center for higher education and more like a crazy sleep-away camp where kids can simulate the feeling of being on their own. People in their late 20's are still tapping Mom and Dad for cash. People in their 30's are moving home, and not strictly for financial reasons. It can be hard to see ourselves as grown-ups in a society that so readily accepts us as children.

We live in a society filled with contradictions. Children are having children. Children dress like adults. Young, semi-naked girls are exploited to market youthful clothing to adults. Tens of thousands of young children run away from home, grown children are living at home, and parents are supporting adult children in unprecedented numbers. Twelve- and 14-year-old boys are tried as adults, apparently based on the notoriety of the crime or the whim of the prosecutor. Adults in their forties, such as Michael Skakel, who was convicted of murder in 2002 for a 1975 murder, try to use the safeguards of the juvenile courts to avoid imprisonment for murder. Young people vote and serve in the military; however, these same young people are arrested for underage drinking. Young adults are not allowed to rent cars. They are prohibited from purchasing adult entertainment, but the U.S. Supreme Court guarantees them access to it on the Internet.

All of these inconsistencies and contradictions create a world in which values are relative, right and wrong are difficult to discern, and it is hard to define adulthood, let alone our expectations for reaching it. No wonder both parents and their adult children are confused. "It's so confusing to me," said 57-year-old Mary Anne. "On the one hand, I know that when my twenty-six-year-old son goes into court, someone's future depends on his competence. On the other hand, he still expects me to go on the Internet to find the cheapest airplane rates on Orbitz, and he doesn't know how to make rice. I ask myself, how is it possible this dichotomy can exist in one person?

"I go back and forth between feeling such pride in his accomplishments and wondering how I could have forgotten to teach him basic life skills. If I had realized how normal it is for these young adults to be competent in some areas and not in others, I wouldn't be blaming myself so much for his shortcomings. I understand why people aren't competent in all areas, but unlike when he was a little boy, now I never know what he can do on his own and what he will depend on me for. I didn't expect this split at twenty-six. Since I was diapering my children, running a household, and directing an alternative school at his age, I assumed, at this age, he also could manage his life without my assistance."

Deborah, the mother of Lisa, a 29-year-old union organizer in Washington, D.C., said, "On an unseasonably hot, early spring morning, I was waiting for my daughter, Lisa, to meet me at my house to go for a run. Lisa parked in front of the house and got out of her car wearing sweat pants and a T-shirt. When I saw Lisa wearing this steam-bath outfit, I said, 'Why are you dressed so warmly?' My jaw dropped when Lisa said, 'You didn't tell me to wear shorts, Mom.'"

Another mother tells a similar story. She said, "My daughter, Karen, who just got her MBA, was supposed to meet her father and me for brunch on Sunday morning. I was surprised to see her at my door an hour earlier than we had arranged to meet, because Karen struggles to be on time. She must have lost ten minutes somewhere along the way, because she's always ten minutes late. When I showed her the time, she said, 'You didn't tell me it was daylight saving, Mom.' This highly educated, responsible young woman was totally clueless that it was daylight saving time. When I gave birth to Karen, I never thought that I would forever be her timekeeper."

Some of our children have trouble with time, choices about clothes, and other everyday decisions. Regardless of how this difficulty manifests, they are all growing up differently from the way we expected and, if not different, certainly later than we anticipated. Without the advantage of conventional wisdom or expert advice, parents need more discussion and knowledge to establish some guideposts for this period. Until this stage of development is more clearly defined and understood, we have to learn from the wisdom of other parents and twentysomethings to give us some answers.

What Markers?

The traditional markers of adulthood are irrelevant to a contemporary assessment of adulthood. As the cost of college skyrockets, more students are forced to rely on loans, and the debt from these loans forces many twentysomethings to move back home with their parents after graduation. Jobs are also more difficult to find, job satisfaction is illusory, progress is stilted, and employer longevity is uncertain (Peterson 2001).

Job insecurity and unemployment also contribute to many of these adult children living at home for extended periods of time. As one focus group parent describes: "The job market has shrunk, producing a lot of anxiety for our kids. They have never lived through a crisis. They have pretty much grown up at a time when if you do the right things, bad things don't happen. They grew up during a 'golden' time." Many of them are unprepared to face the realities of today.

In the past, young couples were able to search for a modest house in a reasonable amount of time, bid on the house, and assume they might be able to move into their dream home someday. Today, the idea of a starter house is no longer realistic. The first-time buyer bids against others in frenzied competition, often purchasing the house without an inspection and for an amount above the asking price. Many twenty-first-century milestones cannot be gauged by the standards of the 1960s and 1970s.

Modern life offers many more sanctioned relationships for our adult children. Now commitments are more culturally diverse, combining race, religion, and culture with much greater frequency. In addition to traditional marriages, some couples commit without marriage. Gay couples "partner" and adopt children. Twentysomething is a stage for which there is no name; therefore, the markers of adulthood need to be redefined.

Making It Up as We Go

In 1950, developmental expert Erik Erikson stated that a transitional phase, a "moratorium," is needed by young adults before they take on adult responsibilities and career choices. In today's world, this incubation period is prolonged because between the ages of 18 and 30, students are spending more time in college and graduate school (Escoll 1987). In addition, twentysomethings are spending more time job-hopping, and they are delaying marriage (Steinberg 2001; Bureau of Labor Statistics 2000; U.S. Census Bureau 2000). As a result of this shift, society is becoming aware that twentysomethings represent a distinct developmental stage, young people who are neither teenagers nor adults, "a group that is identified as 'young adults'" (Escoll 1987, p. 1).

This period is difficult to define because it bridges and overlaps adolescence and adulthood and represents a significant stage of maturation for our children. This phase is very much a result of society's increasing life span. In past generations, when people died in their thirties, twentysomething was practically old age (Escoll 1987), and the preceding generation was mostly gone.

Unfortunately, there is no separate category for 20 to 30, such as the "terrible twos," to reassure parents. Such knowledge would put this period of transition into perspective. Parents could more easily understand that the twenties are merely one stage of development and, like other stages, their children will move through it. Unlike earlier developmental stages, thus far, mental health professionals have not yet characterized ages 20 to 30 as a distinct or unique phase of life. Most psychological literature offers nothing to guide parents past adolescence.

Though Erikson offered no direct information for parents of twentysomethings, his concept of transitional periods that our children eventually grow out of can shed light on this period. Erikson's ideas of "push and pull" (Erikson 1950) are appropriate for this age because, within each stage of life, there are inherent dichotomies that result in a push/pull dynamic. When parents accept the existence of these dichotomies, we can better understand why our children are still in transition during the twentysomething years.

Using the Characteristics of Adulthood as the Standard to Measure Maturity

The traditional markers of adulthood, such as holding a job, marrying, finding a home, or having children are merely circumstantial evidence of adultlike behavior. In the past, we have used these markers as indications of adulthood because it was easy to do; it required little thought or judgment. Since these traditional markers are ineffective measures of adult behavior in today's society, we must shift our perspective. It is the process of achieving characteristics associated with these traditional markers of adulthood that matters. Assimilating characteristics, such as empathy, integrity, and responsibility, is key to being an adult.

As parents, we should encourage development of these types of characteristics of adulthood. We also must expect twentysomethings to behave in adultlike ways, rather than accumulating adultlike trophies. If this process is successful, young adults will internalize the necessary behaviors and then achieve those markers that make sense for them.

Attaining adulthood is a developmental process. Through this process, twentysomethings develop skills that enable them to become more self-sufficient and resilient adults. Adulthood is not obtained by adding birthday candles to a cake. Further, although they are universal and timeless, the characteristics of adulthood will manifest themselves differently for each individual.

The Characteristics of Adulthood

If the traditional markers are not useful to measure maturity, we must look elsewhere for standards to guide us. This is not a loss, for, as stated, we believe these markers are more symbolic than real. They are proxies for a group of characteristics that one social scientist has called "emotional intelligence." In his book *Emotional Intelligence: Why It Can Matter More Than IQ,* Daniel Goleman states that emotional intelligence consists of qualities that include "self-awareness, impulse control, persistence, self-motivation, empathy, and social deftness" (1995). It is these characteristics that enable people to live successful adult lives.

While society tends to define success by career and earning potential, we feel strongly that emotional intelligence is the critical factor in a young person's becoming a competent and healthy adult. Without emotional intelligence, it is difficult to operate effectively in life.

As parents, we have all had experience with children who may not demonstrate their strengths in traditional academic environments but seem to have the wisdom of the ages. They show common sense, and they may be able to motivate themselves, persist in the face of obstacles and frustrations, empathize, and hope. One mother tells the story about her son, who had a number of learning difficulties in school and couldn't wait to be finished with college. Carol said that out of her three adult children, Noah is the one who always knows what she is feeling, knows the right things to say, and always asks how her day went. Carol said, "Noah not only asks about my day, he actually listens to what I have to say. His interpersonal skills are superior, and I know they will carry him in good stead for the rest of his life. My sweet Noah has an old soul."

Children need to understand themselves to be successful adults. They need to create an internal compass. One mother, Jeanine, a 49-year-old psychotherapist, says she'll always remember a certain professor's words: "If you only have a hammer in your toolbox, then everything you see had better be a nail!" We all require a full set of tools to cope with adult life. Emotional intelligence provides the skills to label and understand feelings that lead to greater self-awareness and the ability to establish and maintain positive relationships. Parents should teach their children to listen to their inner voices and to derive satisfaction from their core, rather than respond to the conventional wisdom of what constitutes achievement. When parents overvalue awards and tributes and encourage their children to strive for material gain, their adult children are often surprised at the emptiness they feel when they have acquired all the desired trappings. Emotional intelligence provides the tools to give adults a more balanced and gratifying life.

From our research, discussions with parents and adult children, and our own personal experience, we believe that the characteristics of adulthood include the following:

- empathy;
- personal responsibility;
- independence;
- financial responsibility;
- appropriate boundaries;
- respectful interdependence;
- mature relationships, including marriage or a partnership and perhaps having children; and
- cultural competence.

Parents can determine the extent to which these characteristics have been internalized by observing whether their children have established personal identities, developed reasonable and rationale judgment, have the ability to make independent decisions, behave in a purposeful and responsible manner, and are self-reliant and self-confident. These measures of maturity will come in increments, and they may be packaged differently from what we expect.

We met with many parents representing different circumstances: parents of gay children, parents of children with disabilities, single parents, and working parents. But an overriding principle transcended the diversity of our focus group participants: All parents want similar things for their children, including a sense of morality, spirituality, or faith and personal responsibility that provide the ingredients for becoming loving, healthy, successful, and happy adults.

PART OF GROWING UP IS HAVING EMPATHY AND THINKING ABOUT OTHERS

Empathy is more than understanding the feelings of others; it is also being aware of the impact of one's behavior on others. Empathic attunement is necessary to build a healthy relationship with a significant other or to succeed in the workplace among other things. Twentysomethings are on their way to becoming adults when they can anticipate the impact of their behavior, act for the greater good, and place the needs of others before their own.

When our children were young, we often listened to their grievances and supported them when their feelings were hurt. However, with our adult children, this simplistic approach is not always helpful. Ann, the mother of 26-year-old Jonathon, said, "I remember comforting my son when he came home from the playground complaining about his feelings getting hurt in some squabble. My knee-jerk reaction usually was to assume that Jonathon never deserved the insult and that he needed some positive feedback from me. However, that seems really simplistic now. Now that he's twenty-six and working at an advertising agency, my approach has changed. When he complains about some issue with a coworker, I'm more careful to help him probe and explore another perspective. I don't just say, 'You're right, Jonathon, and they're wrong.' Now that he's older, I try to get him to think about what behaviors in others make him angry to help him realize what he may have done to cause someone else to treat him badly."

Ann has realized that being supportive of her adult child is more complicated than automatically agreeing with his perspective. Complaints about work and arguments with friends provide parents with an opportunity to help their adult children to reflect on how their behavior affects others and to begin to take responsibility for their behavior.

The fact that twentysomethings have obtained some of the traditional markers of adulthood, such as purchasing a house or making a large income, does not necessarily make them adults. One mother shared the following story: "My friend Rita has three grown children. The oldest child, Robin, is twenty-seven years old, has been married and divorced, and owns her own home. Rita's two sons are in their early twenties.

"Last spring, Rita's brother was hospitalized to undergo a series of tests. Rita spent the next day by her brother's bedside. Her two sons rushed to the hospital when they heard the news, but Robin failed to call her mother the entire day to see how her uncle was doing. When she finally called and asked what she could do, Rita's response to her daughter was, 'If you have to ask the question, it's too much energy for me to answer. If you can't figure it out yourself by twenty-seven, I can't help you.' For me, this story illustrates that I didn't stress enough to my own children the importance of thinking about others and anticipating other people's needs. So often it's all about them."

Janice, a 59-year-old mother of two adult children, provides an alternate example: "When your children invite you over to their apartment, plan a menu they know you enjoy eating, and cook dinner for you, they are thinking beyond themselves. When my children initiate an activity, like going to the movies, and include my husband and me in their plans, then I know they are becoming adults."

Parents do agree that we can't expect our children to be mind readers. There is nothing wrong with parents telling children that something is important to them. Edie, a mother of two adult children, explained, "I had trouble telling my son that it was important he come home for Christmas. He asked me whether I cared if he and his wife came home, and even though I was very anxious to see them, I told my son it was their decision. To my great disappointment, they decided to stay home for Christmas. It killed me that they didn't come home, and I regretted that I didn't give them a clear message how important their visit was to me.

"After this experience, I learned that it's okay to tell my children when something really matters to me. If they know my real feelings, I believe they will do their best to please me. If things don't work out, at least I'll know I made my needs clear, and gave my children the opportunity to do the best they could to meet my needs."

There are times when adult children should demonstrate, without being prompted, that they have the skills to act appropriately in response to family and friends during times of stress. And there are times when it is appropriate to tell our children what is important to us. As Joan, a 51-year-old school principal, said, "There are certain times when if you don't do it right, you may not have another op-portunity to redo it." This was the case for Rita and her daughter, Robin. Robin should have known to call her mother as soon as she knew her uncle was in the hospital. Sometimes, however, as with the example of Janice's disappointment at Christmastime, it was Janice's responsibility to let her son know how she felt. Without honest information, it is impossible for children to know when something is really important to their parents.

Barbara, a 58-year-old mother of two adult daughters, agrees: "Children learn to give to others by watching us and by our asking for their help when we need them. Sometimes, they are not really aware of what we need. I found that out the hard way when my hus-band became ill. My daughters had no real clue as to what to do. I finally had to say, 'I need your help. You have to come and help me.'

"There is nothing wrong with telling them you need them. They don't just want to take from us, especially when they get to a certain age. I think that is another marker of adulthood; they really want to be of help. It makes them feel good that you need them." The satis-faction we get from helping our children goes both ways. They also want to experience what it feels like to give.

Another mother, Lauren, laughed when she told the story about her son, Brad, who was living with his girlfriend. Brad received a phone call from his ex-college roommate, and he didn't want to be bothered with returning the call. His girlfriend, Leslie, said, "Brad, you can't do that. How would you like to be the one who doesn't get his phone calls returned?" Leslie is behaving like an adult. In addi-tion, Brad's mother, Lauren, ended with saying, "Writing thank-you notes on their own, without being told, for me that's being an adult!"

Children have to be shown how to treat others in appropriate and sensitive ways, and this ability is one of those intentional les-sons that must be taught by parents. It is also the responsibility of parents to tell their children when something is important to them. We have to provide opportunities for our children to learn how to do the right thing.

PART OF GROWING UP IS
ASSUMING PERSONAL RESPONSIBILITY

Assuming personal responsibility is an essential component of adult competence. Personal responsibility appears in many forms, including accepting responsibility for one's actions and how they affect other people, establishing a moral center that guides one's actions, and following through on commitments, which demonstrates integrity. Parents can assist in this process by modeling appropriate behavior and by allowing their children to accept the consequences of their actions. This is easier said than done, of course.

Neil, a 53-year-old electrician, said, "You know, we make our children incompetent. If I had to, I could paint a house, I could do concrete work, I can lay bricks, I can fix plumbing, and, obviously, I can do electrical wiring. Having these skills makes me feel that I can always put a roof over my head and put food on the table, no matter what I have to do. I know I can take care of myself. I don't know whether I have passed these skills on to my own kids.

"If we constantly do things for them, I think we're doing them a disservice. I tell my children, 'One day I'm not going to be here, and you're going to be standing there with an empty basket trying to catch something that's not coming your way. If you don't have the skills to reach for the ball, you won't ever get it, unless it's coming right at you.'"

It isn't our children's fault if we don't give them the chance to catch the ball themselves and feel ownership of that success or failure. We learn as much from mistakes as we do from success. In fact, sometimes we learn more from mistakes. Christine, a 55-year-old mother, said, "Now that my children are in their twenties, I realize that I neglected to let them learn from the consequences of their actions. By always rescuing them, I was the one who became more competent at their expense. For the last ten years, *I* have applied to college by filling out the forms for my kids, *I* repeated high school by preparing my kids for all their classes, and *I* made excuses for them when they didn't follow through on their commitments. I'll never forget calling the attendance office to say my daughter was sick when she wasn't. She just hadn't studied for her algebra test. What does that teach them?" Personal responsibility is one of those character traits that children learn through experience.

Assuming personal responsibility enables our children to learn their own strengths and abilities as well as their weaknesses and limitations. The first time parents allow their children to accept responsibility and experience the natural consequences of their actions, they may panic and beg for our involvement. However, parents must restrain themselves from jumping in and always saving their children if their children are to develop personal responsibility, move forward, and grow.

As parents, we can help our children understand that they have the competency to be responsible for their own lives. This recognition helps them to avoid blaming others for adverse life experiences and the associated feelings of uncertainty and powerlessness. Bruce, a 56-year-old lawyer and father of 24-year-old Zach, said he recently had an epiphany regarding Zach's career choice. "I always told Zach that he had a ready-made job if he became a lawyer. My practice is very solid, and nothing would give me more pleasure than having Zach join me. Since Zach was a young teenager, I think that I dropped many not-so-subtle hints that this was the best plan for his future. Zach was bright, he was articulate, and I could just imagine him in court making an impassioned plea to a jury. I assumed that what was a perfect fit for me was also for Zach. The fit seemed so perfect that Zach wasn't even in touch with how wrong it was for him.

"In fact, he didn't have any idea that law school was a poor fit until he was well into his second semester of his first year. Zach wasn't at all happy, and my wife and I attributed it to the rigors of first-year law school. But we were wrong. Finally, Zach began asking himself questions that he needed to think about. He stopped assuming that what would make me happy would also make him happy. Zach began taking responsibility for his own choices. Boy, was he right. He went back to school to get a master's degree in education, and today he is a dedicated and innovative high school teacher.

"Because his path was of his own making, Zach is much more able to own his success, knowing that he did it on his own. I'm really relieved that Zach had enough personal strength to tell me that my dream was not his dream. He had never told me to back off and never said, 'Maybe I don't want to be a lawyer.'" In this case, Bruce helped his son by giving him permission to trust his own instincts about what would make him happy. Bruce helped Zach by giving him the freedom to choose, by releasing him from any sense of obligation Zach had felt to follow in his father's path. Now, both Zach's successes, as well as his mistakes, will be his own. Only by making their own choices can adult children build personal responsibility. An important component of adulthood is having the freedom to make, and live with, individual decisions.

Increasing opportunities to accept more and more personal responsibility propel twentysomethings into becoming capable adults. We know how natural it is to want to protect our children; however, as they get older, what was appropriate protection when they were children may become disabling as they enter into adulthood. As parents, we can provide them with our wisdom and insight as they move toward independence—or we can try.

PART OF GROWING UP
IS DOING THINGS ON YOUR OWN

It is impossible to be a capable adult without some degree of independence, which engenders self-confidence and self-reliance. It is important that young adults know that they can take care of themselves. This doesn't mean that twentysomethings have to do everything on their own to feel competent, but rather that they know they can. Unfortunately, many parents respond to their children's reticence to do things on their own by doing things for them. By letting our children know how well we can negotiate life's demands and fix problems, we affirm their lack of confidence. We deny them the opportunity to use their own experience to learn necessary skills. If we make life too easy for them, we discourage initiative. We enable their lack of competence and encourage them to rely on us instead of themselves.

Unlike when we parent younger children, we have to make conscious decisions to let our adult children do things by themselves. This skill requires giving our children more opportunities to do things for themselves instead of doing things for them so that they can become more competent adults. One father, Richard, said, "I know this is trite, but it's trite because it's so true. If you give them a fish, they'll eat for a day; if you teach them to fish, they'll eat for a lifetime."

At one of our focus groups, we posed the question "What behavior by your adult child would convince you that he or she is capable of taking care of himself or herself?" Here are some of the answers:

> "When my son tells me to stop calling at seven-thirty in the morning to make sure he is awake and getting ready for work."

"When my daughter stops calling me every single time she goes to get a haircut to ask how much she's supposed to tip . . . I mean this has gone on for four years!"

"When my daughter no longer asks what she should wear to job interviews, which is always shocking because I wear elasticized pants and she is in the fashion industry."

"When my son, who is a prosecutor and puts people in jail, is no longer afraid to ask for extra ketchup at McDonald's."

"When my daughter asks how my day went."

"When my son can find his own doctor in Chicago, instead of calling me in New Jersey to find a doctor for him. My son is on top of everything, but there are things that I always did for him that he still wants me to do. When I didn't find a doctor, he called and asked, 'What do you mean you haven't found me a doctor yet in Chicago?' He actually took off from work to come home and see our family doctor."

"When my daughter can negotiate systems for herself, and she doesn't have to call her dad to get her car or apartment insurance or get her car fixed."

As Tracy, mother of Jed, said, "He's got one foot in the adult world and the other foot in the sandbox." It is interesting that many of the parents agreed that their adult children are competent in so many areas, which is why they are surprised when this competence breaks down. Christine, a 53-year-old insurance agent, said, "My son, Evan, is larger than life and confident that he can do anything. In fact, he runs political campaigns and can pick up the phone and call corporate executives and local politicians. Yet, he isn't comfortable opening up a checking account without my assistance."

Parents need to stop doing tasks for their adult children that the children should be doing for themselves. If adult children can hold a job, they have the skills to open a checking account without parental assistance. Calling children in the morning to get them up for a job denies them the opportunity to be responsible for themselves and to suffer the consequences if they are not. As one dad put it, "Little kids make little mistakes; big kids make big mistakes." We are well aware of the consequences if our children do not do something well, but this isn't a good enough reason to continue to jump in and take over, because it may backfire. The hardest thing about letting go is allowing children to experience natural consequences when things don't go well. However, we know this is one of the best ways to learn the essential lessons of adulthood.

PART OF GROWING UP IS
BECOMING FINANCIALLY INDEPENDENT

All of the parents in our focus group agreed that twentysomethings can be considered adults when they are self-sufficient, which must include being economically independent. Becoming financially independent provides adult children with some control over their lives. Again, it gives them the opportunity to know they can take care of themselves, which engenders self-confidence and resilience. This doesn't mean that parents can't choose to help their children, but, as one parent said, "I don't want to feel I have to give my son money in order for me to maintain his lifestyle. When I offer money, I want it to be my choice to help him. I don't want to be pressured by his desire to travel to Belize or join the best health club in town." Parents should guide their children toward making a distinction between asking for help with insurance, rent, and health care and paying for lifestyle "needs."

Many parents are willing to contribute money toward something specific that they feel is important to their children's well-being. It's important not to undermine their children's ability to take care of themselves by overdoing or creating dependency. Steven, a 57-year-old retired police officer, said, "When my son, Joey, rented an apartment in the city, he didn't come right out and ask me for any money. I said to him, 'Joey, the smoke is getting thick in the room here. I have to move it out of the way, so I can see. Obviously, you need some money. I'm happy to help you, but consider this a loan. I'm giving you my tax money, and I want you to pay it back.' I knew that Joey needed help," Steven continued, "because to get this apartment in New York City, he needed another sixteen hundred dollars.

"I feel strongly that Joey needed to know this was a loan. Even if I were a multimillionaire, it wouldn't be any different. There is a lesson that my son has to learn. There's no free ride."

Parents should make these choices based on a combination of their strategy for teaching their children financial independence, personal values, and a reasonable assessment of their own means. However, as their assessment of these factors pans out, it is critical that parents be honest and clear about providing financial support. For example, one mom told us, "I'm willing to give on a spot basis." A clear message allows adult children to develop realistic expectations about what they are responsible for and what financial support is available from their parents.

One benefit of targeting assistance is that it allows adult children to be able to take credit for what they can manage independently. Jamie, a 27-year-old graphic designer, said, "My parents helped me a lot in my early twenties. I felt like twenty-four going on twelve. At first, I was totally freaked out when my parents said that my salary should pay for the health club, cell phone, rent, and food. I was overwhelmed and panicked. My parents sat me down at the kitchen table and showed me what I made monthly and how much my bills would be. I earned enough money to cover certain expenses, and they helped me by paying for my car and health insurance. Little by little, I had to learn to live on my salary, by cutting back on hair appointments and eating out. I never thought how proud I would be when I could take care of myself. Now I don't feel guilty when my mom wants to take me shopping."

Barbara, a 55-year-old real estate attorney, told us a story about her daughter, Dana, who was a teacher but had decided to go back to graduate school in social work after three years of teaching. Barbara said, "My daughter accumulated a lot of credit card debt, mostly to maintain a lifestyle that she couldn't afford. I don't know where she developed such fancy taste, a four-dollar triple mocha Frappuccino every morning and pedicured toes that are ready for sandals in snowstorms. We live a pretty modest lifestyle, so this was a surprise to me. In fact, my husband and I pay our bills as they come in and almost never pay credit card interest.

"Dana began her debt in college when credit cards charged twenty-one percent interest. At first, my husband and I kept bailing her out. He doesn't even know the half of what I sent her. When she decided to go back to graduate school, we told her that she would have to support herself on loans and work part-time. When this reality sank in, something shifted for her. Dana realized that if she was going to be living on loans, she wanted to clear her past debt.

"We agreed to lend her money until she got settled in graduate school. Once she started to work and her loans came through, she not only cut back on spending, but she mailed me a check for the money that we lent her. I felt fabulous, because I knew that she was relieved and I no longer felt responsible to maintain her." This experience taught Dana several lessons: Life is a series of compromises, managing living expenses is more important than another cappuccino, and parents have needs and limits.

Parents are not doing their children any favors by supporting them in the style to which they have grown accustomed. If we constantly upgrade their lifestyles, we encourage our adult children to develop a sense of entitlement and discourage them from having goals and working to meet them. Parents also burden themselves with responsibility for their children's financial mismanagement, even when they frequently can't afford to.

We must remind ourselves of the satisfaction and self-confidence we felt when purchasing our first cheap sofa from Ed's Used Furniture. If parents believe that being grown-up requires financial independence, they must tolerate their children's frustrations and allow them to reach this goal on their own by, among other things, being able to pay for what they wish to purchase.

One father put it this way: "Young people have too much. When you work for something, you appreciate it a lot more than when it's handed to you. I knew from an early age that I shouldn't expect to have everything I want. I never really thought about it. I had what I had. I certainly didn't expect to have everything or for my parents to fill in for me." Even when adult children can afford to buy big-ticket items for themselves, in this economy parents worry about their ability to keep up with the payments.

Buying a house or a car for the first time is something only adults can afford to do. For parents, it provides a symbol that their kids can take care of themselves. It also makes parents worry that their kids have a so-called bigger nut to crack. However, twentysomethings believe that doing these adult things makes them "feel more like an adult." Peter, a 29-year-old apartment manager, said, "I remember buying my condominium, realizing that I could finally make holes in my walls and not worrying about forfeiting my security deposit. My parents were really proud. I guess for them it was a big deal because I did it all myself. That makes me feel like an adult; I have finally arrived."

For twentysomethings to develop confidence in their ability to support themselves, parents must demonstrate that they believe in their ability to do so. If we continuously subsidize our children's lifestyles or bail them out of debt, we teach them to live within *our* means rather than *theirs*. We make it more difficult for adult children to become self-reliant if we warp their sense of reality by providing them with a lifestyle they cannot afford on their own. We must teach our adult children the relationship between choices and consequences and the importance of making compromises.

PART OF GROWING UP IS SETTING AND KEEPING APPROPRIATE BOUNDARIES

One of the important tasks of growing up is learning to set boundaries. Boundaries are important issues for both parents and their adult children. They help twentysomethings to establish independent lives and set their own courses. It is difficult for parents, after having been involved in the details of their children's lives when they were younger, to have respect for the independence of twentysomethings. Parents can demonstrate this respect by permitting adult children to express their opinions freely and by showing consideration for their privacy.

One friend relayed the following story: Lana's daughter, Stephanie, had just made an exclusive commitment to her boyfriend, Jason. Stephanie called her mom and mentioned that she and Jason had discussed what they thought of each other when they first met. "So, what did Jason have to say?" Lana asked. "Sorry, Mom. That's my business," Stephanie responded. "Some things are private." Lana asked, "What did Jason say?" Stephanie responded, "Mom, that's my business, some things are private between myself and Jason." Lana asked again, hoping Stephanie would change her mind, but Stephanie held her ground. Lana acquiesced. "You're right, honey, that is your business." Sometimes it takes our children to remind us about the importance of privacy and maintaining appropriate boundaries. And sometimes parents have to set boundaries for themselves.

Anna, mother of 23-year-old Rachel, recalls, "When Rachel

moved into a new apartment, I automatically offered to help set her up. I had done previous apartments and every dorm room she had lived in. I just assumed this was my job. My problem was, Rachel assumed this as well. She called me the day before moving and asked me to bring my cleaning supplies. Rachel told me she didn't want to move into her apartment with dirty floors. On moving day, I found myself on the floor scrubbing the grime off the linoleum in cracks you don't want to know about. I didn't mind pitching in, but I really minded that while I was working like a dog, she was organizing her CD collection and making plans for dinner. In the middle of backbreaking Cinderella work, I stood up and decided I was finished, even though the floor wasn't clean.

"I realized that this wasn't my job anymore and that I had contributed to Rachel's sitting on her rear, while I was on my hands and knees. I had not set appropriate boundaries for me that reflected her new age. How was she ever going to learn to take care of herself if I didn't stop doing for her?" Parents need to be conscious of what works for them as well as what works for their children. Rachel will never have the opportunity to be independent if she continues to rely on her mom for things she should be doing for herself.

Boundaries seem to be less rigid and more diffused with daughters than with sons. It isn't that parents are less interested in finding out the details of their sons' lives; having learned early on that boys generally don't talk, parents are more reluctant to ask them what's going on. We have several examples of parents who feel more comfortable giving advice to and asking their daughters for more information than their sons.

Tina, mother of 26-year-old Matt, said, "My friend asked me how my son and his girlfriend of five years were doing. I answered, 'I think okay, but I don't really know for sure because I don't ask Matt any leading questions. He can smell them coming.'" In cases like this, parents seem to hold their daughters and sons to different standards based on gender.

Anne, a 56-year-old mother of two adult children, said, "My advice to my children was, if they are not going to college they must learn a trade. They must do something to support themselves, because that's what gave me my freedom. It was easier giving that advice to my daughter than my son, because my daughter is much more verbal about her feelings. My son has always been harder to approach. I always thought it was a privacy thing, so I didn't push him to talk to me. I didn't realize until very recently how wounded he had been from his school experience, and how scared he was about what he was going to do with his life. If only I had known that his silence masked his deep insecurities and hurts, I would have figured out a way to talk to him."

Leslie told the following story, which illustrates the possible consequences of setting up gender boundaries with children: "I talk to my daughter, who lives in a different city, every day. I hardly ever speak with my son, who lives forty-five miles from me. He was recently married, and before his marriage he could go months without calling me. I would finally break down and call him, and we would have an interesting conversation, but unless he had something specific to tell me, he would never think to call me. But since he has gotten married, he calls more often, because I think his wife is always saying, 'Call your mother.'"

Like many other parents, Leslie is comfortable calling her daughter frequently. Daughters generally feel comfortable calling their parents often as well. Meanwhile, Leslie's son probably has to be prodded by his wife to call her. An imagined boundary had been established that gave Leslie's son permission to call her, but that didn't give her the same freedom to call him. This invisible boundary says that talking to daughters fosters intimacy and openness, but talking to sons interferes with their privacy. Boundaries should be set to provide respectful and appropriate limits, but they should not be determined by gender.

Boundaries can be set like fences. They can be tight and not let any light through, or they can be loose like lattice. They might be placed too close to the front door or too far away, leaving the occupant feeling open and vulnerable. To be effective, boundaries must be flexible enough to change—depending on the child, the period of development, and the situation. When they work, boundaries provide limits. With limits come safety, trust, and privacy, for both parents and children.

PART OF GROWING UP IS
DEVELOPING RESPECTFUL INTERDEPENDENCE

Albert Einstein spoke of human relationships when he wrote: "Separation is an optical illusion of consciousness, and . . . if we see things only in that framework, we become locked in a prison and lose that capacity to be intimate, compassionate, to know ourselves in the larger sense" (Ornish 1997, p. 177). Adults understand the importance of being both independent and being connected. The goal for parents is to give their adult children opportunities to be independent and autonomous while staying connected.

The role of the family as principal transmitter of connection is described well in *Tuesdays with Morrie*. When facing his death, Morrie Schwartz tells his former student, Mitch Albom, the most important lesson he has learned in his life. Morrie says, "Invest in the human family. Invest in people. Build a little community of those you love and who love you. In the beginning of life, when we are infants, we need others to survive, right? But here's the secret; in between, we need others as well" (Albom 1997, p. 31). We want to impart to our children the value of establishing a community that includes both family and friends. Becoming a grown-up doesn't mean being separate from parents. Connections with family and friends enrich our lives; they don't take away from them.

Diane, a 58-year-old mother of two adult sons, said, "I introduce the image of a patchwork quilt to the foster children I work with. I tell them I don't want to build a safety net for them. Instead, I want to make a patchwork quilt, where there will be all these pieces stitched together with love, providing the warmth they need to envelop them when they need it. For me, this is a different image from a safety net with holes in it. I use this with my family when I think of how we can provide for each other."

Individuals within a family can remain autonomous and still be connected through dialogue. This can be demonstrated by being tolerant of family members, even when you don't necessarily agree with them, and being open to different points of view. Love should not be equated with agreement. Families need to celebrate the fact that they can openly discuss controversial subjects without children worrying about parents' disapproval. Independent thinking is one characteristic that is necessary for our children to become confident adults. Parents' openness and ability to communicate advice and opinions, without conditions, contribute to the development of a healthy, interdependent relationship with their adult children. Connections can come in life's small moments in a variety of ways, as evidenced by the following story:

Bob, a 54-year-old father, said, " I love talking with my adult children. There is a really big difference between saying 'you're wrong' and saying 'I disagree.' I have strong opinions, and so do my kids. My father always said, 'Your judgment is no better than your information.' My kids, Sara and Matt, and I can really disagree and still respect each other. I don't treat them like little kids because they disagree with me. I learned there is a wide spectrum of ideas that are okay. Most things don't matter in the long run. Debating ideas is our family's way of staying connected. We love bouncing ideas off one another. Nothing is better than going to a movie together and having a heated and lively discussion over a bottle of wine and dinner. My wife and I love watching Sara and Matt become independent thinkers who still want to share their ideas with us."

We want our children to flourish as adults, but we also want them to enjoy the connection with their families. This interdependence between adult children and their parents is fuzzy and imprecise and takes on different meanings and challenges for various types of families.

Adult children with disabilities frequently must rely on their parents to help them become independent. This challenge creates a unique relationship between adult children and their parents. In a recent study of young adults with disabilities, the respondents named their parents as key to their achievements and ability to become adults. They cited paid employment and being in control of their own personal assistants as crucial to attaining adulthood. Many of those interviewed preferred living in independent households but realized the difficulty in obtaining this goal. However, adult children voiced other markers of adulthood. For example, Jenny said, "Independence would not necessarily mean leaving home . . . it would mean that I could live my days . . . without having to ask my parents to help me . . . whether that be getting around or using the phone . . . things like that" (Hendey and Pascall 2002, p. 2). For children with disabilities, connection with parents sustain them on their way to becoming adults. The markers to measure maturity are as diverse as the children themselves.

Often when famous people accept awards, they use it as an opportunity to publicly acknowledge the connection they have with their parents. When Arthur Hiller received the Jean Hersholt Humanitarian Award given by the Academy of Motion Picture Arts and

Sciences in 2002, he approached the microphone, looked up, and said, "Thank you, Mama, thank you, Papa." When Sidney Poitier won an Honorary Award for Lifetime Achievement that same year, he said, "My art portrays the dignity of my parents." Being an adult means realizing a sense of family and community as well as independence. As Teddy Roosevelt said, "Connections we make reverberate long after we make [them]."

PART OF GROWING UP CAN BE
DEMONSTRATED BY RAISING CHILDREN

Getting married and having children are traditional markers of adulthood. However, marriage doesn't signal instantaneous adulthood for many twentysomethings. Parents can look at marriage, however, as a passage that provides opportunities for their children to become more mature. This transition provides parents with a wonderful opportunity to treat their children as adults. Many parents shift their expectations because the boundaries created by the new marriage influence new behavior by both parents and their adult children. Having children, however, is an even more defining moment. There is nothing more compelling than creating a life that can't survive without you. Parents have less difficulty viewing their children as adults when those children assume the responsibility of being parents themselves.

One mother said that marriage didn't make her daughter grow up, but having a child certainly did. Lynn, whose grandson is nine months old, said, "Seeing my daughter take care of Matt was amazing. It was a completely transforming experience for her. Kate could never get anywhere on time. I had to constantly remind her of appointments. Now, when she has to take her son to the pediatrician, you can bet that she knows when it's time to go and gets there on time. Kate also has to juggle home and work. She has a schedule that was difficult enough before she had a baby. I think Kate understands priorities in a way she didn't before she had Matt."

Parents report how important, yet challenging, it is to step back and watch their children raise their grandchildren. They realize, slowly, that they are not their grandchildren's parents and they should wait to be asked before they give advice. This is not an easy transition for many parents, although all agree that it is necessary. Suzanne, a recent grandmother, said, "It's really difficult when your kids have children. It is so hard not to say 'Take that thumb out of her mouth,' 'The milk should be warmer,' 'Put a hat on him,' or 'What's wrong with giving cereal so he can sleep through the night?' The hardest thing is keeping my mouth shut, but it's possible. I asked my cousin Minnie, whom I love dearly, for advice. I said 'Minnie, you have such a wonderful family, two married boys and one son very close to being married. They are great guys, and they have such terrific families, and you have such a wonderful relationship with them. How do you do it?' Minnie responded with, 'Suzanne, I bite my tongue until it really hurts, and then I keep right on biting.' I think of that saying so often, but it's still hard to do."

Until you have your own child, you always define yourself first as someone's child. Having children creates a profound change in priorities and perspective. Now, you become first and foremost a mother or a father. Nothing defines being an adult more than becoming a parent.

GROWING UP REQUIRES CULTURAL COMPETENCE

One significant skill that adult children need in order to be successful adults in this diverse, multicultural society is cultural competence—the ability to understand and acknowledge one's own cultural background as well as others'. Twentysomethings must become knowledgeable about, and take into consideration, different standards and operating principles in order to be successful in the world of work and in the community in which they live. Whether adult children will be successful at acquiring these skills depends largely on the lessons they learned from their parents. Children will adopt the values of inclusion and tolerance if their parents model these behaviors at home. The most important teacher a child will ever have is his or her parent.

Ilene, a 52-year-old mother of an adult son, related the importance of acceptance and one parent's reaction to a changing world: "One of my favorite movies is *Guess Who's Coming to Dinner*. I will never forget the discussion between Katharine Hepburn and Spencer Tracy when they find out their daughter is going to marry a Black man. Tracy plays the role of a liberal newspaper editor, who is having trouble accepting his daughter's choice of a mate. Hepburn responds with, 'This is the way we raised her . . . People who think they are better than someone are sometimes stupid, sometimes hateful, but always, always wrong. We didn't say, but don't ever fall in love with a Negro . . .'" Hepburn's character understood how destructive prejudice is, and that tolerance and respecting differences are essential adult characteristics. Twentysomethings need cultural competence to thrive in the twenty-first century.

Adulthood and independence may be defined differently in different cultures. For example, European Americans generally define adulthood in terms of independence significantly more often than people of color. Other racial and ethnic groups generally define adulthood in terms of both independence and *inter*dependence: children are expected to assume greater personal responsibility, but allegiance to family remains the priority and does not stop with adulthood (Lynch and Hanson 1998).

We are aware that different cultures operate under different assumptions, but parents and children have the opportunity to move forward together to create social justice and to celebrate the richness of living in a diverse society. Without the ability to operate in a multicultural society, twentysomethings will be less prepared to be highly functioning adults in both the workplace and their interpersonal relationships.

Finding Common Ground: Maturity Is a Process That Takes Time

In our focus groups we speak with many parents of twentysomethings about markers of adulthood or the lack thereof today. The parents of twentysomethings talk about their first experience in the adult world, often after graduating from either high school or college, when they were inspired by dreams of a better future in a society eager for their contributions. For most of the parents, getting married in their early twenties quickly led to adulthood. Julie, a 55-year-old mother, told us, "For me, becoming an adult was getting married and moving into an apartment with my husband. And then having a baby at twenty-six years old. These passages said to me, 'I must be an adult.' I think the signs are different now, because everything seems to happen so much later for our children."

Twentysomethings certainly are aware of their parents' belief that developing many of the characteristics of adulthood should be completed in a finite, relatively short period. They see us as having pushed them all of their lives. As one twentysomething put it, "I'm racing the clock, and I'm not sure whose clock I'm racing!" Parents can help in this process by identifying, respecting, and supporting their children's individual "clocks."

It is no accident that twentysomethings do not share the experience of the two generations that preceded them. As we discussed in chapter 2, baby boomer parents have wanted to maintain their group image as superachievers with high standards, and they were determined to excel in parenting in the same way. Baby boomers studied child rearing to master it, engaged in constant dialogue with their peers, and competed to produce *perfect* children.

As part of this drive for perfection, baby boomer parents created a family life that produced a different parent-child relationship. We sought closeness and involvement in every aspect of our children's lives. We allowed our children a voice in family decisions that affected them. However, when we were encouraging this closeness, we did not expect that our children would remain so closely tied to us as young adults, or to be as financially, physically, or emotionally dependent.

Despite their different vantage points, many twentysomethings actually understand and internalize their parents' views about maturity. One twentysomething made his case to us: "I'm becoming more and more of an adult, like learning to save money with each paycheck. To me that means I'm becoming more self-reliant. I bought a car, and I'm responsible for the car payments and the insurance, and I am twenty-seven years old. It's one step at a time, and I need to keep moving in that direction."

Twenty-eight-year-old Nicole openly expressed her strong desire to reach her objective of adulthood. "I can't wait to be out of my twenties, to be honest. A lot of my friends are over thirty, and they say, 'Just hold on, it gets so much easier.'" Many twentysomethings believe they will have figured it all out by the time they enter their thirties. As Brett describes, "You start making money, you will have finished school, and you may have a sustaining relationship. Some people may have figured it out earlier, have matured earlier, but we all expect to know something by the time we reach our thirties."

The goal of reaching adulthood by the age of 30 may satisfy some parents and adult children but be unacceptable to others.

However, in our focus groups, we have observed that parents do recognize that their twentysomethings are changing. As one father observed, "I think I've been most surprised by how much they change from twenty to thirty. I kind of thought that when my children reached twenty-one that was who they were going to be, and really they're quite different, growing and changing all the time."

What is crucial is that whatever their differences, adult children and their parents must identify, respect, and build from their common ground. This process begins with focusing on the characteristics of adulthood, rather than on the somewhat misleading traditional markers. Maturity can no longer be measured by the attainment of discrete milestones, such as college graduation, forming committed relationships, or buying a home.

Maturity can be measured meaningfully by observing the process of integrating characteristics, such as empathy, personal responsibility, independence, appropriate boundaries, respectful interdependence, mature relationships, and cultural competence. While identifying the characteristics of adulthood is important, parents must be mindful that becoming an adult is a process whose time frame varies from person to person. Unlike our relationships with young children in which we direct the process, our relationships with adult children must be responsive to their needs and pace.

Take-Home Messages

Learn to measure adulthood by behavioral characteristics rather than by markers or milestones.

Some of the most important characteristics of adulthood are empathy, personal responsibility, independence, appropriate boundaries, respectful interdependence, mature relationships, and cultural competence.

Respect your adult child's pace, while looking for teachable moments.

Be patient with your twentysomething. Maturity is a process that takes time.

6. Lean on Me

WHAT ARE THE DIFFERENCES AMONG ENABLING, HINDERING, AND SUPPORTING ADULT CHILDREN?

I have found the best way to give advice to your children is to find out what they want and then advise them to do it.

—*Harry S Truman, television interview, 1955*

Give a man a fish and you feed him for a day. Teach a man to fish and you feed him for a lifetime.

—*Proverb*

Much of the literature about raising children talks about the concept of "letting go." What does it really mean for parents to "let go" of their children? One father confessed, "I know she's an adult, but she'll always be my child." Sasha, a 29-year-old teacher, confirms this sentiment. She recalls, "While I was sitting in a delayed airplane on my way home to San Antonio from New York, I answered my cell phone. I smiled because my dad was on the phone. I turned to the stranger next to me and said, 'It's my dad; he still

likes to know where I am.' As he always says, he is still my dad."
Adult children can be independent and productive and still remain
close to their parents. However, the twentysomething years are a
time of life when parents must renegotiate their relationships with
their children. For every family, the balance among enabling, hindering, and supporting is different.

The Road to Enabling Is Paved with Good Intentions

Enabling occurs when parents try to protect their children from the
consequences of their actions and, thereby, fail to hold them accountable for their personal behavior. Enabling parents assume responsibilities that their children should assume for themselves. By
engaging in enabling behavior, parents encourage their children to
behave less maturely and to be more dependent. Parents short-
change their children when they do things for them that children
can do themselves. Inadvertently, they deny their children opportunities to learn a crucial adult skill—to be held accountable for their
behavior. Enabling parents give their adult children the unintended
message that they don't have faith in their ability to do things for
themselves.

Enabling parental behavior can be as overt as always bailing a
child out of financial difficulties or as subtle as making plane reservations or researching information on the Internet without being
asked to do so. Overdoing encourages twentysomethings' irrespon-
sibility, dependency, and lack of self-esteem. In contrast, supportive
parenting is a positive form of assistance that encourages children
to develop the skills of adulthood.

Supportive parents teach their children about accountability,
personal responsibility, and boundaries. Parents hold children ac-

countable for their performance and personal behavior. Their goal is to assist their children to become "more able," not "less able" or "unable" to do things for themselves.

For example, one father told us that his 27-year-old daughter, an attorney, asked him to call her car dealership in another state to solve a problem for her. She believed that his running interference for her was supportive. The dad believed that calling the car dealership would enable her to avoid learning how to be responsible for her own life. It certainly is appropriate for parents to help their adult children to solve some of their problems; however, in this instance, the dad could support his daughter best by telling her how to approach the car dealership on her own. By "coaching" her, rather than by solving her problems for her, the dad gave his daughter the opportunity to take care of herself. As parents, we too often challenge our adult children with contradictory expectations, which can take a toll on them. We want to fix things for them and alleviate their anxiety, but we also want them to learn to take care of themselves.

Our fast-paced, 24/7 lives—frequently as single-parent families or families with two working parents—force us to cut corners. We do more things for our children, rather than fewer, because it's quicker and easier than teaching them to do things for themselves. Teaching skills takes time, something we have in short supply. We may be too impatient to let our children perform tasks two or three times until they get it right. We may also do things for our children out of a sense of guilt about our lack of availability. Our intentions are good, but this behavior actually disables our children, denying them the opportunities to learn adult skills and encouraging their increased dependence on us. We instill the expectation that we can take care of things better than they can.

Twenty-five-year-old Ross explained the consequences of parents' doing too much: "There's a fine line between getting too much help from parents and their participating enough so you don't feel overwhelmed. If parents make life too easy, you can lose the sense of why you're working. I know I'm working to be able to live where I want and do what I want; if my parents do everything for me, I won't learn how to do things for myself."

Another twentysomething, Paige, told a similar story: "My brother's ex-girlfriend's parents were paying for this gorgeous apartment, even though she had a good job and could have afforded a nice enough apartment herself. She wound up getting into credit card debt for $15,000. Her parents finally realized how they had contributed to this mess and decided not to bail her out. She had to move out of her apartment and get a second job as a waitress." If this young woman had been living within her means, she may have been able to avoid getting into debt and having to work two jobs to pay it off.

Our children will take advantage of our good intentions when we do too many things for them or bail them out of trouble too frequently. We set up a pattern that is difficult to break. By giving young adults a false sense of reality, we deny them the knowledge of how to minimize the frequency of avoidable mistakes. The process of assisting our adult children to develop the behavioral traits necessary to minimize such mistakes begins with an understanding regarding mutual expectations. This understanding includes both financial and emotional responsibilities that parents and their adult children can be counted on to meet.

Getting in the Way

Hindering is virtually always a negative experience for parents and children. Various synonyms for *hindering* include *obstructing, getting in the way of*, *hampering*, *deterring*, or, at the very least, *delaying development*. Hindering interferes with the maturation process of young adults that would otherwise take place. Assistance that appears helpful in the short term may actually prevent or discourage emotional development over the long term. Hindering can produce an extended nightmare of frustration and antagonism for parents and their adult children.

To determine whether conduct is hindering their adult children, parents must assess its impact on the individual child's ability to function independently. We must honestly ask ourselves whether we are contributing to, or hampering, our children's developing adult behavioral characteristics. As one parent explained, "If, God forbid, anything happened to you, could those kids continue to function?" Another parent told us about her brother whose extended dependency on their parents made him unable to cope well into his forties.

Lily said, "My brother has lived beyond his means because my parents always supplement his income. My parents were on the brink of bankruptcy because of it. I used to be angry with my brother and sister-in-law, until someone said to me, 'Well, maybe your brother doesn't realize the toll on your parents.' And it was like a lightbulb went on. I think my brother thought Dad had the money to give him, and if he did, it was okay to accept. My dad wanted to take care of my brother and sister-in-law, but he was doing a disservice to himself and to them."

Some adult children continue to take money from their parents just because they want it and feel entitled to it and the money seems to be available. Parents have a responsibility to be honest with their children about the sacrifices they are prepared to make to keep them in a certain lifestyle. If they don't set these limits, parents rob their children of the opportunity to challenge themselves and solve their own problems. Parents certainly can still assist their children financially; however, they should always remember that excessive financial assistance can hinder their children's ability to learn the skills necessary to become financially independent.

Parents who have difficulty setting limits may produce adult children who have trouble recognizing and valuing limits. Parents must be very clear about, first, whether they have the money to give, and, second, even if they do have the money, whether giving it will benefit their adult children's development. When parents fail to set appropriate boundaries, they create a barrier to a relationship with their adult children based on respectful interdependence. This barrier facilitates a prolonged dependence and, possibly, dysfunctional behavior by twentysomethings.

As children get older, parents often miss being needed by them. We interpret our twentysomethings' seeking us out for help as evidence that they still value us. Before providing help, parents can support their adult children best by determining whether we wish to help them for their benefit or our own. Obviously, there are ways to identify a form of support that is mutually beneficial. This process allows us to stay involved in our children's lives and help them in a manner that facilitates development of adult behavioral traits. We certainly want our children to come to us when they are in need, and we want to maintain our connection to them; it's how we define *need*, distinguishing it from *want*, that can make the difference between enabling or hindering and supportive.

Lauren reminded us that the considerations of this process vary between children in the same family. "I have a twenty-nine-year-old sister, with a Ph.D., who always lives beyond her means. My parents are furious with her, but my father continues to bail her out of debt. She makes decent money, but she never has a nickel to her name. Although my father is resentful of my sister's dependency, he continues to pay for things my sister can't afford on her salary. As soon as she pays off one car, she will buy another new car. My husband and I only consider used cars, and she's buying new cars on my father's dime." In some families, like Lauren's, one child may be more financially responsible, while the other siblings have more difficulty with limits. For this reason, parents must intentionally make decisions that are not based on "one size fits all." Limits are essential, but they must be tailored to the true needs and characteristics of each child as well as to the circumstances of each situation.

Greg, a 26-year-old graphic designer, agreed: "If I were a parent, I wouldn't pay for everything. I would only help out until the point at which my children could be on their own. And I would only help enough to allow my children to feel like they are responsible and not drowning in expenses. I wouldn't expect my parents to pay for my social life, only for basic living expenses, such as insurance or help with rent."

Enabling and hindering behavior may take a variety of forms. In one of our focus groups, we learned that one mother is referred to by her children as "Concierge Mom." Her children know she is an excellent networker with a fabulous Rolodex, so they call her before looking for information on their own. The extent to which we teach our children to expect us to solve their problems has nothing to do with proximity. Adele received a phone call from her daughter, a financial development specialist for a prestigious private school in another state. She said, "Mom, I don't know whether to get into the shower. The water pipes are making these weird hissing sounds; I'm afraid they are going to explode. What should I do?" Adele replied, "Call your landlord. I'm not a plumber. What do you expect me to do?"

Unfortunately, enabling or hindering may cause adult children to feel guilty and resentful, even though they may ask for our help. Every time parents rescue a twentysomething who doesn't need to be rescued, we give him or her the message that we don't think that the child can survive without us. Most adult children don't want to continue their dependency on us any longer than they have to.

Give Maturity a Chance

Determining the appropriate type and amount of support is tricky. One mother told the story of her son who worked for the local newspaper. She said, "When my son, Jeremy, first started to work on the newspaper, he would often e-mail his articles to me so I could give him my opinion before he would send them to his editor. At first, I was complimented that he valued my opinion, and I wanted to help him make a good impression in his new job. Jeremy had also struggled in school, and I was proud of him for being so persistent and getting this job. But after a while, I felt he was depending too much on my opinion, and it started to feel uncomfortable.

"One night, he called to send me an article. I decided to tell him that I didn't really think I needed to see it, and I was confident he had done a good job. Jeremy responded, 'I know, but Mom, you always help me with the salient points.' At that moment, I knew it was time for him to do his own work. The only way Jeremy would know he could do his own work was for me to stop the pattern. Jeremy wasn't happy, but, more important, he learned how capable he was. That knowledge was worth everything to me."

Healthy support not only differs from family to family but also from child to child within the same family. If we have more than one child, our support and advice should be predicated on what is best for each child. Rigid or dogmatic behavior is less likely to produce the results parents want. Parents should aim to match the prescription or policy with the child and the circumstances.

As one parent explained, "You're always parenting differently, just like you deal with different people differently. You might e-mail one person and call someone else on the telephone because you know the other person doesn't want to be e-mailed." Appropriate support lets our children know we have confidence in their abilities.

Sara, the mother of two twentysomething daughters, said, "My kids are so different that it wouldn't make any sense for me to treat them the same. Emily, my twenty-nine-year-old, is a typical firstborn. She is superorganized, and I can count on her to help me out when I get overwhelmed cooking for thirty-five for Thanksgiving. Jane, my twenty-six-year-old, is easily thrown off balance. I find myself gingerly asking her questions, worried she may take them the wrong way. With Jane, whatever I ask, it seems to be too much. When I think about how Emily and Jane were as little girls, I realize they are not so different now from when they were young. Emily was a contemplative, mini adult, and Jane was gregarious but moody. It's easy to give to Emily because she never takes advantage and only asks for help when she really needs it. On the other hand, I have to hold back more around Jane. If I'm not careful, she will continue to expect me to bail her out of situations that she should be responsible for herself."

The suitability of support also can vary with the circumstances, even for the same child. If help is suitable to the situation and the particular needs of your child, support can encourage self-reliance. Appropriate support contributes to the self-esteem and maturity of adult children. Children feel connected to families that continue to sustain them in positive ways. This support creates respectful interdependence between parents and children. However, for parents to be both appreciated and effective, terms for the support must be negotiated between parents and twentysomethings to preserve mutual respect.

Diane, a 53-year-old mother, told the following story: "My twenty-five-year-old daughter, Tracy, is in women's fashion. She moved from New York to live in Los Angeles, because it's one of the cities where the industry thrives. Tracy went to Los Angeles without a job, and she has been living with three different sets of friends. We are, obviously, augmenting her money until she gets settled. Her first job offer was with a guy who is a sleaze. I could tell through the phone lines that he was no good. My husband also felt it. We told Tracy, 'You know what? There are some situations when a person would have to take that job because they had no alternative. We know you will wait tables or do whatever you have to do to make a living. Don't feel so desperate that you have to take the first job offered to you when you have a bad feeling about working there.'"

Tracy's parents left the decision of whether to take the job up to their daughter, but they let her know what their preference was and that they would support her while she continued her job search. Tracy's parents felt confident that helping their daughter in this situation would not be taking away her capacity to feel "hungry" and succeed.

Kristin, a 27-year-old insurance agent, said, "I think asking for 'too much' is an individual consideration. I don't want to ask for too much. I like to be independent, but I know my mom likes to help, so she gives me money for special things that I wouldn't buy for myself. This arrangement works for her and for me."

Lowell, 26 years old, has a different but workable arrangement with his parents. He said, "I take care of all my expenses, except what my parents give me as gifts. My graduate school gift from my parents was money for car insurance. My parents feel they are helping me 'get on my feet,' and a gift feels better than a loan or having to ask them for money. A gift doesn't injure my self-image as a grown-up; that's why I find it easier to accept."

Twentysomethings and parents alike agree that lending money under certain circumstances, and for a limited period of time, can be viewed as positive support and not disabling. Many parents approach this issue by trying to make a distinction between providing monetary support to pay a portion of graduate school and providing discretionary money to keep them in bar money so they can go out to eat all the time.

Twentysomethings also make a distinction between genuine "needs" and lifestyle "wants." Many twentysomethings in our focus groups felt that helping an adult child who is between jobs for a pre-set limited period is not disabling. Some parents believe that negotiating a formal arrangement regarding the terms and limits for monetary support is useful for establishing clear expectations and boundaries.

Neil, a 58-year-old father of two adult sons, explained the arrangement he made with his 26-year-old son. Neil said, "My son wanted a five thousand dollar loan to buy a cheap, used car. It would have been easy for me to have lent him the money, but, instead, I suggested he go to a bank to get the loan. My friends asked, 'Why are you making him go to the bank for such a small amount of money?' I told them I felt it was important for Bill to go to the bank and learn how to apply for a loan and be responsible for the payments. I told Bill I would be willing to co-sign the loan. He liked the idea because he could establish his own credit. Yet, he knew I would help him with the payments if he couldn't make them." Neil was trying to teach Bill a life lesson by not simply handing over the money to his son. He provided Bill with the opportunity to become more financially independent, which, ultimately, empowered his son.

The question parents must ask themselves before lending or giving money to their adult children is not, *should* they feel comfortable with this decision, but *do* they feel comfortable? Parents have to decide for themselves what the right decision is. Parents also have to factor into the decision whether it's a loan or gift, and whether this is the most supportive decision for their children. Under the right circumstances, a loan can provide an important learning experience for adult children. Repaying a loan in a timely fashion helps adult children to develop personal responsibility, the best antidote to disabling behavior.

Another form of supportive behavior is the process of reflecting reality back to our adult children. When our children ask for our opinions, it is crucial for us to be truthful. Honesty is essential for our children to develop and maintain trust and confidence in an adult relationship. Trust is the foundation of a relationship based on respectful interdependence.

If we always tell our adult children they are perfect, if we only feed back to them what they want to hear, we teach them that they cannot trust our objectivity and judgment. We deny them the opportunity to learn how to analyze situations from a variety of perspectives, which is the basis for empathy. We also deny them the opportunity to learn how to handle disagreements, mistakes, conflict, and failure productively.

Parents have a responsibility to "tell it like it is." We have to be willing to accept our children's reactions, including negative or unpleasant ones. We must also accept the fact that, when we give them the best advice we have, they may choose a different path—their own. This divergence of opinion is not a failure; it's part of the process of learning to assess problems, make decisions, and live with the consequences.

As Melanie, a 58-year-old mother of two adult daughters, described: "We often have intense arguments over issues. When I would disagree with Charlotte, she would respond with, 'You're not listening to me.' And I would say, 'I am listening to you, but I'm not agreeing with you. I am listening to you, but I can't agree with the way you want to do something.'"

Another parent recalled, "I listened very carefully to my son tell me about his plan to travel for six months after graduate school, picking up odd jobs along the way. I think his idea makes sense, but I'm not sure the timing is right, given the downturn in the economy.

I asked him a question about the logistics of implementing this plan. I was really careful, but he said, 'I'm sensing your negativity.' I responded with, 'I don't think I'm being negative.' Because I wasn't cheerleading, he didn't like my response."

Like all people, parents and children need the reassurance of others' agreeing with them about matters they believe to be important. But as our children get older, they usually begin to withhold information. They also stop asking questions if they decide our answers will be different from what they wish to hear.

This separation is not necessarily negative or certain to lead to a poor relationship. Withholding may be a sign of growth and the beginning of setting new and more adult boundaries. We want our twentysomethings to evolve into adults who are capable of making their own decisions. Part of this process is learning to keep one's own counsel and remain private about certain aspects of one's life. We want adult children to be integrated members of our families, but not subsumed by us to such an extent that they fail to develop their individuality, their sense of self. Privacy, as opposed to withdrawal, can be a good thing, as one dad discovered.

Paul, a 48-year-old father of an adult son, said, "My son came home from a camping trip to Wyoming. He hadn't told me that he was going to a pretty deserted area. If he had, I would have counseled him against going there. After my son returned home, he told me about his scary adventure! He said that while he was camping, he came across a bear. He proudly announced that if you put your hands up and stand still, the bear thinks you're bigger, and it turns around and runs the other way. He tells me the whole story. I'm thinking, you know, some children have secrets from their parents. This story is not something I need to know!" Creating a little bit of distance from the family to find one's self is not incompatible with retaining close ties as an adult.

Decisions and Disagreements

As parents, we often forget the power of our opinions. Although our adult children are older, they may still need our approval. It is our responsibility to share our point of view with our adult children in a manner that demonstrates respect. This includes waiting to be asked for advice, listening without judgment, and accepting differences of opinion. As one parent explained, "If we raise our children to be free thinkers and independent, if that's the goal, when they have different opinions, we're just getting what we asked for! I think if we really value that, we need to honor their opinion."

Parents can get into trouble and are more likely to incite needless conflict with adult children when they give advice or guidance dogmatically or without being asked. Once asked for our opinion, it is important to assess the issues presented and determine our children's substantive concerns before we wade in. Parents are better able to give advice about a problem or situation they feel comfortable discussing. However, such discussions may not always be comfortable for us, so we have to do the best we can. The challenge is to give the best advice we have, while being empathetic and respectful of an unwanted response or an outcome that may be different from what we would like.

Giving support is easier when children make choices we agree with; it's more difficult when our children make decisions we don't agree with. As Paula Stanley, a marriage and family counselor, explained, "We all have to find our own way in life, but it's hard for parents to allow children the freedom and support to do that if they choose an unfamiliar path" (DeGeronimo 2001, p. 7).

Depending on values and belief systems, families may view maturity concerns through different lenses. Each family has different standards for accepting or rejecting adult conduct, such as choosing an alternative lifestyle, having premarital sex, or choosing to marry someone from a different faith or race. Families have different views about the relationship between college selection and choosing careers that are either extremely competitive or socially rewarding but are poorly compensated. When addressing these kinds of issues, providing parental support is particularly challenging, and communication between parents and children becomes more problematic.

Theresa, a 56-year-old mother of two adult children, is concerned about her daughter, Karla, who wants to become a stand-up comedian. Theresa said, "My daughter's doing something I'm very upset about. It's not that I disapprove, but it's so unconventional. She's attempting to become a stand-up comedian, and it worries me ad nauseum because I think there's a very low chance she'll make it. So I support her, but reluctantly.

"My husband and I went to see her perform. She was working in a comedy club that was just the dregs. You have to pay to get in, and there's a two-drink minimum. The club was smoky, and people were getting up all the time in the middle of routines. Also, a lot of these comedians are so crude and hard to listen to.

"My daughter got up to perform. Thankfully, she's not crude. She's okay. But it just worries me. Then we were walking down the street after the show, and there is this guy on the corner handing out flyers to come to his show, and Karla says 'hi' to him, in a very familiar way, and I realized that this was her community. It's just tough because her choice of a career doesn't go along with what I had in mind for her.

"Karla also lives in this walk-up apartment. She doesn't make enough money to buy much in the way of food. I went to a grocery store with her, and Karla had to put back a green pepper because she couldn't afford it. And she won't take money from me. I know that is my problem, not hers. She's very happy and supporting herself, barely, with another job."

Once they grow up, we can no longer forbid our children to follow their own paths, even if we are worried sick about it. That doesn't mean we don't try to influence them, but the final decision at this age remains with them, not us. Unlike when we were twenty-somethings, our children tend to be much more adventurous and experimental. This is normal for their generation. It is the time of their lives when they can explore. According to Jeffrey Arnett (2002), research associate professor of human development at the University of Maryland, "A key feature of emerging adulthood is that it is the period of life that offers the most opportunity to explore the areas of love, work and world views." We may not like this change, but at least we can take comfort in the knowledge that we are not alone in trying to adjust to this new developmental stage. Parents still have choices to give their support or not, but we have to be willing to accept the consequences, just as we expect our children to live with the consequences of their decisions and actions.

Adult children choose alternative lifestyles and nontraditional careers and form relationships that are racially, culturally, and religiously different. We can choose to be supportive or we can attempt to stop them from making their own life choices. If we attempt to control or hinder their choices, we should expect a battle that either or both parties may lose. The following story illustrates this point:

Robert, a 24-year-old graduate student, knew in high school (and probably earlier) that he was gay, but by high school he stopped fighting the feelings so much. He was the victim of countless incidents of harassment. Robert just tried to make himself more and more invisible until he could get to college, hoping that he could flourish in a more diverse and, he hoped, accepting environment. Robert believes his parents knew his sexual orientation but chose to ignore it. He holds himself responsible for not sharing his lifestyle with his parents earlier. Robert said, "I finally decided to talk to my parents when I started a relationship with Derek. I wanted to be as respectful of their feelings as possible. I wrote them a letter to give them time to absorb the information. I didn't hear from them for days. I finally couldn't wait any longer, and I called them from school. My mom couldn't talk without crying, and my father refused to talk to me at all. I love my parents, but I have to live my own life. I haven't seen my parents in over a year, but I am still optimistic they will come around.

"Derek's parents have totally accepted us. I go to their house for holidays now, but I miss my own family. I think if my parents understood how much happier I am, they would be more willing to accept me. But, right now, they can't let it in. I know they love me, and I also know they are as hurt as I am over the rift between us. I am still hopeful that, over time, we'll be a family again." Robert's parents' decision not to talk to Robert ended up hurting both parents and child. In spite of large differences, however, there are circumstances in which compromises can work for parents and children.

Laila and Justin come from different religious backgrounds, one Muslim and the other Jewish. When these adult children began to form a relationship, their parents felt the likelihood of a successful union was doubtful. Both sets of parents spoke with their children about the difficulties they would face if they remained together, from both their families and society. There were many discussions about these issues, but Laila and Justin decided to stay together anyway. Their parents mutually decided they could live with this decision, but, at the same time, it wasn't realistic to try to protect Laila and Justin from society or family members who wouldn't approve of the relationship. The young people needed to know what they would face as an interfaith and intercultural couple.

Their parents felt they could insist that family members be respectful, but that was it. They couldn't insist that they embrace a relationship that they disapproved of or that caused them discomfort. Although the parents are accepting of the relationship, they have respectfully warned Laila and Justin to be prepared for their relationship to become a source of family conflict. One can hope their parents' help will prepare Laila and Justin for a society that doesn't accept this kind of mixed marriage.

Parents don't do their children any favors by trying to insulate them from intolerance, which, in any event, is impossible. The most parents can do is to talk honestly about problems they may face and give them a "heads up" if they see potential conflict. Pretending that their culture and or family members will accept Laila and Justin is unrealistic and would set the couple up for disappointment and sorrow.

Parents have a responsibility to support their children by providing them with a realistic understanding of the world they will face. Relatives may disown them, they may not be included in family events, some people may shun them, and their own children may encounter prejudice. Parents and siblings may sustain them, but discussion needs to take place about how they may react when extended family members and, possibly, some siblings treat them rudely, when invitations don't come, or when their own children are excluded from family events. Parents can best support their children by helping them to prepare for the challenges they may face.

For some parents, disapproval of their children's life partners for religious or other reasons may prevent them from giving their children any support at all. It's important to remember that choosing to withhold support can lead to irreparable damage between parents and their children, damage that may take years to overcome.

Safety First

For parents, the overriding consideration in deciding whether to support their children must always be their health and safety, regardless of age. During our focus group discussions, parents repeatedly raised concerns about safety issues. All other considerations aside, there are times when it is appropriate to intervene for safety reasons. If, for example, a child is in an abusive relationship or drinking heavily, parents have a responsibility to take any action necessary to help. When safety is a factor, we can support our children best by getting them the appropriate help. They may not want to hear what we have to say, and they may not cooperate, but we have an obligation to say what needs to be said and do what needs to be done. There are times when we won't win any popularity contests, but they pale in comparison to the harm that may result if we don't become involved.

There are less extreme situations when parents determine, for their own sense of comfort as well as for the safety of their children, that it is appropriate to intervene. Katharine, a 49-year-old mother, told the following story: "My daughter, Anna, at twenty-six years old and after living with us for two years after college, was finally ready to move out of our home. Anna told me, 'Mom, all I can afford for rent is seven hundred fifty dollars, I can't do more than that.' She finds a first-floor apartment in a rough neighborhood of St. Louis. Anna was really excited, but all I could think about was her safety. I'd been encouraging her to move out, wanting her to get her own apartment, and she picks something in a dangerous neighborhood. Now, I say to my husband, how am I going to stop her? Or, am I going to let her go? It was agonizing.

"I asked my husband to go and look at the apartment with me. In the daytime, it wasn't too bad. We went back at night and walked around the place. This was not a safe environment for a single woman to be living in alone. But what should we do about it? We don't want to discourage her independence, and we don't want to make her afraid. But I knew I would never sleep again until she moved out of that apartment. I finally decided to tell her how I felt, but left the decision about whether or not she should rent the apartment to her. I told Anna that I thought it was an unsafe neighborhood but that she should go at night with her boyfriend, walk around, and see how she felt being there. And so she did.

"Anna came back home and said that she wasn't comfortable living there, but she couldn't afford an apartment in a different location. My husband and I told her, for our peace of mind, that we would supplement her money for rent with an additional two hundred dollars per month, until she was making enough to be able to afford a different apartment on her own. Anna at first wasn't happy with that solution, because it made her feel too dependent. But safety became the priority issue, and she found another apartment.

"As soon as Anna could afford to, she took over paying the rent. The extra money also made her more careful about how she spent the rest of her money. So the arrangement worked out, and I could sleep at night. But it is hard. It's very distressing, this wanting them to be independent and on their own, and yet also wanting them to be safe."

It's a struggle to find the right balance of support. There is nothing wrong with voicing our concerns, but, unlike younger children, young adults must weigh the information and come up with their own decisions. Anna was not happy to be taking money from her parents, yet she was less happy about living in an unsafe environment. Learning to make compromises is not a bad lesson, especially when safety is involved.

Holding Twentysomethings in the Balance

Support should be provided without conditions. Whether it is emotional or financial support, if we freely choose to give support, there shouldn't be any strings or "I told you so." At the same time, parents must allow themselves to withhold support when they are uncomfortable giving it. Adult children must also learn to live with the consequences of their conduct when they move in a direction their parents disapprove of. But once support is offered, adult children should expect it to be given free and clear, based on understood and agreed-to terms of support.

Our children appear to be more sophisticated at younger ages, but this is often a superficial maturity. They are exposed to so many images, in the media, through the Internet, and on television. Twentysomethings have had so many different experiences at ages so much younger than many of their parents that we assume they know more and can do things before they actually are ready. One mother said, "I didn't get on a plane until I was nineteen." A father remarked, "My son flew for the first time when he was six weeks old! Things are so different now." As a result of social change, most colleges have eliminated the rules such as curfews and single-sex dorms that they had 20 years ago. Students are left to parent themselves before many of them are actually ready. Having more experiences at a younger age doesn't mean they are more grown-up.

Many twentysomethings enter adulthood having been so overprogrammed and overly controlled by their parents that they are often burned out and unable to think about their future. Some of them expect instant success, and when they find adult life to be more demanding than they anticipated, they develop paralyzing anxieties. One twentysomething shared the following story: "I always worried about my future and never focused on the here and now. This produced a lot of stress. I felt like I was trying to work really hard and was forced to make decisions when I was really young. I am now trying to learn how to relax without all the answers and not feel so rushed." Another young man said, "I have expectations coming from everywhere, my parents, my teachers, and even my friends. Who said I'm supposed to be established in my career by the time I'm twenty-five?"

Parents can help their adult children feel less anxious and less pressured by acknowledging and praising each step toward independence. In addition, parents need to be loving and supportive when their adult children stumble or make mistakes. Less pressure produces less anxiety and gives adult children the freedom to make better choices. The most important question to ask is, What can you do to empower your children to take care of themselves, encourage a sense of well-being, and, simultaneously, sustain a positive relationship based on mutual interdependence?

In speaking with parents and adult children, in an attempt to answer this question, we have come to believe that to be effective parents of twentysomethings, we need to be aware of the line between guidance and interference. There are few tangible guideposts to help parents understand the difference. Rules we have relied on for parent-child relationships have changed as a result of the pressures and expectations of modern life. While love is the cornerstone of any parent-child relationship, we must educate ourselves and be prepared to address in a productive way the moral ambiguities of contemporary culture. We also must be receptive to our children making different life choices than we might prefer. We need to understand ourselves and exercise tremendous patience in order to maintain healthy relationships.

Take-Home Messages

Enabling behavior encourages increased dependency on parents and decreased self-esteem in adult children.

Hindering adult children from doing for themselves what they are capable of doing delays their maturity.

Positive support sustains adult children during their development and maintains the relationship between parent and child.

7. "They're Baack!"

HOW DO YOU LIVE WITH YOUR ADULT CHILD?

We see a closer link between adult children and their parents
now than we have seen since World War II.
—Jeffrey Jensen Arnett, psychologist and author

We have now come full circle. Not since the aftermath of World War II, when many young people moved in with family because of the severe housing shortage, have so many young adults moved back home. This phenomenon may be transitional, but with twentysomethings finding themselves the first generation in America that may not be able to have the same standard of living they had as children, moving back home may become a more persistent pattern.

In increasing numbers, adult children are moving back to live with their parents after college or between jobs. Currently, 18 million 20- to 34-year-olds live with their parents (Paul, 2002). In the 1930s, only 25 percent of those who left home returned. In the mid-1980s, this figure rose to 40 percent, and today, it's as high as 60 percent (Levine 2002, p. B1). Nearly half of emerging adults move back in with their parents at least once (Goldscheider 1997). In response to this trend, a mother jokingly told her son, "Please don't be like our neighbor's son, Seymour, who still lives with his mom at age forty-five." One twentysomething woman agreed: "The only people who should be warned about living with their parents are the unemployed 30- or 40-somethings" (QLC Message Board 2002).

Twentysomethings may move back home for several reasons: they lose their jobs, they find themselves in debt, they're transitioning between job and school, they're still in school, they're trying to save money, or their relationships have ended. Parents have to resist the notion that they failed as parents because their children are moving back home. Rather, they should view this as an opportunity for their children to regroup or start over. Adult children intend for the move to be temporary. They would prefer not to move back home, except in certain cultures in which it is customary for adult children to live at home until they get married.

In a *Newsweek* article, journalist Peg Tyre explains the coming-home phenomenon in the following way: "For their part, these over-grown kids seem content to enjoy the protection of their parents as they drift from adolescence to early adulthood. Relying on your folks to light the shadowy path to the future has become so accepted that even the ultimate loser move—returning home to live with your parents—has lost its stigma" (2002, p. 39). Many parents welcome their children home but are puzzled about what parenting skills still apply. The circumstance here is that it's not a child who is coming home, it's an adult, and that requires more emphasis on guiding the "adult" and not the "child."

As a result of this trend, today's parents of twentysomethings can no longer count on turning that unused bedroom into a den. In fact, many find their empty nest becoming a modern boarding-house, cluttered with girlfriends and boyfriends, unpacked duffel bags, athletic equipment strewn everywhere, ringing phones, blaring music, and half-filled and empty food cartons. Because many adult children have not established a platform of independence and their own touchstone to rely on, they frequently return to the comfort and safety of their parents' home.

Moving back home raises a number of issues between parents and adult children. Adult children may be used to their parents' involvement in their lives, but living under the same roof with them with the same level of involvement is akin to walking a tightrope. Parents may fall back into the pattern of monitoring their children's comings and goings and waiting up for them even though they are adults. When young adults move back home, parents must update the relationship they have with them. Both parents and twenty-somethings must quickly learn to make adjustments, establish new rules, and negotiate responsibilities. The old rules of childhood and adolescence have to be reframed for young adults. Parents need to negotiate different boundaries with adult children, such as privacy issues, curfews, calling home, and financial responsibilities.

Fran, the mother of 24-year-old Nicole, explained, "After being on her own for a year, Nicole came back home when she started to work and wanted to save money. I guess the main issue was she kind of took over again. You know, came in when she wanted, her music versus our music, her television programs versus our television programs. When she was younger, we treated all of this as adolescent angst. That attitude didn't cut it with Nicole as an adult.

"She did all of her own cooking and took care of herself, but we still lived in the same house and adjustments had to be made. It was fun having her at home, after six years away, but worries came back as well. She would come in at three A.M. When Nicole was in Egypt by herself, we didn't know when she came home, and we didn't worry about her. We finally agreed that if Nicole wasn't going to be home until one A.M., she would call us.

"Also, when Nicole wanted her boyfriend to spend the night, we agreed, even though we hadn't allowed her older brother to do it because we had younger children at home at that time. We changed as parents and paid attention to the shifting circumstances of our family life."

Parents react differently to their children's moving back home. The factors that influence this transition include patterns established earlier in the relationship, the amount of time the children want to live at home, and the reasons why they are returning.

Parents offer an emotional safety net. One parent said, "I want my son to be able to make it on his own, and I don't want to push him out before he's ready. I feel like a mother bird and I want him to fly, and not fall out of the nest." This support doesn't end until parents are unable to care for themselves; it just changes. In this chapter, we will explore some of the following issues:

- benefits and challenges of adult children living at home;
- differences between moving in short term and long term;
- impact on younger children who live at home;
- influence of culture on adult children's decisions to live with their parents;
- rules and responsibilities for living at home; and
- what makes moving back successful or unsuccessful.

The Ambivalence of Adult Children Who Return Home

For the most part and regardless of the nature of their relationship with their parents, adult children are ambivalent about coming home, but they are grateful for the safety net. They are also mindful of the trade-offs. One twentysomething expressed her feelings of gratitude and shame about moving back home. Like many twenty-somethings, she is concerned about how her peers will respond. This phenomenon is so common that twentysomethings have created an on-line community for support and advice.

The following is an example of interactions between twenty-somethings who live at home: "I just turned twenty-two years old, and I am still living with my mom. The thing is, I'm working on getting my master's degree, and I have a part-time job at a restaurant. So, I'm not a slacker or anything. Unfortunately, I'm feeling ashamed of living at home. My boyfriend used to put me down about my situation and the opportunities I had. My parents helped pay for my college, and I didn't have to pay rent. My ex didn't have these opportunities, so it could have been jealousy. Even though he's not in my life anymore, his putdowns still haunt me . . . I'm working on my master's degree and working, so I don't feel irresponsible. My parents are also more than happy with our arrangement."

One response: "Don't be so silly, no way should you feel bad about living at home. Enjoy your parents while you can, and spend as much time as you can with them; in a few years, you'll be off doing your own thing. It's great to have such a good relationship with them; after all, having a good family network for support is half the battle in life!"

Another response: "I am twenty-two and I live at home. I even got a job and finished school, but I just have to pay off some loans and get my stuff together before I buy my first home. Hey, you're getting a master's, and you're working at the same time. That's great. Don't worry what others think. Everyone is different, and as long as things are good at home then you're good to go.

"It's really hard to make it on your own these days, that's what I can tell you. I'm twenty-two, work full-time, and still live with my folks, and even with working at $6 an hour, I still can't afford my own place. I'm headed back to school to study computer science, so hopefully I won't be in the hole for too long . . ." (QLC Message Boards 2002).

Twentysomethings can be comforted by the knowledge that they are not alone. Even though moving back home has become more common, it is helpful for twentysomethings to be able to talk with one another about their experiences. It is equally important for parents to normalize the experience. Twentysomethings feel ambivalent about the move; parents can reduce the feelings of failure and shame and emphasize that this transition is not forever.

A Time for Healing

Moving back home as a young adult can provide opportunities to heal a parent-child relationship that was problematic during childhood and the teenage years. Many young adults find that it's easier to get along with their parents than they did during adolescence. One mother said, "Our home was like a war zone. My daughter was learning disabled with severe emotional problems. She was vibrant, yet she was volatile and couldn't function at school. Our relationship was antagonistic and filled with tension. I had resigned myself to this unsatisfactory relationship. However, she is the child who chose to come back after college and live at home. Now, as an adult living at home, she is having the happy childhood she never had. I am enjoying her, too, for the first time."

Ginny Stanley, the mother of three adult children, had a similar story: "Due to a series of unfortunate circumstances, one of my daughters and my eight-year-old grandson moved back home with us. She had left in an explosive way at age fifteen, and now at thirty, she needed our help again. We were all anxious about how well this would work, but it felt like a much-needed second chance. She is warmed by our support and love and is blossoming in a way that is beautiful and gratifying for us all to see.

"There's also a good deal of pushing. This requires a different kind of parenting, one in which we sometimes withdraw our protection and push her to do what she needs to do to grow independently. That's hard because it is obvious that she is often frightened. When she went for job interviews, she felt inadequate and thought she had nothing to offer. We became her own private cheerleaders. She got a job as a waitress with a difficult boss and several times despaired of ever learning the myriad details required.

"When she wanted to quit without having another position, we didn't allow her that option, reminding her that the decision impacted on all of us. To her credit, she stayed in that uncomfortable situation and learned not only the job but also many important life skills which have enhanced her self-esteem" (Stanley 2002, p. 2).

In this case, a loving family environment created the opportunity for the adult daughter to heal and grow. And her parents were able to reconnect with their daughter at a time when she was vulnerable and in need of family support. There is nothing more satisfying for parents than seeing their children transcend adversity and rise to the occasion.

Empty Nest Gone Amok

Many parents experience their adult children's returning home as a step backward, especially parents who have gotten used to living alone in their homes. After years of planning meals, carpooling, and responding to other people's schedules, it is not unusual for parents to find having children underfoot again to be a difficult adjustment.

Carol, whose two children returned home five years after they left, told us, "My husband, Steven, and I were enjoying our freedom. We'd go to movies on weekday nights after work, sometimes eating popcorn for dinner, and it didn't matter because we didn't have to answer to or take care of anyone. Then, in March, our son, Eric, moved home, only to be followed by our daughter, Maggie, in June. First, I took the barbells out of Eric's old room and then dismantled my office to make room for Maggie. Since they came home, I'm finding the kids to be suffocating. Although I love having more adults to relate to at home, it's the transition—the fact that they are neither fish nor fowl—that I have problems with. I don't like being pulled into their unhappiness and conflicts. I developed my own life after my kids left, and I didn't expect to have to consider their wants and needs on an everyday basis. I find it conflicting. I can't help but be pulled into their problems when they are in my face.

"Having both kids at home has interfered with our privacy. Steve and I had regained that spark and felt much freer about expressing intimacy. For now, that's on the back burner. I know the kids came back because they felt that they didn't have any other option. It's horrible, because they aren't happy to be back. After not worrying about certain things, I feel like I have to be available, make sure there is good food, food that they like. All that takes a lot of time. I find that I fall right back into the pattern of serving them and find it hard to change. It drives me crazy when they are sitting around the house doing nothing, but when they help out and dinner is on the table, it improves the situation."

Having your adult child descend on your doorstep can take a toll on the entire family. When adult children are unhappy and expect to be cared for like children, many parents tend to feel resentful. Under these circumstances, it is imperative that the family establishes appropriate responsibilities and expectations, and parents must be clear about what they are willing or unwilling to do. Adult children should be encouraged to continue their process of becoming adults. When adult children move back home, more than anything else, parents want to avoid a deterioration of their relationship. This deterioration is more likely to occur if the period of time children are going to stay is open-ended.

The success of moving back and its impact on the family also depends on what the relationship was like before the child moved out. Jeff, a 26-year-old, said that he was reluctant to move back home, but he had no choice. He was out of money, in debt, and needed his parents to bail him out of some gambling mistakes. Jeff said, "It has never been easy around my house, but I knew that I had no choice but to move back home. I was pretty grateful for my parents' financial support and felt awful that I put such strain on them. I must admit that I was at my lowest point when they bailed me out, and I made a promise to myself that I would take the time to get back on my feet.

"The first few days it was very calm at home, but the resentment my parents felt started to rear its ugly head, and we got into many arguments. When I think back on it, I feel bad that I wasn't able to keep the peace at home. My parents were just too angry. Part of me wanted to stay at home until we all got it right, and the other part of me wanted to beg, borrow, and steal to move out."

Conversations about expectations and the parameters of moving back will help to alleviate some of the problems and antagonisms between parents and their returning adult children. Welcoming or accepting their arrival must be genuine; otherwise, as with Jeff, submerged anger can be very destructive. It's difficult to keep up a false front for too long. The family in the following story decided to handle the challenge of children returning home in a direct manner with a happier resolution.

William, father of 28-year-old Sean, explained, "My son came home for several months between graduate school and starting a job. The job didn't begin for a while after school ended, so it wasn't his fault. I kept telling myself, 'This is great. This is the last chance we will ever have to be with him at home like this. Enjoy it. Enjoy it.' But I knew my wife and I were not looking forward to his schedule again, coming and going, not telling us if he would be home for dinner, the phone ringing, piled-up laundry, and food in his room. We decided to make the best of it, even though I believe it doesn't work anymore to have them move back. When they're adults, they shouldn't be home, although I know that in a lot of situations they have to be.

"My son said we should treat him like a boarder. That's fine, but this isn't a hotel. So we made some compromises. Sean was willing to help, but he asked that we tell him what we needed. We told him he could come and go, but we would agree to have dinner together one night a week. If he wanted to have dinner with us any other night, then he had to tell us."

Sean's parents reminded him that they also had a life and their own schedule. As long as they are respectful of each other, even if parents are hesitant about their children's return home, there is a greater likelihood that they will share good times together. Respect, cooperation, and compromise are key. This experience provides another opportunity to teach our children about the importance of thinking about others.

Revolving Door

One mother described her front door as being like a rubber band—when one child would leave, another would snap back in. Nancy Sigler (2002, p. F1), mother of three adult children, wrote the following for *The Washington Post*: "It wasn't supposed to be this way. My life's script said I would raise my three children to adulthood, then they would begin lives of their own. In their own homes. With their own families. First one child moved out and then two were gone. Those of us left behind absorbed the empty space. Before the middle child could leave, numbers one and three returned. One of them with a dog. The house is a lot smaller than it used to be. There isn't room for everybody anymore. Am I living my life backward?"

Another mother in our focus group said, "I have this situation with my kids coming and going. I can't get rid of them. I have just had the experience of my Carolyn, who's going to be twenty-four, coming home. She left to go camping for a month, and her brother, Ron, came back for an extended visit. This time he brought his girlfriend and cat with him. When they found an apartment, of course, they couldn't have the cat. So, now we take care of the cat! With all the free amenities at Chez Mom and Pop, why wouldn't they all come back?" This trend is especially difficult for baby boomer parents, who probably wouldn't have dreamed of going back to live at home under almost any circumstances.

Janet, a 56-year-old mother of three adult daughters, said, "We never went back and lived with our parents, but my daughter came back to live with us for a year to save money. It's like a revolving door. The kids go out for a while, and if they're not immediately successful, or they need a change, or they need time to accumulate funds to take their next step, they move home in between. I have a lot of friends whose children have moved back home, married, with or without children, in between jobs. Some can't seem to move on with their lives. Also, if it works for one child, then you find yourself with another one who wants to come home for a period of time. This was unheard of when we were in our twenties; we never would have thought to come home again."

Extensive Home Leave

Parents should be very intentional about making the time their adult children live with them productive. A positive outcome is more likely if boundaries are maintained, and the children are expected to assume certain responsibilities. The parents' role is to uphold whatever agreement they reach with their adult children. This understanding is necessary in any kind of a long-term relationship.

Lydia shared the following story about her daughter and granddaughter who came to live with her: "My twenty-eight-year-old daughter, who is living with me, decided her job at a fitness center was intolerable. After agonizing for several weeks, she quit, giving the obligatory two weeks' notice. At the time, she had no lead on another job. I was not pleased with her decision, as our local job market was depressed and she has limited knowledge and skills for that job market. She assured me that her goal was to get back to work as soon as possible and that she would meet all her financial obligations to me. These obligations were significant, about six hundred dollars a month for rent and utilities, plus more than half of the cost of groceries.

"Very soon it became clear to me that getting a new job was going to take longer than she had anticipated. She found herself with extra time on her hands in between sending out her resume and going for interviews. She suggested that if I would hire a friend of hers to help, the two of them would rebuild my brick patio, refinish my wrought iron furniture, and plant a vegetable garden. What a deal for me! Over the next few weeks, the two of them did exactly what she had proposed. Tearing up bricks, disposing of them, and laying new brick was a new experience for my daughter and, as she said, 'Grueling work!' Two months later, I had a beautiful new patio, nicely refinished patio furniture, and a blooming vegetable, flower, and herb garden. However, she still had no job.

"Shortly after that, she found the job she had wanted and started back to work. Although I admit to being anxious at times, she did pay me every cent she owed me. In addition, she took care of three major home projects. Only toward the end did she ask if I'd be willing to give her some financial credit for her work. I was most willing to reduce her rent by a hundred dollars for the next four months."

This experience taught Lydia to let her daughter work at her pace at getting the job she wanted. As long as her daughter met her obligations to Lydia, her job—or the lack thereof—was not Lydia's business. Her daughter learned how long it can take to get a job and how limited opportunities were for someone with her skill set. Her daughter also learned a great deal about home maintenance and gardening. By keeping to their bargain, both mother and daughter benefited from this experience.

As with any stage of parenting, having a sense of humor helps to keep harmony in the home. The unexpected is difficult enough for parents and children; having perspective about the situation can help to make their time together meaningful and fun. One mother has the following sign on her refrigerator: "If you take it out, put it back. If you open it, close it. If you throw it down, pick it up. If you take it off, hang it up." Setting the rules of the house in this way makes them easier to accept, because they are meant for everyone, not just for children who have moved back home.

Make Room for Danny

Having an older sibling move back home can be an added bonus for younger siblings who were too young to have developed a "mature" relationship with their brother or sister before he or she moved out. Parents often forget the potential benefits for others in the family because they are so focused on why twentysomethings are moving back home and for how long. In our focus groups, parents were able to get some distance and look at the big picture. Many parents said that younger brothers and sisters looked forward to the unexpected return of older siblings. This isn't to say that adjustments do not need to be made. Bedrooms may be reorganized, siblings used to having their parents' undivided attention now have to learn to share, and rivalries may reemerge. Once again, resilient families are flexible and are able to figure out how to let twentysomethings feel that they can go home again.

Larry, the father of 24-year-old Danny and 16-year-old Andrew, said, "Danny moved out when Andrew was ten years old. Andrew was too young to be anything but Danny's baby brother. When Andrew moved back, Danny was able to have the relationship that many siblings have by living together when they are closer in age. Andrew was too young to enjoy all the football and hockey games he was dragged to. Danny always underestimated how grown-up Andrew was becoming. Danny's moving back home reestablished their relationship, but in a new way. The boys became friends, because they were able to make up for the time that was lost because of their age difference.

"The boys had the time to share and enjoy many common interests. I would come home from work and see them lying on the carpet in front of the television playing video games. Sometimes, I would hear them in Andrew's room talking about basketball and music. Danny was able to watch and enjoy Andrew play sports firsthand. My wife and I never anticipated how important this hiatus for Danny would be for the boys' relationship. We thought we were the ones helping Danny; we never realized how much we all benefited from his moving back home."

One issue that seems fairly common when twentysomethings move back home has to do with their assuming the role of parent with their younger siblings. They come back from being out in the world and view their parents and siblings from a different perspective. They frequently assume they are more knowledgeable and feel entitled to tell their parents that they are making mistakes with their younger brothers and sisters. Parents tend to be stricter with their older children than they are with their younger ones, and twentysomethings point this out as a disservice to their young siblings. As one mother said, "I learned from the mistakes I made with my first child. I was more relaxed and my younger children benefited." She joked, "I always heard that older children should be like pancakes: you throw the first one out!"

Jackie, the mother of 25-year-old Robyn, 21-year-old Ben, and 17-year-old Rachel, was exhausted from justifying her parenting decisions to Robyn. Jackie said, "My oldest daughter was much more critical of me and my parenting than anybody else. No matter what I did with her younger siblings, she thought I was too lenient or too strict, too indulgent or too uninvolved. Robyn acted like a critical parent. Not only did I get sick and tired of her criticisms, but her brother and sister were angry that she always had something to say about their lives. For me, the final straw was when Rachel was invited to the junior prom and there was an 'after-party.'

"Robyn actually made Rachel cry when she tried to convince us not to let her go, reminding us of the rules we had for her during high school. My husband and I sat down with Robyn and reestablished ourselves as the parents. Her father and I reminded her that we did a fine job raising her, and even if we were doing things differently than she remembers, we are doing a fine job, again, in raising her siblings. We told Robyn that we were confident about our parenting, and she needed to reassume her role as sister, not enforcer. By putting an end to this pattern, we felt we were protecting Robyn's relationship with Rachel and Ben, who were getting pretty fed up with her. They finally told Robyn that the job of mother and father had already been filled."

Boundaries often need to be clarified when older siblings return home. If boundaries are not maintained, what could be a positive experience can turn negative and create added conflict within the family.

As you see, the return home of twentysomethings can have its positives and negatives. Younger siblings get the opportunity to live with their older siblings at an age when they normally would not have had such close contact. This experience can foster closeness and deepen their bonds. On the other hand, moving back home can create resentment if the older sibling assumes the role of parent. It is our job as parents to communicate and maintain appropriate boundaries between our children.

Living at Home from Different Cultural Perspectives

Different cultures respond to adult children's living at home from diverse perspectives. It is helpful to look at how culture impacts young adults' moving back home. This knowledge provides us with a broader framework. For example, studies show that it is more unusual for parents outside the United States to subsidize their children's independence (Cordon 1997). For that reason alone, it is more common in other countries for adult children to be living at home. In Belgium, for example, families who have children who move back home are called "hotel families." In Italy, sons and daughters commonly live at home until they marry and can afford to live separately. In fact, there was a court case in which the judge ordered the parents of a 30-year-old man to continue his allowance. In Britain, a poll showed that one in ten adult children would move home for four different periods before they finally settled in their own homes (Levine 2002; Cordon 1997).

In the United States, it is common in racially and ethnically diverse families as well as in immigrant families for adult children to live at home. The family remains primary, and for economic reasons or tradition, twentysomethings either don't leave home or come back to live after college until they get married. More than one generation, including grandparents, parents, children, and great-grandchildren, often live together in the parents' home.

It is extremely common for parents and other family members to provide support for one another in African American, Asian American, Latin American, and Native American families. In these ethnic groups, it is not unusual for adult children to stay home or return home. Family members live together in many different creative arrangements. They are expected to help one another, and this support can come in the form of financial aid, housing, or providing child care for grandchildren. Interdependence among family members is a very important family value and often takes on more significance than independence (Lynch and Hanson 1998).

Isabella, a Latina, the mother of Sophia, 24, and Daniel, 26, described the traditions in her family. She said, "My family is typical. My children lived at home through college. After college, we all needed to pool our resources. They never even considered moving out of the house. Daniel is just beginning to think about moving out. My mother and the kids help with their younger brothers. We have 'familialism,' a strong sense of family loyalty. I have raised my children to know that family comes before anything else. It is our strongest cultural value. We believe if unmarried adult children live in the same city as their parents, it doesn't make sense for them to live apart."

Another parent shared a similar story. Lola, an African American mother of two adult daughters and two adult sons, said, "I am a single mother living with my children. Two are working, and two are still in school. They know they are always welcome. We depend on each other. I love having them in the house. I can't imagine why they would live on their own until they are married, and, frankly, neither can they."

In European American families, children tend to leave home

early because they often go away to college, so when they return it's a shock to the family. In other cultures, a child's living at home until he or she is married is the norm; even adult children with their own families return to the home of the parents or other relatives if they can't support themselves (Lynch and Hanson 1998). As one African American twentysomething said, "We don't look forward to that move, but there is no stigma attached to it, either." The question for many families is what they can afford. Adult children move out when they can support themselves, without any help from their parents. Gaining a multicultural perspective can help to normalize different cultural experiences.

Rules and Responsibilities

Many parents decide it isn't worth the battle to ask their twentysomethings to assume household responsibilities when their children return home for only a short time. Most emerging adults live a separate life, even when they are living with their parents. Fifty-four-year-old Vicky, mother of 23-year-old Michael, said, "Michael loved moving back to our house. We have a basement room with a separate bath, and he had more privacy there than he had in his apartment with a roommate. I often didn't know if he was home or not. Sometimes I could hear the sound of his music coming up through the vents, but most of the time he came and went as he pleased. I didn't ask him for any financial contribution because he was saving for his own apartment. Michael loves to cook and made dinner for us once a week. Now that he's on his own, I miss his gourmet meals. These were some of the nicest times we had together."

Some parents don't ask for money because they realize that their children moved back home to save money. Other parents insist on it. Two parents in the same home may disagree. One mom told us,

"I want my son to be a guest; my husband wants him to have responsibilities." These issues from childhood keep cropping up, but parents do have to come to some agreement concerning rules and responsibilities when their adult children move back home.

Eileen, a single mom of 25-year-old Gordon, told us the following story: "Gordon lived in London after college and moved back to the states about six months ago. While he was looking for a job, he moved back home. I never worried about what time he came home or whether he came home when he lived in a different time zone across the Atlantic. But when he moved back home, I found myself awake at two in the morning, worrying about his whereabouts.

"One evening he didn't come home and waltzed in early the next morning. I said, 'Gordon, I was worried sick about you.' He explained, 'Mom, I couldn't get home because the Metro shuts down after two A.M. I'm a big boy. I stayed out all night in London, and I can stay out all night here.' Eileen said, 'You know, at two A.M., I almost called your cell phone, but decided not to.' Gordon answered, 'Thank God, I would have been uncomfortable saying to the girl I was with, excuse me, I have to take this call from my mommy. That wouldn't put me on her A list.' I understood his predicament, and yet, I had to figure out a way to get some sleep for the next six months. We decided that he would call my cell phone and leave a message about whether he was coming home. This works for me, because if I wake up and he isn't home, I can call my messages on my cell phone and know whether I have to report my son missing or just go back to sleep.

"We also had a discussion about how he can have a social life with privacy in our home. Gordon laughed when he said, 'Mom, let's just use the towel rule. When I lived in the dorm, we would put a towel around the door knob if the room was occupied. No one would dare open the door with a towel on it.'" The towel rule only works if parents are comfortable with their adult children bringing home assorted girlfriends or boyfriends. Twentysomethings have to be aware of their parents' values when it comes to grown-up sleep-overs. What seems to work for parents and children alike is the understanding that common courtesy and respect for privacy and one another's feelings are appropriate at any age.

Parents may have different perspectives about other household rules. Chores are often a potential battleground with teenagers, and it probably won't be any different when they return as adults. However, parents of adult children can be very creative in encouraging them to help out. Sharon, the mother of two adult sons and one adult daughter, had all three adult children home at one time. She said, "I let the kids decide what chores they would do. They would kind of get on each other about picking up the slack. If someone didn't empty the dishwasher, there was a note on it, 'The dishes are clean.' That would be my note most of the time. I didn't say, 'Empty the dishwasher' or 'Don't empty the dishwasher.' I assumed they would interpret the note and empty the dishwasher, which one of them did most of the time. They operated as a team. If one did it one day, another would do it the next. They helped out a lot more as adults than they did as teenagers!" Another mother left typewriter notes in each of her adult children's rooms when they returned home. "Welcome to Chez Rogers," the note began, followed by a list of rules, including what time breakfast is served, when to prepare their rooms for the cleaning woman, and the parent's schedule during the week. Her children found their mother's hotel-like list of rules humorous. Most important, they followed them.

Dinner often becomes an issue between parents and adult children who are living at home. Usually, all parents want is to be informed about their children's dinner plans. Young children are usually expected to eat dinner with the family. Now that they are young adults, their parents are generally satisfied just being told whether to expect them. Unlike when they were younger, they are no longer expected for family dinner; parents simply want consideration.

Many of the old rules that applied to twentysomethings when they were younger may no longer apply. We have to be conscious of the fact that adults are coming home, not children. Parents need to clarify what their expectations are when their adult children move home and to communicate these rules directly to their twentysomethings. These should be negotiated rules based on their twentysomethings' new status as *adult* children.

Moving Back Home: What Makes It Successful or Unsuccessful?

To avoid unnecessary arguments and resentment, honest conversations about expectations are helpful before adult children move back home. Discussions might include the length of time twentysomethings plan on living at home, the reasons for moving back home, rules and responsibilities, and expected contributions to the family. Whatever decisions are reached initially, flexibility and change should be expected. An important part of the puzzle is the personalities of the players.

Once the newness wears off, parents and adult children must be careful that old habits don't reemerge. Sometimes you get a petulant teenage girl, rather than a grown-up woman, living with you. Sometimes you get that old adolescent argument that parents can't be right; only children are right. Parents have the right to ask for a 30-second phone call from their adult children if that is what they need to make their own plans or to avoid losing sleep. Adults who live in the same house should let one another know when they are coming home. Twentysomethings also can be quiet when they come home late at night (or early in the morning), but some of them, who feel childlike as soon as they get close to home, may need to be reminded of these simple courtesies. Parents have to remember that this is also a hard transition for their adult children, and they may not be moving back home at their best.

For parents, success will depend on how adaptable they are, whether they still think their children are 17, the extent to which they can be friends with their twentysomethings, their ability to step out of their parental roles, their ability to give adult children freer rein, and their ability to refrain from commenting or judging.

For twentysomethings, success will depend on spending productive time at work, helping out at home or in school, respecting the needs of their parents and other siblings, and observing limits. For parents and adult children alike, the time should be used to enjoy one another. If attitudes are positive, the experience is more likely to be successful.

For millions of twentysomethings, moving back home provides one solution to their economic insecurity, emotional dismay, or need for a safe haven, or it may be just a grown-up version of a temporary time-out. For whatever reasons, moving back provides twentysomethings and their parents with an opportunity to reconnect, which has its own rewards. Parents are also able to see firsthand how their adult children have changed and continue to do so. Judy remembers her daughter, Molly, saying to her younger brother, "You don't know how good you have it. I didn't know until I went to college and then was out in the world and started seeing other people's families." Being appreciated never hurts, and after their adolescent years when our very presence annoyed them, it seems worth the wait.

Take-Home Messages

Moving home can provide adult children and their parents the opportunity to reconnect and reframe their relationships.

Adjusting and compromising are essential to avoid resentment and bad feelings.

Learn from other cultures what works and doesn't work when adult children live at home.

Negotiate rules and responsibilities when adult children move back and reevaluate them as needed.

Enjoy the time together; it doesn't last forever.

8. The Wedding Is Over

HOW DO YOU RENEGOTIATE
YOUR RELATIONSHIP WITH ADULT CHILDREN
AND THEIR SIGNIFICANT OTHERS?

> Real freedom comes from choosing interdependence rather
> than the false choice between co-dependence and indepen-
> dence . . . the capacity for love and intimacy—an open heart—
> is so important to having a joyful life as well as to survival.
> —*Dean Ornish, M.D.*

The wedding is over; now what do you do? Many parents find the transition from having single children to children who are living with a significant other or who are married to be an awkward time. One mother of two adult sons said, "I live in dread of my sons' getting married. I probably should have had a girl, too, because I think the relationships with sons after marriage change more dramatically. I love my relationship with my kids, and I don't want it to change." We are much more involved in the lives of our children than our parents were, and for this reason alone, the transition from single to a committed relationship presents a new and sometimes difficult change for our generation of parents.

Our parents only had to deal with future in-laws when the ring was on our finger. Even if we were living together, we kept it from our parents. They were usually the last to know. Today, parents may become involved with significant others and their families long before a wedding takes place, sometimes more than once, given that two-thirds of twentysomethings cohabit before marriage. According to the latest U.S. Census Bureau figures, 4.7 million unmarried couples were living together in 2000 (Smock 2002). Moreover, cohabitation doesn't necessarily end in marriage the way it did for our generation. For many young couples, cohabiting has become an alternative to either marriage or living alone.

Before their children move in with a partner or get married, parents may have felt they had uninhibited access to their sons or daughters. So they may feel tentative, ill at ease, and left out of their children's lives when they begin to form their own families. However, how we respond to this period of adjustment in our children's lives can play a major role in the ultimate success of their newly formed families.

As children focus on their new significant relationship, parents may feel sidelined because of reduced access, lack of control, and possible discomfort with their children's living situation. One mother told us, "Now that my daughter is married, I am no longer the first one to get the information, her husband is!" Another parent said just the opposite: "I am so relieved that I am not in hypergear anymore. I know they can take care of each other." Another mother, Jan, expressed her relief at no longer being the "go to" person, and Laura, mother of a newly married son, said, "I look at my son's apartment and realize that his piles of crumpled clothing and stacked, crusty dishes are no longer my mess." Stepping back and being respectful of an adult child's newly formed boundaries may accompany this sense of relief. Laura added, "Wrestling with this is harder than I thought," so what is best about her son's new status can also be experienced as a loss. She continued, "I realize now that my daughter-in-law, Marissa, is the first to be called when something happens. I can't stop by without calling first."

With marriage, two family systems come together. As a result, "when you decide to marry you are not only taking on a new husband or wife, but you are also taking on a new family. Parents need time, just like the spouse, to adjust to the new in-law relationship" (Breazeale 2001). In all likelihood, one's son- or daughter-in-law has been raised with a different set of behaviors or expectations that may be stated or implied. We have to learn to spot and acknowledge signals of these differences before we can voice our own ideas.

Until we understand these differences and determine whether they are stylistic or substantive, we need to be very careful. Otherwise, we run the risk of alienating the people closest to our children and, eventually, our children themselves. Once we have this understanding, we are in a better position to judge the impact of our words and behaviors. In this new relationship, we certainly can express our feelings, talk to our adult children, and give them information. However, unlike when they were younger, the ultimate decision is now entirely theirs.

In an interview with Dr. Susan Wechsler, a psychologist and mother of two married daughters, she explains, "This is an odd dance that plays out time and time again. Your adult children can go to you for information, and you give them the best you can. At some point, they draw the line, and you're gone. You are 'in and out' before you know it. As baby boomers we didn't go to our parents in the ways that our children come to us; we were left to make our own mistakes" (Wechsler 2003).

Parents have to be respectful of their children's new boundaries.

One parent said, "Sometimes I feel like I am taking crumbs and am at their beck and call." Accommodation is necessary, because every family has its own unique way of doing things. This new relationship is even more challenging when children choose a different lifestyle from what we had hoped. There are bound to be disagreements and even conflicts, but learning about the cultural expectations of one's in-laws can avert some of this discord.

Each culture has its own expectations, and every religion has its own rituals. Each side of the new extended family must learn about the other and then make compromises that will make the whole family more comfortable. In any case, parents still have choices to make. We can make peace with our children or we can go to war with them. We may not have control over their choices, but we do have control over how we respond to those choices.

In one of our focus groups, we spoke with Margaret, whose family is Mormon. She had married Jason, whose family is Methodist. Margaret remembered, "For the first few years of our marriage, my mother would call me before every holiday and ask if I wanted to go to church with her. She just wouldn't accept that Jason and I were not interested. After a while, we decided that we wanted some religious involvement. Jason and I joined a local nondenominational church, and over time our parents began to accept our choice. They showed an interest in our church and began to ask questions about the services and rituals we participated in. We had conversations with our parents about our beliefs and what our ideas were once we had children. Our parents even came with us to several church activities. It turns out, we were strong in our beliefs, but our parents' acceptance was very important to both Jason and me."

It may take some time for each family to accept different religious choices, but these families were able to give each other the time needed and, ultimately, to share in their religious activities. Their relationship took precedence over family religious differences.

Marriage Talk

Marriage is one of those subjects that we intend to talk about with our children, but we often don't get around to it. The complexities and realities of adult relationships are intimidating topics, especially when compared with the seductiveness of the fairy-tale ending ". . . and they lived happily ever after." Parents may make oblique references to committed relationships and the fact that marriage requires hard work, but it is the rare parent who initiates a discussion about the issues to be addressed and the nature of the work to be done. Sheryl Paul, author of *The Conscious Bride: Women Unveil Their True Feelings about Getting Hitched,* in an interview says, "Getting married doesn't solve your problems. Whatever issues, problems or life circumstances you have continue when you get married. What happens, especially during that first year of marriage, does take work." She also says that no one, no matter how perfect things look on the outside, can actually achieve perfection in their relationship (Paul 2003). Parents need to explain to their adult children that getting married is not the ultimate goal, but merely the beginning of working toward an intimate, lifelong relationship with another human being. The operative term here is *work.*

Even with the knowledge that divorce is so common among parents of twentysomethings, we make a misguided effort to protect our children by not exploring this subject with them. Courtney, a 26-year-old stockbroker, said, "My parents never told me why they got divorced. They just said they couldn't live together anymore. This doesn't help me to decide whether or not my boyfriend, Kyle, and I should consider getting married. I wish I had more information. I thought my parents got along well. It makes me question how to make a marriage work." Courtney is one of so many that received no warning about her parents' incompatibility and no guidance about how to avoid their pitfalls. Once again, the key to success is communication.

Wedding Bell Blues

In the life of a couple, "parents are often a major component in the happiness or unhappiness of a marriage. The challenges may begin before the vows, during the stressful time of planning the wedding" (Breazeale 2001). Parents need to stay firmly grounded during the wedding-planning process. The wedding and its preparation can be a joyful experience if both parents and children keep the event in perspective. This opportunity to develop a positive, long-term relationship between both families is much more important than arguing over immediate concerns, such as whether a five-year-old nephew should be the ring bearer. Hard feelings over wedding plans cause injury for years long after the last dance is over. As Sheryl Paul (2003) explains:

> It's critical that parents realize that not only is their daughter [or son] in one of the most important rites of passage of her adult life, but parents are experiencing their own transition. A wedding activates a host of emotions, from grief around letting go to coming face to face with one's own age and mortality. It's important that these emotions are addressed directly so that they don't interfere with our son or daughter's transition process. An engagement and wedding is not a one-sided event, but a complex process that spans the spectrum of human emotion.
>
> Our culture supports feelings of joy and negates the more difficult emotions that surface. Instead of acknowledging these emotions outright, they stifle them or displace them onto the planning. We hint at the separation with rituals like the father

walking his daughter down the aisle and letting go of her hand, but we have no real container that helps parents make sense of their emotional upheaval.

The pressure to create the ideal wedding is enormous. Elaine, the mother of three married daughters, told us, "The wedding industry is a little like the funeral business. I found myself in a position where I was inhibited about setting limits on spending money. When my daughter and I went looking for bridal gowns, we needed to consider the price of the dress as well as what looked best on her. Inevitably, the saleswoman would say, 'But you're only doing this once, and don't you want the best for your daughter?' Meaning that the cost shouldn't be a consideration. I was made to feel that the price of her wedding gown should demonstrate how much I loved her. If we needed to buy a less expensive dress, that meant I didn't love her as much. It reminded me of being talked into a more expensive coffin than what I had intended to spend for my father, as if the cost of the coffin represented my love for my dad."

As Pamela Paul says in her book, *The Starter Marriage and the Future of Matrimony*, "The sheer consumerism of the American wedding is almost enough to convert one into a Marxist by a wedding day . . . Weddings have morphed into massive extravaganzas. In our consumer society, it's almost as if we think that by spending money on our wedding, we'll be able to buy ourselves happy marriages . . ." (2002, p. 63) or prove that we're better parents. Parents can help their children to keep their focus on what's important, which is the couple's relationship and making the wedding a happy occasion.

Boundaries Build
Strong Foundations

Creating a positive balance between your role as a parent and your child's newly formed family is key to your future relationship with your adult child. Again, at every stage, the relationship needs to be renegotiated—first with the couple as a parent, and then, if they have children, as a grandparent. Parents need to understand how important it is for their adult children and their partners to establish their relationship as the primary one in order to create a strong foundation for their new family. Appropriate boundaries should naturally form from the reality that your son or daughter is in the process of creating a home and family of his or her own.

This is a time to step back and take our cues from our children. Once again, this doesn't mean we can't maintain connection and provide support, but we must value the process of their becoming a distinct family unit, first and foremost. Our own experiences should help to prepare us for this process. Steve, a 52-year-old father of two adult children, said, "I was twenty-two years old when I got married. I felt like a hamburger stuck between my parents and my wife. I didn't establish myself as Kate's husband at the beginning of our marriage. Instead, I straddled two identities: Stevie, the son of Joyce and Bill, and Steve, the husband of Kate. My biggest regret is not standing up for myself as Kate's husband. I should have told my parents to stop criticizing us and to stop finding fault with Kate. Most of my fights with Kate during our first years of marriage revolved around my parents. After thirty years, I finally feel comfortable establishing my own priorities. I can finally tell my parents that I don't want to spend an afternoon with Aunt Anne. I wish I had done this earlier in my marriage. I will tell this to my children when they are ready to commit to permanent relationships. I hope I give my children the message that it's okay with me that they are each other's first priorities."

The parental role with married children is mainly one of support, rather than of providing direction. One mother said, "I feel that my son and daughter-in-law are a couple, and I want to be a positive force in that relationship, because it's their relationship and they can't live by my values." Adult children have the right to shape their households and raise their children according to their own values and lifestyles.

Negotiating transitions is often challenging for all concerned. Some young couples must blend different family models, for example, the superautonomy in one family with close family dependence in another, and expect a perfect match. As Alison, a newly married twentysomething, told us with laughter, "I don't understand why my husband doesn't love my parents as much as I do, and want to be around them as much as I want to. I could live with my parents and be terribly happy. It's especially hard because we live close by. We have a 'no dropping by' rule, but my parents would never do that anyway.

"The biggest fights I have had with Brett have been about boundary issues. He is very clear about wanting me-and-you time. There can be me-and-you-and-my-parents time, but Brett wants much more of me-and-him time. It's very hard for me. This is the biggest change. My family was my brother, my parents, and me; that was my family. Now there is Brett and me, and I thought I would just bring him in, so it would be Mom, Dad, my brother, and Brett and me.

"I thought this plan would work, but Brett wasn't so into the plan. He loves my parents, but there are times when he says, 'I can't be with your parents tonight,' and I have to be like, 'Okay, I understand that.' And then I get mad at him. My mom is the one who tells me to 'back off.' She will say, 'He's right; you can't force him to just want to be with us all the time.' And I'm still, 'You know what? Yes, I can!'"

Alison's mother has shown that she understands the importance of setting and keeping boundaries. Alison continued, "My mom will say, 'I'm thinking about coming over tonight; what are Brett's plans? I don't want him to come home from work and see me just hanging out.' It's hard for me to understand that because I'm so comfortable around my family that Brett doesn't feel the same way." The transition from one family to the next is difficult for adult children as well as for their parents. What is significant here is that Alison's mom understands how Brett feels and is able to set and respect new boundaries, even though her daughter would just as soon not have them.

Another twentysomething shared with us how her mother-in-law made the transition easier by also setting and maintaining appropriate boundaries. Melanie, a newly married 25-year-old, said, "I didn't have to set up any boundaries. My mother-in-law, Carol, did that. Neither of our families lives in the area, but I don't really think that matters. Carol is determined to be the best mother-in-law; she makes her own boundaries. While we were engaged, she called me and said, 'I made a dentist appointment for Teddy, is that okay?' I said, 'Of course. He's not going to do it himself, you might as well do it.' She's always mindful of how I will feel. She always says to me, 'Tell me if this bothers you.' I don't think I am ever going to have to say to her, 'Listen, back off.' Because Carol is so respectful of my feelings, I am determined to give equal time to both families. It also makes me want to try and look at things from Teddy's perspective as far as in-laws are concerned. My mother-in-law has made it easy for me to talk to her, and Teddy and I have made a rule to always talk about issues as well." This is a wonderful opportunity for parents to be positive role models for their newly married children.

Most parents know from their own experiences as young married couples that there are lines that parents shouldn't cross. Marion, a

53-year-old mother of two adult married children, said, "My parents crossed boundaries when they thought that, after I had two children, my husband and I were not going to have any more. So, while I was at work one day, my parents gave away all of the baby furniture and baby clothes. I was furious and pitched a huge fit. I will never be so intrusive with my adult children." Parents certainly should not make assumptions about their adult children's plans or decisions and act without first discussing the situation, especially because parents' assumptions are rarely free of their own biases and expectations.

Creating boundaries must be a conscious process, and it can't be one-sided. Both parents and adult children need information to give them perspective. In our focus groups, parents said over and over again, "I need to know, not guess." Clear and honest communication is key to successfully navigating the new relationship. One mother shared the following story concerning her daughter and the changes in their relationship after her daughter had a child: "Rebecca has become more assertive now that she has a child. She asked me to stop insisting that Lily needed cereal at one month of age to sleep through the night, and she tells me when I've overstepped my bounds. Her husband is also very vocal when we've crossed his boundaries. Their decisiveness makes it easier for me to assert my needs as well. I don't have to worry about saying or doing too much. They let me know when I've crossed the line. I only pick the battles that I think are important. I know they will respond honestly, and we are both careful to respect each other's wishes."

Advice or Vice

How do you know when to give advice and when not to? This is an easy question when everything is going well, but what do you do when you see problems? The simplest rule is to offer your married children advice only when you are specifically asked for it. Even then, try to frame your advice as suggestions for discussion or consideration that the couple can think about and then either accept or reject. We all see our children making choices we wouldn't make. Throughout our children's lives, one of the most difficult challenges for parents is to allow them to learn by failing, even when we know the possible consequences. One mother explained this challenge: "Sometimes we can see them about to veer off course, and we have to hold ourselves back from grabbing the wheel because the wise part of us knows that they need to experience the consequences for themselves." Of course, this is easier said than done.

Joanne, a 57-year-old mother of two adult children, remembered when she was newly married, some 30 years ago. She told us, "When I was first married, I got into the biggest fight of my life with my mother-in-law on how to make gravy for Thanksgiving dinner. And through some divine intervention, I realized fairly quickly that this was not a fight over gravy, but over 'I'm a grown-up. This is my house, and my mother-in-law is trying to take charge over my house.' But I came to the conclusion that, you know what, I don't really care. Maybe if I lived in the same town it would drive me crazy, but if she comes three or four times a year and she wants to clean cupboards in my kitchen, I don't really care." Joanne had the maturity to understand limits, what she could live with and, for her, what issue wasn't worth a battle. Perhaps a different set of rules and understanding based on firm boundaries would be necessary when parents and their adult children live near one another.

Another mother, Barbara, agreed about the importance of picking one's battles when it comes to interacting with her newly married son. Her advice is, we "don't say anything. My son found his soul mate. Both of them don't care if the clothes get washed. They'll pick something off of the floor and say, 'I'll wear it one more time.' They are both wonderful, brilliant kids, but they have no sense.

They don't complain, and they are very happy with each other. If they come to our house and we have food or don't have food, they really don't care. She doesn't like to cook, so he really does all the cooking. And she does her thing, but they keep meshing and there's no lack of compatibility. Other people might look at the way they live and say, 'Ohhh!' But we don't say a word. People ask us how we do it. We don't say anything because my daughter-in-law is just like my son, and we can't believe they found each other."

Barbara knows that keeping quiet is a wise choice because her son and daughter-in-law aren't starving or homeless. Her children have developed their own lifestyle, and she realizes that it has to be right for them, not her. This mother doesn't expect her son and daughter-in-law's lifestyle to mimic her own standards and values, and she avoids this potentially destructive battle.

Divorce

Watching a child go through a divorce is a painful experience for parents. Divorce can also produce a formidable test for the relationship between parents and children. How do you help divorced children? "When my daughter's husband divorced her, he described it as 'breaking up,' as if they were pinned or going steady, rather than ending a marriage," said Ellen.

Frequently, parents are at a loss about how to help their children survive the end of a marriage. Parents of the divorcing couple may feel all the emotions that their own children are feeling, including anger, sadness, disappointment, and anxiety, about their future. To be helpful, parents must keep in mind that the divorce is not happening to them, but to their children. A parent's job is to stay calm and be as good a listener as possible. Parents should try to share their own fears and frustration with others, not with their children.

Adult children who are going through a divorce may also need more than emotional support; they may need financial and child-care help as well. Parents must be clear with their children about what support they are able to offer because unrealistic expectations will only serve to do further harm to their children and to the relationship.

One mother whose daughter was going through a divorce said, "Nothing we do is right. My daughter is dealing with her own anger, and we have to support her without showing our anger. It's hard. It's hard not to call my son-in-law names, but I stop myself, because if they get back together, I'm the one who will suffer. One thing I am really careful about is not making any negative comments about Noel in front of my grandchild. We are trying to stay out of their financial dispute. Sharon is so bitter, and so is Noel. I know she depends on us because we are the constancy in her life. We do a lot of listening and less talking, and that seems to console her, for a while, and then she gets angry again."

Divorce is especially difficult if grandchildren are involved. As much as possible, it is crucial for grandparents to maintain the same positive and supportive relationships they had with their grandchildren before the divorce. Sometimes this goal can be elusive, particularly when the divorcing parents have strong and bitter feelings toward each other. Grandparents can experience the genuine loss of limited contact with their grandchildren; however, they must try to communicate their feelings to them in some way, whether by phone, cards, gifts, or E-mail. By doing this, they may keep the door open for more contact as the grandchildren grow older. Reassuring their grandchildren that whatever they feel is okay and normal is an important role for grandparents to play during a divorce.

Grandchildren

When our adult children have children, once again, parents are presented with changing dynamics for the parent-child relationship. When twentysomethings become parents, they are thrust into adulthood. We can see our children as adults more easily because this event reminds us of when we were young parents. We believed that once people became parents, they automatically entered adulthood. Certainly, having children changes the self-focus of twentysomethings to their children. Seeing your children with their children does make it easier to accept them as adults. But it is still hard for us when we see them make parenting decisions we disagree with. The parents with whom we spoke generally agreed that it is harder to not intervene with grandchildren, but at the same time, they agreed that unless the child is in danger it is still better not to.

When do you step in, and when do you keep out? Everyday concerns, such as snacks, presents, and how your grandchildren are dressed, should be decided by their parents, unless you are asked for advice. This question is more difficult to answer when an adult child who has a child of his or her own is in trouble. One parent faced this challenge. Judy, a 59-year-old mother of two adult children, shared the following story: "My son, Michael, twenty-nine, is hearing impaired and has severe learning disabilities. He functions at a below-average level. He drives, can hold a job, and manage his money, more or less. At the same time, he does not care well for himself or his property, and can make bad decisions that cause him no end of trouble.

"He and his live-in girlfriend, who is also cognitively limited, had a baby, something that both of them wanted. It became clear early on that they were having difficulty caring for their newborn. They lived out of state, away from all family. Various family members came to their aid, sending money and basics for the baby. Although I sent one large box of clothing, toys, and other layette items to my grandson, Andrew, I refused to provide anything else or any money. I felt that Michael and Katie wouldn't know if they could actually raise a child until they had to do it on their own.

"As events transpired, Michael and Katie were not caring appropriately for their baby. Michael's father and I started a chain of events that resulted in the state social services agency removing Andrew from the home and placing him in foster care for several months. I tried to persuade both of them to place Andrew up for adoption. Michael was somewhat amenable to the idea, but Katie was not. They wanted Andrew back so much that they got married, without telling anyone, just to strengthen their perceived capacity as parents.

"The agency eventually returned Andrew to them. However, after a serious incident of abuse, Michael took Andrew back to social services for the baby's own safety, which was a very good move on Michael's part. To my relief and that of other family members, Andrew is now in a loving, permanent home. Michael seems relieved that Andrew has a wonderful family. It's unclear whether he still harbors any anger toward his father or me for our intervention, but I don't see any evidence of it."

In contrast, the following story deals more with the anxieties of the grandparent than the potential damage being done to the child. While parents should be on the alert for potential health problems, they need to approach the situation respectfully. Nancy, the grandmother of one-year-old Alex, told the following story: "I see that the baby is hungry. I think he needs more food, but my son keeps telling me, 'Mom, he's right on target, give me a break, I'm a pediatrician!' I don't know if I can survive all of the 'targets' he's hitting, because I'm so worried he won't grow. I also think that the baby should be reaching for things more. I think they should be handing him things, but they don't really do that. So, when he's with me, I do it all the time. I just think they need to talk to him and play with him more. I don't say anything to my son, I just do it. But it's hard. It's really hard to know when to speak and when not to."

Sometimes our anxieties get in the way of rational thought. As baby boomers, we tend to think that the only right way to do things is our way. This grandmother should find some comfort in the fact that her son is a pediatrician. He should know something about raising small children.

Connection: Keeping an Eye on the Prize

A learning curve takes place when adult children form relationships with others. Your adult child's place now belongs to the two of them. You may feel this young couple is calling the shots, and this is true to a certain extent, especially about issues that concern only them. Parents can still get their needs met by communicating appropriately with their children. It is our hope that the relationship works to the benefit of all parties, but if there is a difference of opinion, the young married couple has a right to set their own course.

One mother said, "My daughter and I talk all the time. Alan, her husband, will make fun of us and get on the phone and say, 'Now, she's cooking dinner, next she's putting the dishes away,' and so on. When my husband gets on the phone, my kids give him the big picture. I will often hear him say, 'Here's your mom; you can give her the details.' Alan comes from a family with four other brothers; he is amazed at the communication that we have."

Many of the focus group mothers who had adult daughters commented that the men in their daughters' lives were surprised by the number of phone calls between parents and daughters. Alan is comfortable with the relationship between his wife and her parents, so it works. However, if one of the members of the couple expresses discomfort with the frequency of phone calls, the couple should come to some agreement, and the parents should honor it. It helps to remember that we are not, as one mother put it, "partners with my daughter, I am her mother."

The message is "Let them be." As the saying goes, "If you love something, let it go; if it comes back, it is yours forever." The best thing we can do for our children when they form committed relationships is to let them solidify those relationships the best they can. Again, this is easier said than done. What makes this adjustment easier is the knowledge that the foundations our married children develop at the beginning of their relationships will help sustain them through the trials and tribulations of a lifelong commitment.

This new stage in your relationship with your adult child will require all of the flexibility you have developed as a parent. The patterns you have established need to be reassessed to match the needs of the grown-up couple, whose first priority is forming their own relationship with each other. Although we are filled with wisdom to impart, it is really in everyone's best interest that we wait to be asked. This isn't a bad thing; it's just different from what we're accustomed to. Spending time with your children and not being responsible for their well-being is a plus. You can enjoy their company and relax.

Roberta Maisel, author of *All Grown Up: Living Happily Ever After with Your Adult Children*, explains in an article about avoiding pitfalls of parenting adult children: "We now have the opportunity to have an adult friendship with our adult children, which is something that can bring us great peace and happiness" (Steffens 2002, p. 2). In addition, with all of the negative jokes about in-laws, "the good news is that more and more parents are determining within themselves that they will be good in-laws. A good in-law relationship can be almost as strong as the parental relationship. It can bring a great deal of joy to both parent and child" (Breazeale 2001). Again, nurturing and caregiving don't end when your child reaches adulthood, they just change.

Take-Home Messages

Understand that your married children's lifestyles and values may not reflect your own, and avoid judging them by your standards.

Respect the sanctity of the new family that your married child has formed.

Enjoy the opportunity to form a friendship with your married child.

9. "ET Phone Home"

WHAT ARE THE BEST STRATEGIES TO MAINTAIN CONNECTION WITH ADULT CHILDREN?

> If we like the people our children become, then we have to give ourselves credit.
>
> —*A focus group parent*

As people who have prided ourselves for twenty-some odd years on being loving and supportive parents, it can be overwhelming to realize we don't yet have all the parenting skills needed to parent a twentysomething. Becoming an adult is a learning process, and so is developing a positive and nurturing new way of parenting your adult child. Parenting demands constant adaptability and vigilance to determine what is appropriate and necessary to meet our children's needs as well as our own. As baby boomers, many of us have created a family life that features a close parent-child relationship, but the level of involvement has to be renegotiated as they become adults.

However, from this common ground, adult children and their parents can learn to respect one another and build loving and nurturing adult relationships. Most important, our message is, your adult children will be okay. This period of enormous change, the transition from childhood to adulthood, is normal and to be expected. Your children will soon be able to manage their own lives. Part of them still wants advice, but they also want to learn to stand alone. You need to *believe* they will be okay.

Some Basic Principles for Parenting Adult Children

Based on our personal and professional experience, research, and the wisdom offered by the parents and adult children in our focus groups, we have developed some overarching principles to assist parents in finding their own answers. Every family is different, but these principles transcend most of those differences and should be considered when making decisions about twentysomethings. These principles include:

- Address your adult child in a manner that encourages effective communication and respectful interdependence.
- Nurture your child's development and maturity, rather than supporting his or her wants and lifestyle preferences.
- Base decisions on the individual needs of each adult child, rather than on his or her sense of entitlement.
- Make decisions based on respect for your child's emerging adulthood and your own needs.
- Avoid imposing solutions on your adult child or capitulating to his or her demands.
- Make a decision based on the lessons you would like your adult child to learn, not on the results you want.
- Be open to the choices your adult child makes, even when those choices may not be the ones you would make.

To implement these principles, we provide the following strategies for you to consider. We believe that they should provide tools to establish your own road map so you can guide your child appropriately toward independence, without forfeiting the ability to stay connected. In applying these principles and strategies, always keep your eyes on the prize, on what you can do to empower your child to take care of him- or herself, encourage a sense of well-being, and, at the same time, sustain a positive relationship, based on mutual interdependence.

Strategies for Parents: A Baker's Dozen

1. HAVE REASONABLE EXPECTATIONS FOR YOUR CHILD'S ACHIEVING INDEPENDENCE.

• Expect an extended period of dependence. This transition period will be less problematic and can be approached more objectively and diplomatically if you know it is only temporary.
• Respect and appreciate that your child has grown up and has the skills to figure things out. Trust that he or she can figure things out and be supportive and nonjudgmental when she or he hits snags.
• Understand that the process of becoming independent occurs in stages and takes time.
• Acknowledge and praise each step toward independence. This will help your adult child to feel less anxious and less pressured. Try to remember that, even as adults, children tend to seek parental approval.
• Expect your children to connect to your values and culture. Therefore, they are more comfortable relying on you for your opinions. Unlike many of us, they didn't grow up adopting values or lifestyles just because their parents would disapprove.

• Relax! Don't think that your children are going to be totally competent when they reach 22.

2. FLEXIBILITY IS BETTER THAN
HARD-AND-FAST RULES AND EXPECTATIONS.

• Count on change. Acknowledge that it's normal for parents and children to feel confused during this period. This acknowledgment can normalize this stage of development and help to make this period less overwhelming for both parents and adult children.

• Don't misinterpret this transition as a crisis, like a midlife crisis, which is more myth than reality.

• Try to remember what it was like for you to live with the uncertainties of emerging adulthood. Be mindful that your child has grown up in a world defined by ambivalence.

• Share concerns about your adult child with friends and family. This can be comforting and increase your capacity to respond appropriately to your twentysomething's issues. Discussing the commonality of experience will help to lessen the anxiety and self-doubts you and your child may be experiencing.

• Tolerate differences and be flexible. Parents can help to create an adult child who is more self-directed and is not defined by one rigid set of cultural values or expectations.

• Don't hesitate to treat each adult child differently. Children take different paths and require different forms of guidance and support.

• Avoid overidentifying with your child's successes and failures and avoid competition.

• Don't sweat the small stuff. Don't worry about anything that isn't permanent. This advice works for children of any age.

3. FIRST, LET YOUR TWENTYSOMETHING SPEAK.
AFTER LISTENING, TALK.
THEN HAVE FAITH THAT HE OR SHE HAS
HEARD WHAT YOU'VE SAID.

• Do more listening than talking. Don't react until your child has finished describing his or her problem. Suspend judgment. Try not to give advice unless you are invited to do so. Remember, being invited to give information does not mean that your child will use it. As hard as it may be, as parents we have to learn to let go of the outcome.

• Tell the truth. A certain amount of exploration is appropriate for twentysomethings. Be supportive of and encourage experimenting with new jobs and adventures. However, some kids move aimlessly from one job to the next, or one graduate program to the next without any focus or goals. It is our job to help our children distinguish the difference between "meandering" and "exploration." Try to remember, it is our children's job to make the choice.

• Have faith that your child is listening to you. Many parents feel they are not being listened to because they don't get a timely response from their adult children. Don't assume your adult child has not heard you or assimilated family traditions. One mother told us, "I was invited to my daughter's house for dinner. We were eating with her boyfriend, Tony, and his five-year-old daughter. We sat at the dinner table and started to eat before saying grace. My daughter said to Tony, 'Don't you say grace or anything before you eat? My family always said a blessing before we ate. It's important to show your daughter that we appreciate what we have.' I can't tell you how surprised I was and how satisfying that moment was to me."

4. MEASURE MATURITY BASED ON THE ACQUISITION OF EMOTIONAL CHARACTERISTICS ASSOCIATED WITH ADULTHOOD, RATHER THAN ON THE TRADITIONAL MILESTONES OF PAST GENERATIONS. THESE CHARACTERISTICS INCLUDE:

- having empathy and thinking about others;
- assuming personal responsibility;
- having the confidence to do things on one's own;
- becoming financially independent;
- setting and keeping appropriate boundaries;
- developing respectful interdependence;
- establishing competent marriages or partnerships and raising children; and
- obtaining cultural competence.

- Understand the emotional characteristics of maturity. Parents can determine the extent to which these characteristics have been internalized by observing whether their children have established personal identities, developed reasonable and rational judgment, have the ability to make independent decisions, behave in a purposeful and responsible manner, and are self-reliant and self-confident.
- Be patient. Maturity comes in increments and may be packaged differently from what we expect. Also, the time frame varies from person to person.
- Teach empathy by "holding," by staying present and communicating that you understand your child's experience. Holding is unconditional. We have to hold our adult children in a way that we stay "bigger." This is tricky when they are in pain, when it is even more important that we are able to manage our own feelings.
- Don't jump in too early with advice and problem-solving. Guide

your child to figure out for him- or herself how to go about solving a problem, issue, or concern.

• Continue to look for teachable moments, using everyday experiences as a way to teach your values.

• Be responsive to the needs and pace of your adult child. Unlike our relationships with young children in which we direct the process of growing up, in our relationships with adult children we must be responsive to them.

• Assist in the process of becoming an adult by helping your child understand that he or she has the competence to be responsible for his or her own life.

5. TRUST YOUR INSTINCTS ABOUT WHAT YOU KNOW IS RIGHT FOR YOUR CHILD. BE PREPARED THAT HOWEVER RIGHT YOU ARE, YOUR CHILD MAY NOT AGREE WITH YOU.

• Update your parenting advice to match this stage of development. This doesn't mean that you can't continue to rely on guideposts that have worked for you in the past. There will be new challenges, so take a breath, give yourself time to regroup, think the problem through, and then respond. If you follow this process, your guidance will be more appropriate for this stage.

• Have faith in your feelings. Frequently, no one knows your child better than you do.

• Be mindful that you can choose to support or not support your child's choices. Expect adult children to live with the consequences of their decisions and actions in order to learn from their own mistakes.

• Give support without conditions. If you choose to give support freely, there shouldn't be any strings attached, or "I told you so" remarks, especially if your child makes decisions that you disagree with.

6. CONTINUE TO FEEL GOOD ABOUT PARTICIPATING IN YOUR TWENTYSOMETHING'S LIFE, WHILE ALSO RESPECTING HIS OR HER PRIVACY AND YOUR OWN BOUNDARIES.

• By all means, remain available. As they say, "Bigger kids . . . bigger problems." Your twentysomething still needs you. Be available to listen when your child is ready to talk.

• It's important for both parents and their adult children to set boundaries. With limits come safety, trust, and privacy for both parents and adult children.

• Be clear about what you can and cannot contribute, both financially and emotionally. Come to a mutual understanding that includes your adult child's own responsibilities.

• Provide only appropriate help. Safety is the overriding consideration when determining whether to get involved in the life of your adult child when you have not been asked to do so. If a child is in an abusive relationship or has an addiction to drugs or alcohol, or if a grandchild is in danger, parents can best support their children by getting them the appropriate help and not enabling destructive behavior.

• Give "guilt-free" advice. Your child should be able to decide what is best for him or her without guilt.

7. "COACH" YOUR ADULT CHILD ON HOW TO DO THINGS RATHER THAN "DOING" THEM FOR HIM OR HER.

• By doing things for our adult children, by always fixing their problems, we run the risk of affirming their lack of confidence. We deny them the opportunity to develop necessary skills and to learn from their own successes and failures.

• Teach your child about accountability, personal responsibility, and boundaries. Provide your child with as many opportunities as possible to practice the skills needed to take care of him- or herself.

• Be mindful that when you rescue your child and make things easier, you aren't necessarily making them better.

8. GUIDE YOUR CHILDREN TOWARD BECOMING FINANCIALLY INDEPENDENT. THIS GIVES THEM THE OPPORTUNITY TO KNOW THEY CAN TAKE CARE OF THEMSELVES, WHICH ENGENDERS SELF-CONFIDENCE AND RESILIENCE.

• Before lending or giving money to your adult child, ask yourself: *Do* you feel comfortable, not *should* you feel comfortable, with this decision?

• Don't bankrupt yourself to support your adult child financially. Parents undermine their children's ability to take care of themselves by overdoing or creating dependence.

• Teach your child to live within *his* or *her* means rather than *your* means. If we continuously subsidize our children's lifestyles or bail them out of debt, we give them false expectations about what they can afford.

• Guide your child toward making a distinction between asking for help with insurance, rent, and health care and paying for lifestyle "needs."

• Target a specific type of financial assistance to allow your child to be able to take credit for what he or she can manage independently.

9. PREPARE YOUR TWENTYSOMETHING FOR THE CULTURAL CHANGES HE OR SHE WILL FACE.

• Accept gender-role changes in your adult child. Mothers no longer are solely responsible for nurturing and taking care of the children, and men are increasingly focusing on their families. In most cases, men and women work outside the home, so the skill sets of both home and work are critical to their family's future well-being.

• Adopt the values of inclusion and tolerance and model these behaviors at home. The most important teacher a child will ever have is his or her parent(s). Without the ability to operate in a diverse society, twentysomethings will be less prepared to be highly functioning adults in the workplace and in their interpersonal relationships.

• Teach tolerance and tell your children about the harm caused by the intolerance of others. For children who choose to live with or marry someone outside their faith or from a different racial or cultural group, or choose a same-sex partner, parents do not do them a favor by trying to insulate them from the perils of intolerance. The most that parents can do is to talk honestly about problems their children may face and give them a heads up if they see potential conflict.

• Express your concern tactfully, but clearly, if your child chooses an alternative lifestyle. Understand that the manner in which you approach your child will influence your relationship positively or negatively. This doesn't mean that you can't be upset. Try to "ask questions that would help you better understand rather than blame. Engage in a conversation with your adult child by thinking about the conversation you would have if you were talking to a friend who told you he or she was going to make a drastic lifestyle change. In that case, you could probably be less self-centered and emotional and focus on your friend's decision and the reasons for it" (DeGeronimo 2001, p. 14).

10. BE PREPARED THAT YOUR TWENTYSOMETHING MAY COME BACK HOME AT SOME POINT.

• If your adult child comes home to live for a while, assure him or her of your love and support during this transition.

• Know why your child is moving back home. If your child does not have any goals, help him or her to develop some.

• Be explicit about your expectations. Tell your child what you need. Mutual respect, cooperation, and compromise are key. Uphold whatever agreement you and your child reach.

• Reframe the old house rules of childhood and adolescence to meet the changing needs of an emerging adult.

• Encourage independence.

• Distinguish between serious problems and irritations. Some issues require intervention and others don't. If your child seems depressed, sleeps all the time, demonstrates dramatic changes in eating habits, or doesn't experience pleasure from the things that used to bring enjoyment, he or she may have a serious problem that does require intervention. However, many things fall under the category of annoyances, such as leaving the outside lights on, ignoring dirty dishes in the sink, or keeping "Count Dracula's hours." These are irritants that may or may not improve. Take a deep breath and acknowledge that your child won't be living with you forever.

• Confirm your adult child's role as a sibling, rather than allowing him or her to parent younger brothers and sisters.

• Permit yourself to ask your adult child to make "courtesy calls" when he or she plans to come home for dinner or stay out exceptionally late. Everyone in the family is expected to do the same; adult children should not be treated any differently.

• Enjoy the time you have together.

11. PARENTS MUST RENEGOTIATE THEIR RELATIONSHIP WITH THEIR MARRIED CHILD OR A CHILD WHO IS IN A COMMITTED RELATIONSHIP.

• View the fact that your child is in a committed relationship as even more of a reason to treat him or her as an adult.

• Reexamine boundaries to include the new person in your child's life.

• Begin conversations about the changes with married children well before the wedding. The engagement, as well as a time to plan practically for the wedding day, is also a time to prepare emotionally for the marriage and address the difficult and sometimes painful task of separating from one's identity as single as well as loosening attachments to family of origin. Parents can either facilitate or hinder this process.

• Don't give advice unless you are specifically asked for it.

• Let your child live his or her life and provide space and time to allow your child to develop his or her own distinct family unit.

• Try not to say, "Here's how I would do it" or "We did it this way" or "You should . . ." when your child has his or her own family, without being asked. In addition, when you are with your children, avoid reprimanding your grandchildren; leave that job to their parents.

• Don't rush to judgment; don't criticize your son or daughter-in-law in front of your grandchildren during or after their divorce. Stay in touch with your grandchildren and decide what level of support you are emotionally and financially able to give your child.

12. CONVEY THE VALUE OF ESTABLISHING A COMMUNITY THAT INCLUDES BOTH FAMILY AND FRIENDS. CONNECTIONS WITH FAMILY AND FRIENDS ENRICH OUR LIVES; THEY DON'T DETRACT FROM THEM.

- Value connection. Avoid making your child embarrassed about feeling a continued need for his or her family.
- Celebrate friendship. One mother told of her experience with her women friends at the bridal shower of a friend's daughter. Judy said, "For decades, our close-knit sisterhood-of-mothers has been a busy hive of love and community for our children. The phone lines light up with our cross-town chats. We trade worries and console each other with endless optimism. Unflagging support is a constant—even when it feels like we are failing miserably at our most important job—being a good mother. As fledgling nurturers, we asked: 'Do you think she's talking too late? What happens if he *never* gets potty trained?' We shared names of the best pediatricians, helpful tutors, and savvy college advisors. And we're always on call to dispense down-home prescriptions for all manner of medical ills. We are women who are as different as snowflakes, yet astonishingly identical, in one sacred way. Our kids are priority number one."
- Expect a more mutual and equal relationship. This adult relationship should bring pleasure to both you and your adult child. As one twentysomething told us, "I don't feel like a little kid in my parents' house anymore. When I go over to their house, and I am cooking dinner, my mom will ask what spice she should put in something. It's a different relationship in a really fun way."
- Enjoy your adult child's company. Dale suggested, "I think it's very important for us to gather as a family on a regular basis. We do it with family trips and we do create a lot of 'hoopla' when they come

home, even if it's just for the weekend. It's always obvious to them how happy we are to spend time with them."

13. COMMUNICATE, COMMUNICATE, COMMUNICATE . . . BY E-MAIL, CELL PHONE, LETTER, TELEPHONE, AND VISIT.

• Find the method of communication that works best for you. Former President Bill Clinton frequently talks about one of his favorite subjects, his own daughter, Oxford grad student Chelsea. He recently said they keep in close touch, but not by E-mail. "Still don't do that," he said, explaining that as the president he worried that someone— an independent counsel, perhaps?—would read his private E-mails. The former president continued: "She's a night owl like me. So we talk at all hours of the day and night. I called her on the way here tonight. We talk a lot and I try to get over to see her. I saw her three times between October and January" (Grove 2002, p. C3).

• Keep the lines of communication open. How you start the conversation sets the tone for the interaction that follows.

• Talk to your adult child as you would talk to a friend. If your friend comes into your house with muddy boots, you wouldn't say, "What are you doing walking around with those muddy boots?" You would use more tact.

• Stay calm and get a grip on your own intensity and reactivity to pave the path for conversation. Being less reactive gets better results.

• When you talk to your adult child about your concerns, identify feelings and talk with "I" statements, such as "I am frustrated . . . ," rather than with "You" statements, such as "You make me nuts . . ."

• Assume that what your child has to say is as important as what you have to say. Learning is a two-way street. Paying attention to what our children are telling us can help us to guide them in a more appropriate way. It also helps us to continue to grow.

- Stay in the present and avoid reverting to dated behaviors, rekindling past hurts, and unpacking old baggage.
- Let your child know that *you* also need him or her.
- Share your family history with your child to provide continuity and connection.
- Keep your sense of humor!

Enjoy Them—You've Earned It

Raising children takes parents on a long and frequently intricate path. Unlike our parents, we still may not know where our children are headed in their twenties. In spite of living with some ambiguity, now is the time to relax a little and reap the benefits. Tricia, mother of five adult children, recalled, "My most vivid memories of all those early years was standing, holding a baby, nursing, and scrambling an egg carefully over the stove so that I wouldn't burn the baby's head. The school bus was coming, the lunches were waiting to be assembled, and my husband was out of town. It was unbelievably chaotic.

"But they still grew up. They were so close together in age that all of a sudden, they were just older, together. I have a wonderful relationship with my kids and I love it. It's terrific. I don't begrudge those early years, but I am really enjoying them now." Having your children as friends can be a joy.

One father of two twentysomethings said, "Our family went to Vermont for Christmas. At night we sat around and played Scrabble. It was the best family vacation we've ever had. It's so much fun with adult children. We related like friends who really enjoy each other's company." Relationships with adult children finally become more mutual. Not only can you enjoy each other, but you can also depend on each other.

As we were finishing the book, I (Susan) was driving home to help my son, Seth, prepare to return to college after winter break. He was going into Manhattan first to look at schools for a possible transfer before making his way back to upstate New York. I was concerned about his completing all of the tasks necessary to prepare for his interviews, driving in the worst winter we've had in three years, and getting where he needed to be on time, even though he assured me he had everything under control. All of a sudden, I realized that I could call my older daughter and ask her to check in with Seth during his stay in New York City, even though I knew that she was overwhelmed with her graduate studies and planning a surprise birthday party for her boyfriend. I realized how grateful I was that I could call and tell Elizabeth that I needed something, and she was finally in a position where she could focus on her own needs and mine as well.

I was so appreciative that my children were becoming adults and I could depend on them, and they could depend on each other in ways that they have always depended on me. I felt that I could let go. When I arrived home, Seth sensed I was feeling emotional about his leaving, and he put his arms around me and hugged me. At that moment, all of the struggles—and there have been many—seemed worth it. I felt I must have done something right.

Often we are concerned that there is a danger in being too close to our adult children. This awareness makes us devalue what we think of as normal, healthy closeness and connection. Many parents worry that they shouldn't be supporting their adult children for fear of hindering their independence. This is a reasonable concern; however, we believe that valuing connection is an essential part of health and survival and can be accomplished without interfering with our children's development.

Becoming an adult does not require separating from those who love you. This new stage does involve negotiating new boundaries and new definitions, however. You have to regroup at each stage of your child's development. The beginning of each new stage may seem overwhelming, but you eventually find yourself relaxing and feeling more confident. With twentysomethings, the surprise comes because you feel you should have already completed all the more complex stages of parenting. We were led to believe that once our children reached their twenties, our job would be finished. We now understand that we can expect an extended period of involvement in the lives of our children during this period of exploration.

The lives of twentysomethings may be unsettling, but at the same time it is important to keep in mind that this transitional age is filled with possibilities. This time provides a perfect opportunity for them to explore their world. Twentysomethings have more freedom than at any other time of their lives. As parents, we can provide them with our wisdom and insight as they move forward toward independence.

Just when you think children are on smooth and solid ground, it shifts. Parenting is an ongoing process. Launching our children is a timeless experience; so is letting go.

After many years of separation from their tumultuous childhood, Jacob and Esau are reuniting. In Genesis 33:12, we find Esau saying to Jacob, "Let us start on our journey, and I will proceed at your pace."

For many of us, our families consist of many trials and tribulations, tests that challenge our ability to understand and support and, sometimes, even to love our loved ones. What we must remember is this biblical quote, since it reminds us that no matter what has gone on in our families; the strife and arguments, the conflict and stress they cause, we must allow room for reconciliation.

Our children must go from us and begin their journeys alone, learning and doing for themselves what we cannot do for them.

By *stepping back* from enabling them, our children will *step up* to growth and maturity. And then, when our children come to us, seeking our support and guidance, let us say to them, "Let us start on our journey [meaning let's do this together], and I will proceed at your pace."

Let your child come to you.
Let your child lead you.
Let your child need you.

—A *midrash* (interpretation) by Rabbi Joui Hessel

References

Albom, M. *Tuesdays with Morrie*. New York: Doubleday, 1997.

American Youth Policy Forum. *The Forgotten Half Revisited*. Washington, D.C.: AYPF, 1998.

Apter, T. *What Teenagers Need from Parents to Become Adults*. New York: Norton, 2001.

Arnett, J. "Emerging Adulthood: A Theory of Development from the Late Teens Through the Twenties." *American Psychologist* 55: 469–80; 2000.

———. Interview, Nov. 21, 2002.

Bartleby.com. "Oscar Wilde." www.bartleby.com; 2003.

BlackBerry advertisement. *Newsweek*, Sept. 16, 2002.

Bombeck, E. "Quotes from Erma Bombeck." www.geocities.com; 2003.

Breazeale, L. "Family, Youth & Consumer News." www.msucares.com; 2001.

Brewster, K., and I. Padavic. "No More Kin Care? Change in Black Mothers' Reliance on Relatives for Child Care, 1977–94." *Gender & Society* 16 (4): 546–63; Aug. 2002.

Browne, I., ed. *Latina and African American Women at Work: Race, Gender, and Economic Inequality*. New York: Russel Sage Foundation, 1999.

Bureau of Labor Statistics, www.bls.gov; 2000.

Codrington, G. "Yesterday, Today, Tomorrow." www.tomorrowtoday.biz; 1998.

Cohn, D. "Single Father Households on the Rise." *Washington Post*, Dec. 11, 1998, pp. A1, 6–7.

Coontz, S. *The Way We Really Are: Coming to Terms with America's Changing Families*. New York: HarperCollins, 1997.

Cordon, J. "Youth Residential Independence and Autonomy: A Comparative Study." *Journal of Family Issues* 18: 576–607; 1997.

DeGeronimo, T. *How to Talk to Your Adult Children About Really Important Things.* "Alternative Lifestyles," pp. 7–31, New York: Wiley, 2001.

"Divorce Stats." www.divorcelawyers.com; 2003.

Doherty, W. *The Intentional Family: How to Build Family Ties in Our Modern World.* New York: Addison-Wesley, 1997.

Ehrensaft, D. "The Kindercult." In *Working Families: The Transformation of the American Home,* ed. A. Hersh and N. Marshall, 305–22. Berkeley: University of California Press, 2001.

Emert, C. "Fledging Investors, Despite Dot-Com Roller-Coaster Ride, Most Twentysomethings Remain Pragmatic, Optimistic About Stocks." *San Francisco Chronicle,* Sept. 1, 2002, p. G1.

Erikson, E. *Childhood and Society.* New York: Norton, 1950.

Escoll, P. "Prologue: The Psychoanalysis of Young Adults." *Psychoanalytic Inquiry* 7 (1): 1–29; 1987.

Federal Interagency Forum on Child and Family Statistics, www.childstats.gov; 1999.

Fleming, A. "Textbook Cases." *Washington Times,* July 22, 2002.

Fox, M. Reuters. www.reuters.com; 2002.

Fraenkel, P. "Beeper in the Bedroom." *Psychotherapy Networker,* March–April 2001, pp. 22–30.

———. Conference on Contemporary Families, New York City, Apr. 26, 2002.

Galinsky, E. *Ask the Children: The Breakthrough Study That Reveals How to Succeed at Work and Parenting.* New York: Morrow, 1999.

Gard, L. "Am I Going Through a Quarter-Life Crisis?" *Lifesmart Solutions Magazine,* Jan. 20, 2002. www.lifesmartsolutions.com.

Garreau, J. "Cell Biology Like the Bee, This Evolving Species Buzzes and Swarms." *Washington Post,* July 31, 2002, p. C1.

Gillis, J. *A World of Their Own Making: Myths, Ritual, and the Quest for Family Values.* New York: Basic Books, 1996.

Goldscheider, F. "Recent Changes in U.S. Adult Living Arrangements in Comparative Perspective." *Journal of Family Issues* 18: 708–24; 1997.

Goleman, D. *Emotional Intelligence: Why It Can Matter More Than IQ.* New York: Bantam, 1995.

Gottman, J., and J. DeClaire. *The Heart of Parenting: Raising an Emotionally Intelligent Child.* New York: Simon & Schuster, 1997.

Graham, L. *The Future Homemakers of America.* New York: Warner Books, 2002.

Grove, L. "The Reliable Source: It's a Family Affair." *Washington Post,* Feb. 8, 2002, p. C3.

Gutmann, S. "The Abyss Yawns." *New York Times,* Jan. 13, 2002.

Halstead, T. "A Politics for Generation X." *Atlantic Monthly,* Aug. 1999.

Hendey, N., and G. Pascall. "Becoming Adult: Young Disabled People Speak." Joseph Roundtree Foundation. www.jrf.org; 2002.

Hessel, Rabbi Joui, E-mail interview, Jan. 14, 2003. Washington Hebrew Congregation, Washington, DC

Kadlec, D. "You're On Your Own." *Time,* Jan. 28, 2002, pp. 24–28.

Kalter, N. *Growing Up with Divorce.* New York: Free Press, 1990.

Kersten, D. "The Daily Grind, Twentysomethings Adjust to Life in Recession." *USA Today* Careers Network, www.careers.usatoday.com, 2002.

Leposky, G. "Boomerang Disconnect." www.ampersandcom.com; 2002.

Levine, S. "All Grown Up with No Place to Go." *Washington Post,* June 4, 2002, p. B1.

Lewis, M. "The Way We Live Now." *New York Times Magazine,* June 4, 2002, p. 21.

Lindsay, D. "Kids Just Wanna Have Fun." *Washingtonian,* Sept. 2002, p. 74.

Lynch, E., and M. Hanson. *Developing Cross-Cultural Competence.* Baltimore: Brookes Publishing, 1998.

Maslow, A. *Dominance, Self-Esteem, Self-Actualization: Germinal Papers of A. H. Maslow.* Belmont, Calif.: Wadsworth Publishing, 1973.

Miller, D. "Reflections from the Rise and Fall of the Internet Economy." The Players, working paper, 2002, pp. 1–47.

Mintz, S. "Ten Lessons Every Social Scientist, Journalist, and Social Provider Should Learn from the History of Childhood." Paper presented at Council of Contemporary Families, New York City, Spring 2002.

Moore, H. "My Deep Dark Secret? I Miss My Family." *Newsweek,* Jan. 14, 2002, p. 14.

Moore, K., R. Chalk, J. Scarpa, and S. Vandivere. "Family Strengths: Often Overlooked, But Real." www.childtrends.org; 2002.

Morin, R. "Much Ado About Twentysomethings." *Washington Post,* Jan. 31, 1994, p. 27.

Morris, E. *The Rise of Teddy Roosevelt.* New York: Modern Library, 2001.

National Association of Student Financial Aid, 2001.

The National Marriage Project. "Sex Without Strings, Relationships Without Rings." www.marriage.rutgers.edu, 2002.

Oprah.com; 2002.

Ornish, Dean. *Love and Survival.* New York: HarperCollins, 1997.

Patchett, A. "The Age of Innocence." *New York Times Magazine,* Sept. 29, 2002, p. 19.

Paul, P. "Echoboomerang." *American Demographics,* June 6, 2002.

Paul, S. E-mail interview, Jan. 8, 2003.

————. *The Starter Marriage and the Future of Matrimony.* New York: Villard, 2002.

Peterson, K. "The 'Dark Side' of Age 25." *USA Today,* Sept. 9, 2001.

QLC Message Board, 2002.

Real, T. *How Can I Get Through to You?* New York: Scribner, 2002.

Sears, W., and M. Sears. *The Successful Child: What Parents Can Do to Help Kids Turn Out Well.* New York: Little Brown, 2002.

Shaffer, E. "Sisterhood Is Powerful." Paper prepared for American Women's History, 1890–Present. Providence, R.I.: Brown University, 1996.

Shapiro, J. "Keeping Parents Off Campus." *New York Times,* Aug. 22, 2002, p. A23.

Shoom-Kirsch, D. Telephone interview, Dec. 5, 2002.

Sigler, N. "Life Is Short: Autobiography as Haiku." *Washington Post,* Oct. 6, 2002, p. F1.

Skolnick, A., and J. Skolnick. *Family in Transition.* New York: Longman, 1997.

Smock, P. Population Studies Center. www.psc.isr; 2002.

Stanley, G. "Unchartered Territory: Parenting Adult Children." Mountains and River Order. www.mro.org; 2002.

Steffens, S. "Avoiding Pitfalls of Parenting Adult Children." Knight Ridder Newspapers, Sept. 19, 2002.

Steinberg, A. "Coming of Age in 2002: Jobs for the Future." In *Margins to the Mainstream,* position paper prepared for the Northeast regional meeting, Boston, Mass., Apr. 25–27, 2001.

Stepp, L. (A) "A Distant Passage: Is Adolescence Growing Longer, or Does It Just Seem That Way?" *Washington Post,* Jan. 22, 2002, p. 1.

————. (B) "Generation Hex: Stereotypes Hurt Today's Teens." *Washington Post,* Jan. 31, 2002, p. C10.

Strauss, W., and N. Howe. *Generations: The History of America's Future, 1584 to 2069.* New York: HarperPerennial, 1993.

Tyre, P. "Bringing Up Adultolescents." *Newsweek,* Mar. 25, 2002, pp. 38–40.

U.S. Census Bureau. www.factfinder.census.gov; 2000.

U.S. Department of Labor, www.dol.gov; 2000.

Vogt, P. "The Internet Offers More 'Humanity' Than We'd Thought." Posted on the Internet, Nov. 6, 2001.

Washington Post Magazine, Advertisement, Jan. 5, 2003.

Wechsler, H., and B. Wuethrich. *Dying to Drink: Confronting Binge Drinking on College Campuses.* Emmaus, Penn.: Rodale, 2002.

Wechsler, S. Telephone interview, June 30, 2003.

Wilhelm, T., D. Carmen, and M. Reynolds. "Kids Count. Digital Divide: Connecting Kids to Technology: Challenges and Opportunities." www.aecf.org.

Bibliography

COHABITATION/DATING/INTIMATE RELATIONSHIPS

Bryant. C., R. Conger, and J. Meehan. "The Influence of In-Laws on Change in Marital Success." *Journal of Marriage and Family* 63 (3): 614–26; 2001.

Christopher, F. S., and S. Sprecher. "Sexuality in Marriage, Dating, and Other Relationships: A Decade Review." *Journal of Marriage and Family* 63: 999–1017; 2000.

Collins, N. L., and S. J. Read. "Adult Attachment, Working Models, and Relationship Quality in Dating Couples." *Journal of Personality and Social Psychology* 58 (4): 644–63; 1990.

Feeney, J. A. "Romantic Bonds in Young Adulthood: Links with Family Experiences." *Journal of Family Studies* 5 (1): 25–46; 1990.

Fischer, J. L. "Transitions in Relationship Style from Adolescence to Young Adulthood." *Journal of Youth and Adolescence* 10 (1): 11–23; 1981.

The Gottman Institute. Twelve-year study of gay and lesbian couples. www.gottman.com/research/projects/gaylesbian, p. 1. 2001.

Popenoe, D., and B. D. Whitehead. "The State of Our Unions, 2002." Report of the National Marriage Project, Rutgers University. www.marriage.rutgers.edu. 2002.

Robak, R. W., and S. P. Weitzman. "The Nature of Grief: Loss of Love Relationships in Young Adulthood." *Journal of Personal & Interpersonal Loss* 3 (2): 205–16; 1998.

Robinson, L. C. "Interpersonal Relationship Quality in Young Adulthood: A Gender Analysis." *Adolescence* 35 (140): 775–84; 2000.

Rose, S., and S. Zand. "Lesbian Dating and Courtship from Young Adulthood to Midlife." *Journal of Gay & Lesbian Social Services* 11 (2–3): 77–104; 2000.

Sprecher, S., R. Cate, and L. Levin. "Parental Divorce and Young Adults' Beliefs About Love." *Journal of Divorce and Remarriage* 28 (3–4): 107–20; 1998.

Steffens, S. "Avoiding Pitfalls of Parenting Adult Children." Knight Ridder Newspapers. Sept. 19, 2002.

Trinke, S. J., and K. Bartholomew. "Hierarchies of Attachment Relationships in Young Adulthood." *Journal of Social and Personal Relationships* 14 (5): 603–25; 1997.

Whitehead, B. D., and D. Popenoe. "Why Wed? Young Adults Talk About Sex, Love, and First Unions." Report of the National Marriage Project, Rutgers University. www.marriage.rutgers.edu. 2002.

CULTURE/ETHNICITY

Brewster, K., and I. Padavic. "No More Kin Care? Change in Black Mothers' Reliance on Relatives for Child Care, 1977–94." *Gender & Society* 16 (4): 546–63; Aug. 2002.

Browne, I., ed. *Latina and African American Women at Work: Race, Gender, and Economic Inequality.* New York: Russel Sage Foundation, 1999.

Carter, B. "Mom, Dad, and the Kids Reclaim TV Perch." *New York Times,* Oct. 15, 2002, pp. C1 and C6.

Fuentes Pressman, S. *Eat First—You Don't Know What They'll Give You: The Adventures of an Immigrant Family and Their Feminist Daughter.* Washington, D.C.: Sonia Pressman Fuentes, 1999.

Furstenberg, F., and J. A. Kmec. "Racial Differences in the Transition to Adulthood: A Follow-Up Study of the Philadelphia Youth Study." Unpublished manuscript. Philadeplphia: University of Pennsylvania, 2000. www.ksg. harvard.edu.

Hutter, M. *The Family Experience: A Reader in Cultural Diversity.* New York: Macmillan, 1991.

Lynch, E., and M. Hanson. *Developing Cross-Cultural Competence.* Baltimore: Brookes Publishing, 1998.

Rich, F. "Mr. Ambassador." *New York Times Magazine,* Nov. 3, 2003, pp. 52–57.

Salant, K. "Roommates Can Be a Rude Shock to Children Who've Always Had Their Own Rooms." *Washington Post,* Nov. 23, 2002, p. H5.

FAMILY STUDIES

Amato, P., and A. Booth. *A Generation at Risk: Growing Up in an Era of Family Upheaval.* Cambridge: Harvard University Press, 1997.

Apter, T. *What Teenagers Need from Parents to Become Adults.* New York: Norton, 2001.

Aquilino, W. S. "From Adolescent to Young Adult: A Prospective Study of Parent-Child Relations During the Transition to Adulthood." *Journal of Marriage and Family* 59 (3): 670–86; 1997.

Aquilino, W. S., and K. R. Supple. "Parent-Child Relations and Parents' Satisfaction with Living Arrangements When Adult Children Live at Home." *Journal of Marriage and Family* 55 (1): 13–27; 1991.

Armistead, L., R. Forehand, S. R. H. Beach, and G. H. Brody. "Predicting Interpersonal Competence in Young Adulthood: The Roles of Family, Self, and Peer Systems During Adolescence." *Journal of Child and Family Studies* 4 (4): 445–60; 1995.

Coontz, S. *The Way We Really Are: Coming to Terms with America's Changing Families.* New York: HarperCollins, 1997.

Cordon, J. "Youth Residential Independence and Autonomy: A Comparative Study." *Journal of Family Issues* 18: 576–607; 1997.

Dalton, P. "Let Go, Already," *Washington Post,* Dec. 29, 2002, p. B1.

DeGeronimo, T. *How to Talk to Your Adult Children About Really Important Things.* New York: Wiley, 2001.

"Divorce Stats." www.divorcelawyers.com.; 2003.

Doherty, W. *The Intentional Family: How to Build Family Ties in Our Modern World.* New York: Addison-Wesley, 1997.

Ehrensaft, D. "The Kindercult." In *Working Families: The Transformation of the American Home*, ed. A. Hersh and N. Marshall, Berkeley: University of California Press, 2001.

Elkind, D. *Ties That Stress: The New Family Imbalance.* Cambridge: Harvard University Press, 1994.

Fraenkel, P. "The Place of Time in Couple and Family Therapy." In *Minding the Time in Family Experience: Emerging Perspective and Issues*, ed. K. J. Daley, 283–310. London: JAL, 2001.

———. "Beeper in the Bedroom." *Psychotherapy Networker,* March–April 2001, pp. 22–30.

———. Conference on Contemporary Families: New York City, April 26, 2002.

Frain, B., and E. Clepp. *Being a Wise Parent for Your Grown Child: How to Give Love and Support Without Meddling.* Oakland, Calif.: New Harbinger Publishers, 1997.

Galinsky, E. *Ask the Children: The Breakthrough Study That Reveals How to Succeed at Work and Parenting.* New York: Morrow, 1999.

Gillis, J. Conference on Contemporary Families: New York City, April 26, 2002.

Glenn Nakano, E., G. Chang., and L. Forcey, eds. *Mothering: Ideology, Experience, and Agency.* New York: Routledge, 1994.

Gore, A., and T. Gore. *Joined at the Heart: The Transformation of the American Family.* New York: Holt, 2002.

Gross, E. "Are Families Deteriorating or Changing?" *Journal of Women and Social Work* 7 (2): 7–22; 1992.

Jacobs, J., and K. Gerson. "Overworked Individuals or Overworked Families? Explaining Trends in Work, Leisure and Family Time." *Work and Occupations* 28 (1): 40–63; 2001.

Lipsitz, G. *Practical Parenting: a Jewish Perspective.* Baltimore: KTVA Publishing, 1997.

Moore, K., R. Chalk, J. Scarpa, and S. Vandivere. "Family Strengths: Often Overlooked, But Real." *Family Strengths Child Trends,* Aug. 2002, www.childtrends.org.

The National Marriage Project. "Sex Without Strings, Relationships Without Rings." www.marriage.rutgers.edu.; 2002.

Pogrebin, L. *Family Politics: Love and Power on an Intimate Frontier.* New York: McGraw-Hill, 1983.

Rich, D. *MegaSkills: How Families Can Help Children Succeed in School and Beyond.* Boston: Houghton Mifflin, 1988.

Risman, B. *Gender Vertigo: American Families in Transition.* New Haven: Yale University Press, 1998.

Roberts, R. E. L., and V. L. Bengtson. "Affective Ties to Parents in Early Adulthood and Self-Esteem Across 20 Years." *Social Psychology Quarterly* 59 (1): 96–106; 1996.

———. "Relationships with Parents, Self-Esteem, and Psychological Well-Being in Young Adulthood." *Social Psychology Quarterly* 56 (4): 263–77; 1993.

Rubin, L. *Families on the Fault Line: America's Working Class Speaks About the Family, the Economy, Race, and Ethnicity.* New York: HarperPerennial, 1995.

Sears, W., and M. Sears. *The Successful Child: What Parents Can Do to Help Kids Turn Out Well.* New York: Little, Brown, 2002.

Skolnick, A., and J. Skolnick. *Family in Transition.* New York: Longman, 1997.

———. *Embattled Paradise: The American Family in an Age of Uncertainty.* New York: Basic Books, 1991.

Stanley, G. "Unchartered Territory: Parenting Adult Children." Mountains and River Order. www.mro.org.; 2002.

Thorne, B., and Y. Yalom. *Rethinking the Family: Some Feminist Questions.* Boston: Northeastern University Press, 1992.

GENDER STUDIES

Cohen, H. "The Baby Bias." *New York Times Education Life,* Aug. 4, 2002, pp. 24–25 and 30–33.

Ehrenreich, B. *Hearts of Men: American Dreams and the Flight from Commitment.* Garden City, N.Y.: Anchor Books, 1983.

Findlen, B., ed. *Listen Up: Voices from the Next Feminist Generation.* Seattle, Wash.: Seal Press, 1995.

Gerson, K. "Children of the Gender Revolution: Some Theoretical Questions and Findings from the Field." In *Restructuring Work and the Life Course,* ed. V. Marshall, W. Henz, H. Krueger, and A. Verma, Toronto: University of Toronto Press, 2001.

————. "Moral Dilemmas, Moral Strategies, and the Transformation of Gender Lessons from Two Generations of Work and Family Change." *Gender and Society* 16 (1): 8–28; 2002.

Howard, C. *I'm No Sleeping Beauty, You're No Prince Charming and There's Not a Fairy Godmother in Sight.* Nashville: Dancing Dragon, 1996.

Johnson, A. *The Gender Knot: Unraveling Our Patriarchal Legacy.* Philadelphia: Temple University Press, 1997.

Kimmel, M. *The Gendered Society.* New York: Oxford University Press, 2000.

Lewin, E. *Lesbian Mothers: Accounts of Gender in American Culture.* Ithaca, N.Y.: Cornell University Press, 1993.

Lofas, J., and J. MacMillan. *He's OK She's OK: Honoring the Differences Between Men and Women.* Sacramento, Calif.: Tzedakah Publications, 1995.

Lorber, J. *Paradoxes of Gender.* New Haven: Yale University Press, 1994.

Mann, J. *The Difference: Growing Up Female in America.* New York: Warner Books, 1994.

Salmelà-Aro, K., J-E. Nurmi, T. Saisto, and E. Halmesmaeki. "Women's and Men's Personal Goals During the Transition to Parenthood." *Journal of Family Psychology* 14 (2): 171–86; 2000.

Shaffer, E. "Sisterhood Is Powerful." Paper prepared for American Women's History, 1890–Present. Providence, R.I.: Brown University, 1996.

Shaffer, S., and L. Gordon. *Why Boys Don't Talk and Why We Care: A Mother's Guide to Connection.* Washington, D.C.: Mid-Atlantic Equity Consortium, 2000.

Tannen, D. *Talking from 9 to 5: How Women's and Men's Conversational Styles Affect Who Gets Heard, Who Gets Credit, and What Work Gets Done at Work.* New York: Morrow, 1994.

———. *You Just Don't Understand: Women and Men in Conversation.* New York: Ballantine, 1990.

HISTORY

Gillis, J. *A World of Their Making: Myth, Ritual, and the Quest for Family Values.* New York: Basic Books, 1996.

Goldscheider, F. "Recent Changes in U.S. Adult Living Arrangements in Comparative Perspective." *Journal of Family Issues* 18: 708–24; 1997.

Halstead, T. "A Politics for Generation X." Aug. 1999, www.theatlantic.com.

Morris, E. *The Rise of Teddy Roosevelt.* New York: Modern Library, 2001.

Roszak, T. *The Making of a Counter Culture: Reflections on the Technocratic Society and Its Youthful Opposition.* Garden City, N.Y.: Doubleday, 1969.

Strauss, W., and N. Howe. *Generations: The History of America's Future, 1584 to 2069.* New York: HarperPerennial, 1993.

PSYCHOLOGY

Arnett, J. "Are College Students Adults? Their Conceptions of the Transition to Adulthood." *Journal of Adult Development* 1: 154–68; 1994.

———. "Emerging Adulthood: A Theory of Development from the Late Teens Through the Twenties." *American Psychologist* 55: 469–80; 2000.

Barry, C. M., L. J. Nelson, and S. Badger. "Distinguishing Features of Emerging Adulthood: The Role of Self-Classification as an Adult." Poster presented at the biennial meeting of the Society for Research on Adolescence, New Orleans, La., April 2002.

Beck, K., and L. Dockett. "Facing 30." www.newharbinger.com.

Belsky, J., S. Jaffee, K. Hsieh, and P. A. Silva. "Child-Rearing Antecedents of Intergenerational Relations in Young Adulthood: A Prospective Study." *Developmental Psychology* 37 (6): 801–13; 2001.

Best, K. M., S. T. Hauser, and J. P. Allen. "Predicting Young Adult Competencies: Adolescent Era Parents and Individual Influences." *Journal of Adolescent Research* 12 (1): 90–112; 1997.

Blos, P. *On Adolescence: A Psychoanalytic Interpretation.* New York: Free Press, 1962.

Bluestein, J. *The Parent's Little Book of Lists: Do's and Dont's of Effective Parenting.* Deerfield Beach, Fla.: Health Communications, 1997.

Brown Mikel, L., and C. Gilligan. *Meeting at the Crossroads: The Landmark Book About the Turning Points in Girls' and Womens' Lives.* New York: Ballantine, 1992.

Carbery, J., and D. Buhrmester. "Friendship and Need Fulfillment During Three Phases of Young Adulthood." *Journal of Social and Personal Relationships* 15 (3): 393–409; 1998.

Chesler, P. *Woman's Inhumanity to Woman.* New York: Thunder's Mouth Press/ Nation Books, 2001.

Côté, J. *Arrested Adulthood: The Changing Nature of Maturity and Identity.* New York: New York University Press, 2000.

Dalton, P. "Let Go, Already." *Washington Post,* Dec. 27, 2002, p. B1.

Deluca, P. *The Solo Partner: Repairing Your Relationship on Your Own.* Point Roberts, Wash.: Hartley & Marks Publishers, 1996.

Dubas, J. S., and A. C. Petersen. "Leaving Home: Understanding the Transition to Adulthood." In *New Directions for Child Development* (San Francisco: Jossey-Bass, 1996), p. 71.

Erikson, E. *Childhood and Society.* New York: Norton, 1950.

Escoll, P. "Prologue: The Psychoanalysis of Young Adults." *Psychoanalytic Inquiry* 7 (1): 1–29; 1987.

Floyd, F. J., T. S. Stein, K. S. M. Harter, A. Allison, and C. L. Nye. "Gay, Lesbian, and Bisexual Youths: Separation-Individuation, Parental Attitudes, Identity Consolidation, and Well-Being." *Journal of Youth and Adolescence* 28 (6): 719–39; 1999.

Friel, J., and L. Friel. *The 7 Worst Things Parents Do.* Deerfield Beach, Fla.: Health Communications, 1999.

Frymier, J. "Developing a Sense of Responsibility." In *Teaching Students to Be Responsible,* ed. J. Frymier, 9–16. Bloomington, Ind.: Phi Delta Kappa, 1996.

Gibbs, N. "The EQ Factor." *Time,* Oct. 2, 1995, pp. 60–68.

Ginott, H. *Between Parent & Child.* New York: Avon, 1961.

Goleman, D. *Emotional Intelligence: Why It Can Matter More Than IQ.* New York: Bantam, 1995.

Hartling, L. "Strengthening Our Resilience in a Risky World: It Is All About Relationships." *Research & Action Report: Wellesley Centers for Women* 24: 4–7, Fall/Winter 2002.

Lewis, S. K., C. E. Ross, and J. Mirowsky. "Establishing a Sense of Control in the Transition to Adulthood." *Social Forces* 77: 1573–99; 1999.

Maslow, A. *Dominance, Self-Esteem, Self-Actualization: Germinal Papers of A. H. Maslow.* Belmont, Calif.: Wadsworth Publishing, 1973.

Neyer, F. J., and J. B. Asendorpf. "Personality-Relationship Transaction in Young Adulthood." *Journal of Personality & Social Psychology* 81 (6): 1190–1204; 2001.

Nissinen, S. *The Conscious Bride: Women Unveil Their True Feeling About Getting Hitched.* Oakland, Calif.: New Harbinger Publishers, 2000.

Nurmi, J. "Self-Definition and Mental Health During Adolescence and Young Adulthood." In *Health Risks and Mental Health During Adolescence and Young Adulthood,* ed. J. Schulenberg and J. Maggs, New York: Cambridge University Press, 1997.

Prend Davis, A. *Claim Your Inner Grown-Up: 4 Essential Steps to Authentic Adulthood.* New York: Plume, 2001.

Real, T. *How Can I Get Through to You?* New York: Scribner, 2002.

Riggs, S. "Response to Troxel v. Granville: Implication of Attachment Theory for Judicial Decisions Regarding Custody and Third-Party Visitations." *Family Court Review* 41 (1): 39–53; 2003.

Roberts, B. W., A. Caspi, and T. E. Moffitt. "The Kids Are Alright: Growth and Stability in Personality Development from Adolescence to Adulthood. *Journal of Personality and Social Psychology* 81: 670–83; 2001.

Roberts, R. E. L., and V. L. Bengtson. "Affective Ties to Parents in Early Adulthood and Self-Esteem Across 20 Years." *Social Psychology Quarterly* 59 (1): 96–106; 1996.

SOCIOLOGY

Albom, M. *Tuesdays with Morrie.* New York: Doubleday, 1997.

American Association of University Women Educational Foundation. *Gaining a Foothold: Women's Transitions Through Work and College.* Washington, D.C.: AAUW Educational Foundation, 1999.

Arnett, J. "Learning to Stand Alone: The Contemporary American Transition to Adulthood in Cultural and Historical Context." *Human Development* 41: 295–315; 1998.

Barker, O. "8 Minutes to a Love Connection." *USA Today,* Dec. 12, 2002, pp. 1D and 2D.

Bombeck, E. "Quotes from Erma Bombeck." www.geocities.com; 2003.

Codrington, G. "Yesterday, Today, Tomorrow." www.tomorrowtoday.biz; 1998.

Dankers, M. "Facing the Not-So-Empty Nest." *AARP,* Jan. 30, 2002. www.aarplifeanswers.com/empty.html.

Dowd, M. "The Boomers' Corner." *New York Times on the Web,* Nov. 24, 2002.; www.NYTimes.com.

Emert, C. "Fledging Investors, Despite Dot-Com Roller-Coaster Ride, Most Twentysomethings Remain Pragmatic, Optimistic About Stocks." *San Francisco Chronicle,* Sept. 1, 2002, p. G1.

Fleming, A. "Textbook Cases." *Washington Times,* July 22, 2002. E-mail from Marjorie Heberlee.

Furstenberg, F. F. "The Sociology of Adolescence and Youth in the 1990s: A Critical Commentary." *Journal of Marriage and the Family* 62 (4): 896–910; 2000.

Gard, L. "Am I Going Through a Quarter-Life Crisis?" *Lifesmart Solutions Magazine,* Jan. 20, 2002. www.lifesmartsolutions.com.

Gardner, M. "The Disappearing Generation Gap." *Christian Science Monitor,* May 29, 2002. www.csmonitor.com.

Garreau, J. "Cell Biology Like the Bee, This Evolving Species Buzzes and Swarms." *Washington Post,* July 31, 2002, p. C1.

Goldscheider, F., C. Goldscheider, P. St. Clair, and J. Hodges. "Changes in Returning Home in the United States, 1925–1985." *Social Forces* 78 (2): 695–720; 1999.

Goldscheider, F. K., and L. J. Waite. "Nest-Leaving Patterns and the Transition to Marriage for Young Men and Women." *Journal of Marriage and the Family* 49 (3): 507–16; 1987.

Graber, J. A., and J. S. Dubas. "Leaving Home: Understanding the Transition to Adulthood." *New Directions for Child Development* 71; 1996.

Grove, L. "The Reliable Source: It's a Family Affair." *Washington Post,* Feb. 8, 2002, p. C3.

Gutmann, S. "The Abyss Yawns." *New York Times,* Jan. 13, 2002. www.NYtimes.com.

Hendey, N., and G. Pascall. "Becoming Adult: Young Disabled People Speak." Joseph Roundtree Foundation, www.jrf.org; 2002.

Johnson, H., and C. Schelhas-Miller. *Don't Tell Me What to Do, Just Send Money: The Essential Parenting Guide to the College Years.* New York: St. Martin's/Griffin, 2002.

Kadlec, D. "You're On Your Own." *Time,* Jan. 28, 2002, pp. 24–28.

Kalter, N. *Growing Up with Divorce.* New York: Free Press, 1990.

Karbo, K. "We Obsess, Therefore We Buy," Mar. 1, 2002; www.salon.com.

Kersten, D. "The Daily Grind, Twentysomethings Adjust to Life in Recession." *USA Today* Careers Network, www.careers.usatoday.com.; 2002.

Klimkiewicz, J. "The Angst of the 20s." *Philadelphia Inquirer Magazine,* July 24, 2001.

Leposky, G. "Boomerang Disconnect." www.ampersandcom.com.; 2002.

Levine, S. "All Grown Up with No Place to Go." *Washington Post,* June 4, 2002, p. B1.

Lewis, M. "The Way We Live Now." *New York Times Magazine,* June 4, 2002, p. 21.

Lindsay, D. "Kids Just Wanna Have Fun." *Washingtonian,* Sept. 2002, p. 74.

Miller, D. "Reflections from the Rise and Fall of the Internet Economy." The Players, working paper, 2002, pp. 1–47.

Mintz, S. "Ten Lessons Every Social Scientist, Journalist, and Social Provider Should Learn from the History of Childhood." Paper presented at Council of Contemporary Families, New York City, Spring 2002.

Moore, H. "My Deep Dark Secret? I Miss My Family." *Newsweek,* Jan. 14, 2002. p. 14.; www.inq.philly.com.

Moran, G. *A Grammar of Responsibility.* New York: Crossroads Publishing, 1996.

Morin, R. "Much Ado About Twentysomethings." *Washington Post,* Jan. 31, 1994, p. 27.

National Research Council. *Realizing the Information Future: The Internet and Beyond.* Washington, D.C.: National Academy Press, 1994.

Patchett, A. "The Age of Innocence." *New York Times Magazine,* Sept. 29, 2002, p. 19.

Peterson, K. "The 'Dark Side' of Age 25." *USA Today,* Sept. 9, 2001.; www.usatoday.com.

———. "Twentysomething Angst." www.detnews.com.; Sept. 18, 2001.

Pogrebin Cottin, L. *Among Friends: Who We Like, Why We Like Them, and What We Do With Them.* New York: McGraw-Hill, 1987.

Polsky, C. "Making Them Comfortable—But Not Too Comfortable." www.newsday.com.; May 23, 2002.

Raymore, L. A., B. L. Barber, and J. S. Eccles. "Leaving Home, Attending College, Partnership and Parenthood: The Role of Life Transition Events in Leisure Pattern Stability from Adolescence and Young Adulthood." *Journal of Youth & Adolescence* 30 (2): 197–223.

Schneider, E. "Giving Students Voice in the Classroom." *Educational Leadership* 54 (1): 22–26; 1996.

Seibert, M., and M. Willets. "Changing Family Forms." *Social Education* 64 (1): 42–47.

Shapiro, J. "Keeping Parents Off Campus," *New York Times,* Aug. 22, 2002, p. A23.

Sigler, N. "Life Is Short: Autobiography as Haiku." *Washington Post,* Oct. 6, 2002, p. F1.

Smith, L. "Staggering into Adulthood." *Los Angeles Times,* Sept. 3, 2001, p. C10.

Steinberg, A. "Coming of Age in 2002: Jobs for the Future." In *Margins to the Mainstream,* position paper prepared for the Northeast regional meeting, Boston, Mass., April 25–27, 2001.

Stepp, L. "A Distant Passage: Is Adolescence Growing Longer, or Does It Just Seem That Way?" *Washington Post,* Jan. 22, 2002, p. 1.

———. "Generation Hex: Stereotypes Hurt Today's Teens." *Washington Post,* Jan. 31, 2002, p. C10.

———. "Goodbye 101: Help for Anxious Parents When the Kids Go Off to College." *Washington Post,* Sept. 2, 2002, pp. C1 and C8.

Strauss, G. "The Bridget Jones Economy." *The Economist,* Dec. 22, 2001, pp. 68–70.

———. "Good Old Boys' Network Still Rules Corporate Boards." *USA Today,* Nov. 1, 2001, pp. 1B and 2B.

Thompson, B. "The Good Divorce." *Washington Post Magazine,* Nov. 24, 2002, pp. 14–20 and 25–28.

Thornburg, D. *The New Basics: Education and the Future of Work in the Telematic Age.* Alexandria, Va.: Association for Supervision and Curriculum Development, 2002.

Turkle, S. *Life on the Screen: Identity in the Age of the Internet.* New York: Simon & Schuster, 1995.

Tyre, P., "Bringing Up Adultolescents." *Newsweek,* Mar. 25, 2002, pp. 38–40.

Tyre, P. "Bringing Up Adultolescents." *Newsweek,* Mar. 25, 2002.; www.newsweek.com.

Vogt, P. "The Internet Offers More 'Humanity' Than We'd Thought." Post on the Internet, Nov. 6, 2001.

Wechsler, H., and B. Wuethrich. *Dying to Drink: Confronting Binge Drinking on College Campuses.* Emmaus, Penn.: Rodale, 2002.

Wilhelm, T., D. Carmen, and M. Reynolds. "Digital Divide: Connecting Kids to Technology: Challenges and Opportunities." www.aecf.org.

STATISTICS

American Youth Policy Forum. *The Forgotten Half Revisited.* Washington, D.C.: AYPF, 1998.

Bureau of Labor Statistics, 2000. www.bls.gov.

Centers for Disease Control and Prevention. "2001 Youth Risk Behavior Survey." www.cdc.gov.

Federal Interagency Forum on Child and Family Statistics, 1999. www.childstats.gov.

Fox, M. Reuters, 2002. www.reuters.com.

National Association of Student Financial Aid, 2001.

Paul, P. "Echoboomerang." *American Demographics,* June 6, 2002.

Smock, P. Population Studies Center, 2002. www.psc.org.

U.S. Census Bureau. "Profile of General Demographic Statistics," 2000. www.factfinder.census.gov.

———. "Race Data," 2003. www.census.gov.

U.S. Department of Labor. "Labor Force Statistics from the Current Population Survey," 2003. www.dol.gov.

Index

About the Authors

LINDA PERLMAN GORDON, LCSW-C, M.ED., is a clinical social worker, family therapist, and trained mediator. She has directed a court-mandated seminar for divorcing parents and, as a member of the Montgomery County Divorce Roundtable, developed the Supervised Visitation Program for Montgomery County, Maryland. Ms. Gordon has been invited to several Judicial Institutes to speak on issues related to children and divorce. She is a graduate of the Family Therapy Practice Center and has advanced degrees in social work and education. Ms. Gordon has taught seminars on the subject of families, and has developed programs concerning mental health issues for children. She has a private psychotherapy practice in the Washington, D.C., area treating individuals, couples, and families. Ms. Gordon is the mother of two twentysomethings.

SUSAN MORRIS SHAFFER is currently the Deputy Director and Director of Gender Equity Programs at the Mid-Atlantic Equity Center. Ms. Shaffer is nationally recognized for her work in the development of comprehensive technical assistance and training programs on educational equity and multicultural gender-related issues. She has authored or coauthored several publications related to gender equity, mathematics and science education, women's history, multicultural education, and disability. She has managed a number of grants from the U.S. Department of Education and has spent more than 30 years teaching and working in public schools. Ms. Shaffer holds an undergraduate degree in history and a graduate degree in education from the University of California, Berkeley. She also is the mother of two twentysomethings.

Linda Gordon and Susan Shaffer are coauthors of *Why Boys Don't Talk and Why We Care: A Mother's Guide to Connection,* and the forthcoming *Why Girls Talk and What They Are Really Saying.* As a result of this work, they have spoken to parent groups and educators nationally and have been the subject of numerous interviews and articles in print, radio, and television. They were invited to participate at the White House Conference on Teenagers.

Susan Schaffer   Linda Gordon